I0519373

The Enlightened Quest

*Blending Neuroscience with Spiritual
Pathways to Self-Realization*

Shawn Christian, M.D.
Steve and Stella Christian

Awnian Media Group

Free Bonuses

As a surprise bonus to assist you on your quest, we're thrilled to offer you some complimentary bonuses! These include the Smart Goals Worksheet, a set of 25 Powerful Affirmations applicable to all facets of life, and the Analyze Your Fear Worksheet – all available for free, but only for a limited time. Simply download othem by visiting https://www.confidenceiatry.com/freebonuses.

TABLE OF CONTENTS

Part Two
Unlocking the Secret Code

Part Three
Inner Realms Explored

Part Four
Transformation and Growth

Part Five
Synthesis of Wisdom

Part Six
Awakening the Senses

Part Seven
Inner Practices and Reflections

Part Eight
Convergence: Paths to Universal Consciousness

Part Nine
Practical Applications and Tools for Transformation

Part Ten
Additional Examples, Tips, and Resources

Disclaimer & Copyright

Usage Rights

This book is provided for your personal use only. You are allowed to read, reference, and share the content for educational or review purposes with proper attribution. No other rights are granted.

Copyright Notice

This book is protected by international copyright law. Any form of copying, reproduction, distribution, or creation of derivative works requires explicit permission from the publisher. The publisher and authors retain full copyright ownership of this book.

Accuracy Disclaimer

The authors have made every reasonable effort to ensure the accuracy and completeness of this book's content. However, due to the rapidly evolving nature of the subject matter, the information may not always be up-to-date. The publisher, authors, and resellers disclaim responsibility for any errors, omissions, or misinterpretations contained herein.

Inadvertent Offense

Any inadvertent offense towards individuals, groups, or organizations is entirely unintentional. We are committed to addressing and rectifying any such issues brought to our attention.

Educational Purpose

This book is designed for educational purposes and does not guarantee income, sales, success, or specific outcomes. The content is solely informational and is not a substitute for legal advice from an attorney, financial guidance from an accountant, or the diagnosis, treatment, prevention, or cure of any medical condition.

Health and Safety Disclaimer

Engaging in any exercise or diet program, including those outlined in this book, carries inherent risks of injury. To minimize these risks, consult with a medical professional or healthcare specialist before commencing any exercise or diet regimen. The publisher, author, and resellers cannot be held liable for any unsatisfactory results or injuries that may arise from implementing the techniques or adherence to the guidelines presented in this book.

Trademark Disclaimer

Any mention of product names, websites, or company names within this book signifies the trademarks or copyrighted properties of their respective owners. The author, publisher, and resellers have no affiliations with endorsements from, or approvals by these product names, websites, or companies, nor do these entities sponsor or support this product in any manner.

Contact Information

For any questions or concerns related to this book, please contact support@awnian.com.

Copyright © 2022 - 2024 by Shawn Christian, M.D., Steve Christian, and Stella Christian

All rights are reserved worldwide.

Reproduction of any portion of this book, whether by electronic, mechanical, or any other means, including storage and retrieval systems, is strictly prohibited without the written authorization of the author. The sole exception is for incorporating brief quotations in book reviews.

Published by Awnian Media Group

www.awnian.com

Paperback ISBN: 978-1-953726-03-2

eBook ISBN: 978-1-953726-04-9

Our Mission

Our mission with "The Enlightened Quest" is to empower readers from all walks of life, offering them a comprehensive guide that transforms static knowledge into dynamic wisdom. We are dedicated to providing a platform that equips individuals, regardless of their background, with the tools they need to navigate life's challenges and opportunities, fostering personal growth and meaningful connections within a seamless journey.

Dedication

To my beloved parents, Steve and Stella Christian, whose unwavering commitment to truth, integrity, support, and love has been the bedrock of my existence. Your guiding light has illuminated my path and inspired me to embark on this transformative journey.

To my cherished readers, whose presence infuses this book with purpose and meaning. Your curiosity and willingness to explore alongside me have made this effort even more fulfilling.

And to the tapestry of life experiences that have graced my days, each one a brushstroke on the canvas of my soul. Through your trials and triumphs, you have already revealed the profound effectiveness of the path I seek to illuminate within these pages.

With heartfelt gratitude and boundless love.

Preface

Dear Reader,

Welcome to an exceptional odyssey of self-discovery and exploration—a journey that unveils the wonders of the human mind, the essence of spirituality, and the priceless gift of life itself. With immense joy and eager anticipation, I extend my invitation for you to embark on this transformative adventure within the pages of "The Enlightened Quest: Blending Neuroscience with Spiritual Pathways to Self-Realization." Inside these pages lie numerous hidden treasures. Once you unearth them, they will seamlessly integrate into your life, becoming an integral part of your journey.

This book is the culmination of a lifelong fascination with the intricate workings of the mind and the profound spiritual dimensions that shape our existence. As a passionate advocate of mindfulness, neuroscience, and personal growth, I have been fortunate to witness the transformative power of these practices in my life and the lives of those around me.

"The Enlightened Quest," is not just a collection of scientific facts and philosophical musings; it is a heartfelt endeavor to bridge the gap between the worlds of science and spirituality. Within these pages, you will find a harmonious blend of evidence-based research, personal anecdotes, and practical exercises that aim to ignite a spark of curiosity and inspiration within you.

Throughout this journey, we will delve into the fascinating realm of neuroplasticity—the brain's ability to adapt and change—which underscores the inherent potential for growth and transformation that lives within each one of us. We will explore the art of mindfulness, unlocking its secrets to find serenity amidst life's storms and discovering its profound impact on our emotional well-being.

But this is not a journey of solitary introspection; it is an invitation to connect with the world and the surrounding people. Within these chapters, we will embrace gratitude and compassion as potent forces that nourish our souls and create meaningful bonds with others. We will witness the ripple effect of love and empathy, cultivating resilience and understanding in our shared human experience.

As we navigate the interconnected realms of science and spirituality, I encourage you to embark on this journey with an open heart and a curious mind. Allow yourself to immerse in the wisdom of the ages and the latest scientific revelations, discovering the symphony of insights that unite our global heritage.

This book is not a mere guide; it is an invitation to integrate these practices into your daily life, forging a path towards self-awareness, purpose, and fulfillment. You hold the key to unlock your true potential, and I hope that "The Enlightened Quest: Blending Neuroscience with Spiritual Pathways to Self-Realization" becomes a guiding light on your transformative voyage.

As we embark on this journey, I want to express my heartfelt appreciation to all who have played a role in shaping this book— mentors, researchers, the wisdom of ancient and modern literatures, personal encounters, kindred spirits, and fellow seekers who have generously shared their insights and understanding. To you, cherished reader, I extend my gratitude for joining me on this odyssey.

Your presence enriches these pages, infusing them with significance, and I am humbled to have you as my companion along the way. With warmest wishes and an eagerness to explore.

Best wishes,

Shawn Christian, M.D.

Introduction

Embarking on a Journey of Self-Discovery and Spiritual Illumination

Welcome to the profound and comprehensive exploration of the intricate relationship between human consciousness, spirituality, and the complex workings of the mind and body in "The Enlightened Quest: Blending Neuroscience with Spiritual Pathways to Self-Realization." Within the pages of this transformative odyssey, we extend an invitation to embark on a voyage of self-discovery, unraveling the profound wisdom that transcends time, space, and tradition.

As you embark on this extraordinary quest, you'll traverse a path that leads from the foundational understanding of the mind and body to the inner realms of consciousness and self-realization. This book skillfully weaves together the threads of ancient wisdom and modern scientific insights, providing a holistic perspective that effortlessly unifies seemingly disparate realms of knowledge.

Throughout this enlightening journey, you'll encounter chapters that delve into the significance of breath, sound vibration, symbolism, and the harmonious fusion of science and spirituality. It's important to note that we have intentionally crafted this book in a simple, easy-to-understand language, avoiding delving too deeply into medical terminology or delving excessively into the details of one specific religion, as these aspects are beyond the scope of this book. Each chapter serves as a key, unlocking an additional dimension of understanding, enabling you to navigate the intricate tapestry of human experience and recognize the profound connection between the physical and metaphysical.

Yet, this book is more than a mere repository of insights—it is an empowering guide, urging you to cultivate mindfulness, navigate your emotions, and unearth your purpose and fulfillment. It stands as a testament to the shared values that resonate across diverse traditions, reminding us of the universal truths that unite humanity.

As you turn the pages of "The Enlightened Quest," you embark on a journey of self-discovery and spiritual illumination that possesses the potential to reshape your perspective, enrich your understanding, and kindle the spark of transformation within. This is not merely a book; it serves as a catalyst for awakening, a roadmap to forging a deeper connection with yourself and the world around you. With an open heart and a curious mind, let us embark together on this once-in-a-lifetime journey to self-understanding.

In the expansive realm of spirituality and philosophy, numerous paths beckon, each offering unique insights into life's meaning and purpose. These paths encompass diverse religions such as Christianity, Islam, Buddhism, and Hinduism, as well as philosophies like Stoicism, Existentialism, and Confucianism.

Visualize these paths as distinct rivers, all flowing toward the same ocean of understanding. They share a common quest for answers to fundamental questions about existence, ethics, and the human condition.

To navigate this diverse landscape, begin with self-reflection and exploration. Familiarize yourself with various paths and contemplate what resonates most with your beliefs and values. Just as different rivers converge into the same ocean, multiple paths can lead to personal growth, wisdom, and a deeper understanding of both yourself and the world.

Ultimately, your journey is unique. Embrace elements from different paths that empower and enrich your life. Your personal synthesis of wisdom will guide you toward your own understanding and purpose.

What You'll Discover

This book covers a wide range of topics related to ancient wisdom, modern science, and spirituality.

Here are some topics or keywords out of many that appear in the Book:

- Mystical Practices
- Ancient Wisdom and Current Knowledge
- The Brain and Mind
- Chakra System
- Prayer Hands Position
- Neuroplasticity
- Breath and Consciousness
- Sound Vibration and Symbolism
- The Power of Light
- Mind-Body Connection
- Forgiveness
- Judgment
- Faith
- Belief
- Responsibility and Destiny
- Energetic Essence
- Soul
- Spirit
- Self
- Love and Harmony

- The Theory of Karma
- Non-Violence
- Artificial Intelligence (AI) Technology and Human Life
- New World Order
- New Consciousness
- Energy of Life

These topics cover a diverse range of subjects, including neuro-science, spirituality, mindfulness, ancient wisdom, technological advancements, and many more. This book provides a comprehensive exploration of how these different aspects intersect and contribute to personal growth and understanding.

<u>WARNING</u>

The content within this book holds tremendous power. It offers a pathway towards transformative personal growth, self-discovery, and confidence. Understanding the interconnection between the mind, spirit, and the journey towards self-realization is a profoundly powerful realization. Should you acquire this book, I encourage a commitment to employing these powerful tools solely for the ultimate good. Never should these techniques and knowledge be used for any form of wrongdoing.

Maximizing Learning

To get maximum benefit from this book, I recommend you read this book multiple times. Research studies have shown that most people only retain 10% to 30% of the material they read. The specific percentage can differ based on the complexity of the material, the reader's level of interest, their prior knowledge of the subject, and the reading strategies employed. Rereading the same material can enhance retention, comprehension, and reinforcement of concepts. Each subsequent reading can reveal additional details, reinforce key points, and solidify understanding. However, it is important to note that the increase in retention rates with each reread can vary and might not follow a linear progression. Therefore, to fully grasp and remember the content, it is recommended to read this book multiple times, enhancing the benefits it offers.

As we conclude this introduction, our quest now extends into the realm of Part I: Foundations of Understanding.

Part One

Foundations of Understanding

Step into the convergence of science and spirituality, where an enigmatic code holds the secrets to the human mind and consciousness. "Foundations of Understanding" extends an invitation to an exhilarating intellectual expedition where the fabric of existence is laid bare, and the distinction between science and spirituality dissolves into a wondrous amalgamation of knowledge. Prepare for a thought-provoking journey that will push the boundaries of your beliefs, broaden your perspectives, and stir the wisdom within. Are you prepared to decode the Mind-Consciousness code and venture into an extraordinary exploration that challenges beliefs while awakening your inner sage?

Chapter 1

Cracking the Mind-Consciousness Code: Science & Spirituality

I n this chapter, we embark on a quest to unravel the profound
connections between the intricate realms of neuroscience, spirituality, and the precious gift of life. By blending scientific
knowledge with insights from ancient spiritual practices, our goal is
to provide readers with a deeper understanding of the human mind,
the power of mindfulness, and the transformative effects of spiritual
techniques on your well-being. Ultimately, our aim is to inspire
readers to undertake a journey of self-discovery, unlocking their true
potential, finding purpose in life, and embracing the wonders of
existence.

The voyage we're embarking on in this chapter will take us on an
enlightening journey through the inner workings of the human brain
and consciousness. We'll start with an engaging exploration of the
complex field of neuroscience, uncovering the brain's remarkable
adaptability and its influence on our thoughts and emotions.

Our exploration then delves into the realm of spirituality and
mindfulness, shedding light on the scientific foundations of these
ancient practices. You'll gain insights into how spiritual experiences

impact our mental and physical well-being, and discover how mindfulness techniques can ease stress, nurture inner peace, and heighten our awareness of the present moment.

As we progress on this journey, the profound significance of the gift of life will come into sharper focus. We'll delve into the deep meaning of something as simple yet profound as breath and its connection to the very essence of existence. We'll also explore the art of meditation, providing various methods to help you cultivate a heightened sense of self-awareness and spiritual growth.

During this expedition, we will seamlessly integrate scientific discoveries with practical exercises, encouraging you to apply your newly acquired knowledge and insights. Our aim is to encourage the cultivation of gratitude, compassion, and mindfulness, promoting personal development, enhancing your relationships, and rejuvenating your sense of purpose.

On this transformative journey, we encourage you to probe your consciousness, connect with your inner self, and unearth the boundless potential that lives within you. By the end of this journey, you will possess a comprehensive understanding of the human mind, a deeper appreciation for the invaluable gifts of life, and the motivation to continue your pursuit of wisdom and contentment.

"The Enlightened Quest" is an empowering journey that equips you with the tools to unlock the enigmas of your own existence, reigniting your appreciation for the beauty of life and nurturing the seeds of personal transformation that will continue to flourish long after you've turned the final page.

Exploring the Fundamental Questions of Human Existence: Identity, Free Will, and the Quest for Truth

The fundamental questions of human existence have captivated thinkers, philosophers, and seekers throughout history. During this exploration, we break down these questions, offering insights and reflections:

- **Who Are We**? This question delves into human identity and existence. Biologically, we are Homo sapiens, a species with advanced cognitive abilities. Psychologically, we are individuals with unique personalities, thoughts, and emotions. From a spiritual or philosophical perspective, answers vary widely, encompassing beliefs about humans as spiritual beings or complex biological entities.
- **Free Will:** Are We Born with It? The complexity of free will is debated by philosophers. Some argue that it's an illusion, as our decisions may be influenced by unconscious processes or external forces. Others contend that while constraints exist, humans possess free will, allowing them to make meaningful choices.
- **The Role of Critical Thinking:** Critical thinking is highly encouraged in the modern age. It involves questioning, analyzing, and evaluating information and beliefs rather than accepting them blindly. With abundant information available, individuals can explore various perspectives, challenge traditional beliefs, and seek evidence-based knowledge.
- **Seeking the Truth:** Pursuing truth involves rational inquiry, evidence-based reasoning, and a willingness to revise beliefs based on new information. It encourages open-minded exploration of identity, purpose, and belief.
- **Finding Your Path:** The path to deeper understanding and self-realization is personal. It may involve self-reflection, exploration, education, and dialogue with others who offer diverse perspectives. Embracing your unique journey fosters a more profound sense of identity and purpose.

In conclusion, the questions of human identity and free will are profound and complex, lacking definitive answers. Embracing the quest for knowledge, critical thinking, and open-minded exploration can help individuals navigate these questions and find their own paths to understanding and self-realization.

Chapter 2

Unveiling the Human Brain

Delving into the intricacies of the human brain and its role in our journey

This part of the book is all about taking a good look at our brain, which is like a supercomputer. We want to figure out how it's built and how it works so we can understand how we think and feel. It's like opening the door to a cool subject called neuroscience, where we learn about the brain. Get ready to dive into the fascinating world of our awesome brain and discover its hidden secrets!

The human brain is an amazing organ that controls all our actions, thoughts, and emotions. It is a highly intelligent biological machine that handles lots of information and various bodily functions. Here's a simple way to understand how the brain works:

Neurons and Communication

The brain comprises billions of nerve cells called neurons. These neurons communicate with each other through electrical and chemical signals. When a neuron is activated, it sends an electrical signal down its long, slender projection called an axon. At the end of the axon, there is **a small gap called a synapse**, where the signal is transmitted to another neuron using chemical messengers called neurotransmitters.

Information Processing

Neurons work together in vast networks, forming circuits and pathways. *When you see, hear, smell, taste, or touch something, sensory information is sent to specific areas of the brain responsible for processing that sense.*

Brain Regions and Functions

Different regions of the brain have specific functions. For example:

- **The frontal lobes engage** *in decision-making, planning, and personality.*
- **The parietal lobes process** sensory information like touch and knowing where things are around us.
- **The occipital lobes manage** vision.
- **The temporal lobes manage** hearing and memory.

Memory and Learning

The brain has an incredible capacity for memory and learning. *As you experience new things, your brain creates and strengthens connections between neurons. This process, known as synaptic plasticity, allows you to learn and remember information.*

Motor Control

When you want to do something, like walk or pick something up, your brain sends messages to your muscles through your spinal cord and nerves to make sure all the right movements happen.

Emotions and Feelings

The brain's limbic system plays a crucial role in emotions and feelings. It includes structures like the amygdala (associated with fear and emotional responses) and the hippocampus (involved in memory and emotions).

Thinking

Higher-order cognitive functions, such as problem-solving, reasoning, and critical thinking, are managed by the cerebral cortex—the outer layer of the brain responsible for complex thoughts.

Consciousness

The brain's ability to be aware of ourselves and our surroundings is known as consciousness. Scientists are still studying this profound aspect of brain function.

Overall, the human brain works as a highly coordinated network of neurons and brain regions, processing information, regulating bodily functions, and giving rise to our thoughts, emotions, and behaviors. It's an endlessly fascinating organ and understanding how it functions can help us appreciate the wonders of the human mind and the complexity of our existence.

Decoding Neuroscience: Multidisciplinary Brain Exploration

Neuroscience encompasses a multidisciplinary realm, blending biology, anatomy, physiology, psychology, physics, and other scientific disciplines to delve into the workings of the nervous system, particularly the intricate complexities of the brain. The subsequent overview sheds light on the mechanics of neuroscience and its pivotal methodologies.

1. **Research Strategies**: Neuroscientists deploy a spectrum of research techniques to explore the nervous system's intricacies, spanning from individual neurons to intricate cerebral networks.

2. **Imaging Techniques**: Tools such as Functional Magnetic Resonance Imaging (fMRI) and Positron Emission Tomography (PET) scans in neuroscience help us see what the brain is doing and map out which parts of the brain are linked to different jobs.

3. **Electrophysiology**: By recording neuronal electrical activity, techniques like Electroencephalogram (EEG) and single-cell recordings unveil patterns within brain dynamics.

4. **Optogenetics**: Using altered neurons sensitive to light, scientists examine neural pathways and control brain functions.

5. **Neuropsychology**: Understanding brain function involves studying how brain injuries or diseases affect behavior and thinking.

6. **Analytical Levels**: Neuroscience works with different layers of analysis to reveal the intricate aspects of the brain.

7. **Molecular and Cellular Level:** This is about understanding the tiny parts of brain cells and how they talk to each other.

8. **Synaptic and Neural Circuit Level:** This means looking at how brain cells communicate through connections and figuring out the complicated paths they create.

9. **Systems Level:** Here, we study how groups of brain cells work together to help us do things like see, move, and remember.

10. **Behavioral and Cognitive Level:** This is about studying how our thoughts, feelings, and actions come from what's happening in our brains.

11. **Interdisciplinary Collaborations:** Scientists from different fields, like psychology, biology, and math, work together to solve tricky brain questions.

12. **Neuroplasticity:** This is the idea that our brains can change and learn new things at any age. It's important for memory and healing after brain injuries.

13. **Computational Modeling:** Scientists use computer programs to mimic and understand how our brains create different behaviors and functions.

14. **Clinical Implications:** All this brain research helps us understand and treat brain and mental health issues like Alzheimer's, Parkinson's, and depression.

In summary, neuroscience harnesses an amalgam of research methodologies, interdisciplinary synergy, and systematic exploration across diverse levels of nervous system analysis. This concerted approach unravels the enigma of the brain's structure, function, and its influence on human behavior, cognition, and well-being.

The Brain-Computer Analogy: Unveiling Cognitive Similarities

The human brain is an amazing and complex organ that's really good at handling a lot of information quickly. Even though it's different from computers because it's a living thing, we can compare it to computers to understand how it processes information.:

1. **Neural Networks and Circuits:** The brain is like a big web of connected cells that talk to each other. This helps it share and work with information, kind of like how computers have their own connected parts.

2. **Information Processing:** The brain gets information from our senses, like what we see and hear. It looks for patterns, changes, and reacts to things. Computers also get information, use rules to work with it, and give answers.

3. **Parallel Processing:** The brain is good at doing lots of things at once. Different parts work together to handle different kinds of information. Computers also do this by breaking tasks into smaller pieces and working on them at the same time.

4. **Learning and adaptation:** Our brains can learn from what happens and adapt to new situations. They do this by changing how they work. Computers can also learn and change their behavior based on what they're told.

5. **Memory Storage:** The brain stores different types of memories, like short-term and long-term. Computers use things like hard drives to store all kinds of data.

6. **Pattern Recognition:** The brain and computers are both good at recognizing patterns. The brain does this for things like recognizing faces and understanding language. Computers do it with things like pictures and speech.

7. **Speed and efficiency:** Our brain cells send messages very fast, but computers are quicker in terms of raw speed. Our brain is efficient because it can do many things at once, while computers are fast because they're very powerful.

8. **Hierarchical Organization:** The brain has different areas for different jobs. This is a bit like how computers have different parts that each do their own thing but work together.

It's important to understand that our brains are very different from computers. While they both handle information, our brains are special because they can think, feel emotions, and be creative. Our brains work kind of like advanced computers in how they process information, using networks, doing many things at once, learning, remembering, and recognizing patterns. But what makes our brains truly amazing is that they're alive and can do things no computer can do.

The Interplay of Cosmic Energy and Neuronal Communication: A Comparative Exploration

The universe, often referred to as the Absolute, is described as a vast reservoir of Energy in constant motion and vibration. Similarly, in neuroscience, the human body contains billions and trillions of neurons, which are like energy particles, communicating with each other through intricate electrical, magnetic, and chemical signals.

Just as these energy particles in the universe communicate with known and possibly unknown systems, neurons in our body transmit signals to other neurons and various systems within our body.

The constant vibration and communication of these energy particles sustain the functioning of our body and everything in the universe. When we inhale, we draw in this life-giving energy, which rejuvenates us and empowers our bodily functions.

It's interesting because there are similarities between how we breathe and how brain cells (neurons) work. When we finish breathing in, there's a little pause, and during that pause, things happen inside our bodies. In neuroscience, which is the study of the brain, neurons also take short breaks between sending messages.

When brain cells send messages to each other it does so in multiple impulses and takes a little break in between each impulse. Much like sending messages between brain cells, when we breath we also pause in between each inhalation and exhalation. During this pause, the energy within us, just as in the universe, seems to connect with a broader life force.

To put it simply, the way energy flows in the universe, which we might call cosmic energy, has a pattern where it moves and then takes a little break. Similarly, in the study of brain cells (neurons), they also have a pattern of sending energy and then taking a pause. These similarities between the really big (macrocosm) and the very small (microcosm) show us how everything in the world is connected. It gives us interesting things to think about and study.

Self-Love and its Neurological Correlations

Neurological quantum science explores the intricate relationship between the brain's neurological processes and the fundamental principles of quantum physics. In *"love thyself,"* this connection emphasizes the profound impact of self-love on our neurological functioning and overall well-being.

In neurological quantum science, it's understood that our thoughts and emotions are intricately linked to the brain's neural pathways and electromagnetic fields. When we practice self-love, our brain's neural networks respond by releasing neurotransmitters (aka messangers) and neuropeptides (aka regulators) associated with positive emotions. This not only influences our mental state but also affects our physical health, immune system, and overall vitality.

The quantum aspect comes into play through the principle of interconnectedness. Quantum physics suggests that all matter is interconnected through a field of energy, which implies that our thoughts and emotions have a ripple effect not only within our own neural network but also in the broader quantum field.

By cultivating self-love, we create a positive feedback loop in our neurological and quantum systems. This leads to a state of coherence, where our thoughts, emotions, and physiological responses are aligned and harmonious. As a result, practicing self-love not only improves our mental and emotional well-being but also influences the quantum field around us, potentially contributing to a more positive and harmonious reality.

In summary, the connection between neurological quantum science and "love thyself" underscores the profound influence of self-love on our brain's neurological processes and its potential to create positive effects at both the individual and collective quantum levels.

Exploring the Interconnection: Self-Love, Neurological Quantum Science, and the Concept of God

Here's how these elements can be interconnected:

Self-Love

When we practice self-love, we acknowledge our inherent worthiness and embrace ourselves with compassion and acceptance. This act of self-love aligns with the idea that we are divine creations deserving of love and care. By loving ourselves, we recognize our connection to a greater source of love and life.

Neurological Quantum Science

This scientific approach acknowledges the deep interrelation between our thoughts, emotions, and the quantum field. When we cultivate positive emotions like self-love, our brain's neural networks respond by creating harmonious patterns of neural activity. This coherence resonates with the concept of alignment and harmony found in spiritual and religious teachings.

Connection to God

Many spiritual traditions teach we are all interconnected with a higher power or divine source. In this context, the practice of self-love can be seen as a way of honoring the divine within us. By loving ourselves, we align with the inherent love and wisdom of the divine. Neurological Quantum Science adds a scientific perspective by suggesting that our positive intentions and emotions contribute to the interconnectedness of all things, which aligns with spiritual concepts of divine unity.

The connection between self-love, Neurological Quantum Science, and the concept of God illustrates how various aspects of our understanding—scientific, spiritual, and personal—can come together. By practicing self-love and recognizing our connection to a larger whole, we create a bridge between our own well-being, the scientific exploration of consciousness, and our spiritual relationship with a higher power or divine presence.

Seeking the Kingdom Realistically

Jesus said, "Rather, Kingdom is inside of you, and it is outside of you. When you come to know yourselves, then you will become known, and you realize it is you who you are, the son of the living father. It's a state of consciousness where you experience the divine within and around you. ***"When the consciousness principle is realized, one finds the individual consciousness and cosmic consciousness is one."***

The verse from the Bible that contains the statement "I and my Father are one" is found in the New Testament, specifically in the Gospel of John. The verse is John 10:30 (John 10:30, ESV).

Unity and Oneness

The statement highlights the idea of unity and oneness. In consciousness, there are philosophical and spiritual traditions that emphasize the interconnectedness of all beings and the idea that, at a fundamental level, everything is one. This concept aligns with the idea of oneness in spiritual consciousness, where individual identities can be transcended to recognize a shared essence or universal consciousness.

Transcendence of the Self

Many spiritual practices and paths emphasize transcending the ego or the individual self to connect with a higher or universal consciousness. Jesus' statement can be seen as an expression of transcending the personal self to unite with the divine. In consciousness studies, this relates to experiences of self-transcendence and expanded states of awareness.

In the statement "I and my Father are one" from the Bible (John 10:30), interpreting "I" and "my Father" can vary depending on theological and philosophical perspectives. In consciousness and spirituality, these terms can be understood in various ways:

"I" Represents the Individual Self or Ego:

In consciousness, "I" can represent the individual self or ego—the sense of personal identity, self-awareness, and individual consciousness. This is the self that experiences thoughts, emotions, and perceptions in everyday life.

"My Father" Represents the Divine or Higher Self:

"My Father" in this context can represent the divine or higher self, which is often seen as a transcendent aspect of consciousness. It is the aspect of self that connects with or realizes its oneness with a higher or universal consciousness, often associated with God or a divine source.

When interpreted in terms of consciousness and spirituality, "I" represents the personal, egoic self with its individual thoughts, desires, and perceptions.

"My Father" represents the transcendent or higher self, which is often associated with a deeper, more universal awareness or consciousness.

The statement can be seen as an affirmation of the unity or oneness between the individual self (ego) and the higher or divine self (universal consciousness). It suggests that, in a state of spiritual realization or awakening, there is a recognition of the inherent unity between the personal self and the higher self, leading to a profound sense of oneness and connectedness with the divine or universal consciousness.

This interpretation aligns with spiritual and mystical experiences where individuals report a profound sense of unity and interconnectedness with all of existence, transcending the boundaries of the individual egoic self. It's important to note that interpretations of this statement can vary among different religious traditions and spiritual schools of thought.

The statement "I and My Father are one" from the Bible and the phrases "I am God," "I am Shiva," "I am Buddha," and "Aham Brahmasmi" from various spiritual traditions share some common themes related to spiritual realization, oneness, and the recognition of a deeper, universal consciousness. While the language and cultural context differ among these phrases, they convey similar spiritual and philosophical ideas.

While the language and cultural expressions differ, the underlying spiritual insight is similar—that of recognizing the unity of the self with a greater reality. These phrases are expressions of profound spiritual experiences and realizations and convey the idea that we can transcend our limited identities and recognize our connection with the divine or the ultimate source of existence.

In conclusion, this chapter delves into the intricacies of the human brain, unveiling the wonders of neuroscience. It explores how our brain, much like a supercomputer, manages our thoughts, feelings, and behaviors. This intricate system comprises billions of communicating neurons, networks, and distinct regions handling various tasks. From sensory processing to complex thinking, memory, emotions, and even consciousness, the brain's workings resemble a cosmic dance of energy, echoing the vibrancy of the universe. This knowledge not only fuels scientific questioning but also ties into broader spiritual ideas, like the connection between self-love, brain processes, and the concept of a universal consciousness. The merging of neuroscience with spirituality reflects the deep unity found in various religious teachings, suggesting that by delving into the depths of our minds, we uncover not just neurological complexities but also paths to understanding our link to the cosmos and a potential connection with a divine essence.

Chapter 3

The Mind-Body Connection

Exploring the profound relationship between mind and body

The **mind-body connection** refers to the interrelationship between our thoughts, emotions, beliefs, and attitudes (the mind) and our physical health and well-being (the body). It suggests that the state of our mental and emotional health can have a significant impact on our physical health, and vice versa. Our thoughts and feelings can influence our physical condition, and the state of our body can affect our mental and emotional state.

Here are some aspects of the mind-body connection:

- **Stress and Physical Health**: When we experience stress, anxiety, or negative emotions, our body can respond with physical symptoms like tense muscles, headaches, digestive issues, and even weakened immune function.

- **Placebo Effect**: The placebo effect is a well-known example of the mind-body connection. When people believe they are receiving a treatment (even if it's a placebo with no active ingredients, for example, a sugar pill), their belief in the treatment's effectiveness can lead to actual improvements in their condition.
- **Mind's Influence on Healing**: Positive thoughts, optimism, and a hopeful mindset can contribute to faster recovery from illnesses and injuries, as well as better outcomes in medical treatments.
- **Psychosomatic Illness**: Certain medical conditions can be influenced or aggravated by psychological factors. For example, chronic stress or emotional distress might exacerbate conditions like irritable bowel syndrome or tension headaches.
- **Mental Health Impact on Physical Health**: Mental health disorders like depression and anxiety can have profound effects on physical health, leading to issues like insomnia, appetite changes, and even cardiovascular problems.
- **Mindfulness and Pain Management**: Mindfulness practices are effective in managing chronic pain conditions, as individuals learn to cope with pain by changing their perception and response to it. Emotional Release and Physical Well-being: Expressing emotions healthily can positively affect physical health, as repressed emotions can sometimes manifest in physical symptoms.

Recognizing and understanding the mind-body connection allows us to appreciate the holistic nature of health and well-being. It emphasizes the importance of addressing both mental and physical aspects of health to achieve overall wellness. Practices like meditation, yoga, and relaxation techniques can help foster a stronger mind-body connection, leading to improved overall health and a better quality of life.

Improving the mind-body connection involves enhancing communication and synergy between your mental and physical well-being. A strong mind-body connection can lead to better overall health, reduced stress, improved emotional well-being, and enhanced self-awareness. Here are some ways to enhance and cultivate this connection:

- **Mindful Awareness and meditation**: These activities help you pay better attention to your thoughts, feelings, and how your body feels. Mindfulness lets you notice what your body is telling you and respond in a thoughtful way.
- **Regular Physical Activity**: Engage in regular exercise or physical activity that you enjoy. Exercise releases endorphins, which are neurotransmitters that contribute to a positive mood and mental well-being. Pay attention to how your body feels during and after exercise.
- **Deep Breathing and Relaxation Techniques**: Practice deep breathing exercises, progressive muscle relaxation, or other relaxation techniques. These methods can help reduce stress, lower blood pressure, and promote a sense of calm.
- **Healthy Nutrition**: Eat a balanced diet rich in nutrients. Nutrient-dense foods can have positive effects on your brain function and mood. Avoid excessive caffeine, sugary foods, and highly processed meals, as they can negatively affect mental clarity and energy levels.
- **Adequate Sleep**: Prioritize good sleep hygiene to ensure you get enough restorative sleep. Sleep is crucial for cognitive function, emotional stability, and overall

well-being.

- **Positive Self-Talk**: Cultivate a positive inner dialogue. Pay attention to your thoughts and replace negative self-talk with affirming and constructive statements.
- **Mindful Eating**: Eat mindfully, paying attention to the taste, texture, and smell of your food. This practice encourages you to be present during meals and can help regulate eating habits.
- **Journaling**: Keep a journal to express your thoughts, feelings, and experiences. Journaling can provide insights into your emotions and promote self-reflection.
- **Body Scans**: Practice body scans, where you concentrate your thoughts on different parts of your body and notice how they feel. This practice promotes body awareness and relaxation.
- **Yoga and Tai Chi:** Engage in practices like yoga or Tai Chi, which combine physical movement with mindfulness and breath awareness. These practices promote flexibility, balance, and a sense of tranquility.
- **Seek Professional Guidance**: If you're struggling with mental health issues, consider seeking guidance from a mental health professional. Therapists can help you explore the mind-body connection and develop strategies for improved well-being.
- **Social Connections**: Maintain healthy relationships and engage in meaningful social interactions. Positive social interactions can have a significant impact on mental and emotional health.

Remember that improving the mind-body connection is a gradual process that requires consistent effort. Different practices may resonate more with you than with others, so it's important to explore and find what works best for your individual needs and preferences.

In the next chapter, we'll dive into the Sanskrit concept of the seven-chakra system, which is an integral part of Indian (Bharatia) spiritual and philosophical traditions, especially within Yoga and Tantra. This system is seen as a way to understand the energy centers in the human body that link to specific functions in our nerves and glands. While it has been used historically for spiritual growth, it's now being explored for its potential benefits in modern health and wellness. In this upcoming chapter, we will give you a detailed look at the chakra system, its connections, and what modern science has to say about its possible advantages.

Chapter 4

Ancient Wisdom

Exploring the Integration of the "Seven Chakra System" into Modern Western Health

The seven-chakra system is called the "**Seven Energy Centers**" or "**Seven Energy Wheels**" in English. This system is a concept derived from various spiritual and esoteric traditions, particularly within Hinduism and certain branches of yoga and meditation, where the body is believed to contain seven major energy centers that correspond to different aspects of physical, emotional, and spiritual well-being. Each of these centers is associated with specific qualities and attributes.

1. Muladhara (Root Chakra)

- **Location**: Base of the spine
- **Neurophysiological Association:** Connected to the coccygeal plexus and the adrenal glands.

- **Endocrine Association**: Adrenal glands produce stress-related hormones like cortisol and adrenaline.
- **Modern Relevance:** Imbalances in this chakra might contribute to issues related to stability, survival, and stress. Techniques to balance this chakra might help manage stress-related disorders and promote a sense of security.

2. Svadhisthana (Sacral Chakra)

- **Location**: Lower abdomen, below the navel
- **Neurophysiological Association:** Connected to the sacral nerves and reproductive system.
- **Endocrine Association:** Influences the gonads (ovaries and testes)
- **Modern Relevance:** Balancing this chakra may aid in addressing issues related to sexuality, creativity, and emotional expression. It might play a role in addressing reproductive health and emotional well-being.

3. Manipura (Solar Plexus Chakra)

- **Location**: Upper abdomen, near the stomach
- **Neurophysiological Association:** Associated with the solar plexus, digestive system, and sympathetic nervous system.
- **Endocrine Association:** Linked to the pancreas and adrenal glands.
- **Modern Relevance**: Balancing this chakra might contribute to better digestion, stress management, and self-confidence. Techniques targeting this chakra might help with digestive disorders and stress-related illnesses.

4. Anahata (Heart Chakra)

- **Location**: Center of the chest
- **Neurophysiological Association:** Associated with the cardiac plexus and heart.
- **Endocrine Association:** Thought to influence the thymus gland.
- **Modern Relevance:** Balancing this chakra may affect emotional well-being, compassion, and heart health. Techniques targeting this chakra might aid in managing emotional disorders and promoting cardiovascular **health.**

5. Vasudha (Throat Chakra)

- **Location**: Throat region
- **Neurophysiological Association:** Connected to the cervical plexus and the throat.
- **Endocrine Association**: Linked to the thyroid gland.
- **Modern Relevance:** Balancing this chakra might influence communication, self-expression, and thyroid health. Techniques targeting this chakra might help address thyroid-related issues and improve communication skills.

6. Ajna (Third Eye Chakra)

- **Location**: Between the eyebrows
- **Neurophysiological Association:** Associated with the pineal gland and the hypothalamus.

- **Endocrine Association:** Influences the pituitary gland, often referred to as the "master gland" that regulates other endocrine glands.
- **Modern Relevance:** Balancing this chakra may affect intuition, perception, and hormonal regulation. Techniques targeting this chakra might play a role in managing hormonal imbalances and promoting mental clarity.

7. Sahasrara (Crown Chakra)

- **Location**: Top of the head
- **Neurophysiological Association**: Associated with the cerebral cortex and the central nervous system.
- **Endocrine Association:** Not directly associated with a specific gland but thought to influence the overall endocrine system.
- **Modern Relevance:** Balancing this chakra might relate to spiritual connection, higher consciousness, and overall well-being. Techniques targeting this chakra might contribute to stress reduction, mental clarity, and spiritual growth.

Connection to Modern Illness and Wellness: While there is limited scientific evidence directly linking the chakra system to modern illness and wellness, there is growing interest in exploring the potential connections. *Many proponents of alternative and holistic medicine suggest that imbalances in the chakras might manifest as physical, emotional, or psychological issues.* Balancing these energy centers through practices like meditation, yoga, and energy healing techniques could promote overall well-being by addressing potential underlying causes.

The number seven holds significant mystical and symbolic importance in the Bible.

It is frequently used throughout the Scriptures to convey various spiritual and symbolic meanings. Here are some key aspects of the significance of the number seven in the Bible and where it is used:

- **Completeness and Perfection:** Seven is often associated with completeness and perfection. In the biblical narrative of creation, God rested on the seventh day, signifying the completion and perfection of His work (Genesis 2:2-3).
- **Covenant and Promise:** Seven is used to represent divine covenants and promises. For example, in the Abrahamic tradition, circumcision was to be performed on the eighth day, indicating a connection with the perfection of the covenant (Genesis 17:12).
- **Days of Creation:** The first chapter of Genesis describes the creation of the world in seven days, with each day representing a different aspect of creation. This structure highlights the idea of divine order and completeness in creation.
- **Seven Churches:** In the Book of Revelation, *there are seven letters written to seven churches*, each with its commendations and admonitions. This symbolism signifies the complete message to the entire Church (Revelation 2-3).
- **Seven Seals, Trumpets, and Bowls:** In the Book of Revelation, seven seals, seven trumpets, and seven bowls are described as part of the events leading to the end times. These series of sevens indicate a sequence of divine judgments and events that culminate in the fulfillment of God's plan.

- **Feasts and Festivals:** The Jewish calendar includes
  several feasts and festivals with seven-day durations, such
  as the Feast of Tabernacles (Sukkot). These observances
  are rooted in the biblical significance of the number seven
  and serve as reminders of God's provision and
  faithfulness.
- **Sabbath**: The seventh day of the week, Saturday, is
  observed as the Sabbath in the Jewish tradition. It is a day
  of rest and worship, emphasizing the idea of spiritual
  completeness and renewal.
- **Seven Spirits of God**: In the Book of Revelation,
  there is mention of the seven spirits of God, symbolizing
  the fullness of the Holy Spirit's presence and attributes
  (Revelation 1:4; 4:5; 5:6).
- **Seven Miracles and Parables:** Throughout the
  Gospels, Jesus performed seven miracles on the Sabbath,
  emphasizing the divine nature of His ministry.
  Additionally, there are seven parables in the Gospel of
  Matthew, often referred to as the "Kingdom Parables,"
  conveying spiritual truths about the reign of God.

Metaphorical Connection Between "Many Mansions" and the Seven Chakras

The statement from John 14;2, "In my father's house are many
mansions," could be connected to the Indian seven chakra or seven
energy systems in a symbolic and metaphorical way. The seven
chakras, often referred to as "wheels" or "energy centers," are integral
to various Indian spiritual and yoga traditions.

Here's a way to make a symbolic connection:

- **The Many Mansions:** In John 14:2, the phrase "In
  my father's house are many mansions" suggests a place of

abundance and diversity in the afterlife. Each mansion can be seen as a unique space or state of being.

- **The Seven Chakras:** In Indian spiritual philosophy, the seven chakras are vital energy centers within the body. They represent different aspects of human consciousness and well-being, from the more physical and instinctual at the base (Root Chakra) to the more spiritual and transcendent at the crown (Crown Chakra).
- **Symbolic Connection:** You can draw a symbolic parallel by viewing each chakra as a kind of "mansion" space within your spiritual and energetic self. Each chakra represents a different dimension of your inner world and can be seen as a unique mansion within your own being.

For example:

- **Root Chakra:** This can be seen as the foundational mansion, representing your connection to the physical world and survival instincts.
- **Heart Chakra:** It might be considered the mansion of love and compassion, symbolizing your emotional and interpersonal capacities.
- **Crown Chakra:** This is the mansion of spiritual connection and enlightenment, symbolizing your connection to the divine.

In this interpretation, the "Father's house" is not just a place in the afterlife but is within you, representing the richness and diversity of your inner spiritual landscape. Each chakra is a unique mansion of consciousness within your spiritual self, waiting to be explored and harmonized.

This connection is metaphorical, bridging Christian and Indian spiritual concepts, highlighting the richness and diversity of inner spiritual experiences and journeys.

In summary, the number seven in the Bible is a symbol of completeness, perfection, and divine order. It is used in various contexts to convey spiritual and symbolic meanings, and its recurrence throughout the Scriptures underscores its significance in the biblical narrative.

Chapter 5

The Significance of the Prayer Hands Position

Exploring Its Meaning in Prayer

Keeping the Prayer Hands gesture (known as in Sanskrit Anjali Mudra) near the heart chakra (Anahata chakra) holds deep significance in various spiritual and cultural traditions. The heart chakra, known as "Anahata," in Sanskrit, is associated with love, compassion, emotional balance, and connection to oneself and others. Placing the hands in this position during prayer enhances the symbolism and impact of the gesture. Let's explore the significance of keeping the Prayer Hands near the heart chakra:

1. **Connection to Emotions:** The heart chakra is considered the center of emotions and love. Placing the prayer hands near the heart chakra during prayer signifies a deep emotional connection to the divine, others, and oneself. It symbolizes the intention to open one's heart and connect on a profound level, allowing for a more heartfelt prayer experience.

2. **Compassion and empathy**: The heart chakra is associated with compassion and empathy. When the Prayer Hands are near the heart center, it reinforces the idea of approaching prayer with a compassionate and empathetic mindset. It encourages us to cultivate understanding and kindness, both towards ourselves and others, as we engage in prayer.

3. **Self-Reflection and Self-Love:** Placing the hands near the heart chakra encourages self-reflection and self-love. It reminds us to turn inward, acknowledge our own emotions, and embrace our true selves. This gesture encourages a sense of self-acceptance and a desire to nurture our emotional well-being.

4. **Unity and Harmony:** The heart chakra is associated with unity and harmony, symbolizing the interconnectedness of all beings. By bringing our hands close to the heart center, we acknowledge our connection to the larger human family, nature, and the universe. This gesture promotes a sense of unity and oneness.

5. **Spiritual Devotion**: Keeping the Prayer Hands near the heart chakra signifies a deep devotion and reverence for the divine or higher power. It reflects a genuine intention to connect spiritually and cultivate a sincere relationship with the sacred.

6. **Balance and Healing:** The heart chakra is believed to be a point of balance between the physical and spiritual realms. Placing the hands near this chakra can help harmonize and balance energies within the body, promoting emotional healing and well-being.

7. **Activation of Energy**: In yogic philosophy, the heart chakra is associated with the flow of energy and prana (life force). Bringing the hands near the heart chakra is thought to activate this energy center, allowing for a more vibrant and powerful connection during prayer.

Incorporating the Prayer Hands gesture near the heart chakra adds a layer of intention and symbolism to the act of prayer. It amplifies the emotional and spiritual aspects of the practice, fostering a deeper connection to oneself, others, and the divine. This gesture encourages an authentic and heartfelt engagement with prayer, aligning with the themes of love, compassion, and unity associated with the heart chakra.

Namaskar: The Art of Greetings, Salutation, or Hello

The Indian (Bharatia) word "Namaskar" is a beautiful and deeply meaningful gesture that carries a rich symbolism. When someone brings the palms of their hands together in front of their heart center and says "Namaskar," they are engaging in a traditional Indian greeting or salutation. Here's a detailed explanation of the term and its significance:

- **Physical Gesture:** The physical aspect of "Namaskar" involves joining the palms of the hands together with fingers pointing upward. This hand gesture is known as "anjali mudra." The hands are typically placed in front of the chest, close to the heart center. This gesture is often accompanied by a slight bow or nod of the head.
- **Heart-Centered**: Placing the hands at the heart center signifies a deep respect and acknowledgment of the divine presence within oneself and the person you are greeting. It's a way of saying, "The divine in me recognizes and honors the divine in you."
- **Symbolism**: The word "Namaskar" itself carries significant meaning. It is derived from two Sanskrit

words: "Namah" and "kar." "Namah" means "I bow" or "I honor," and "kar" means "to do" or "to make." So, "Namaskar" can be interpreted as "I bow to you" or "I honor you."

- **Spiritual Connection**: Beyond a mere greeting, "Namaskar" embodies a spiritual connection. It reflects the Indian belief in the divinity present in all living beings. By using this gesture, individuals are not only acknowledging the external presence of others, but also recognizing the universal spirit that unites all of humanity.

- **Cultural Significance**: "Namaskar" is deeply ingrained in Indian culture and is a common way of showing respect, gratitude, or reverence. It is used in various contexts, from everyday interactions to religious ceremonies and yoga practices.

- **Yoga and Meditation**: In yoga and meditation, "Namaskar" is often incorporated into the practice as a way of centering oneself, showing respect to the practice, and connecting with a sense of inner peace and spirituality. Practices like "Namaste Yoga" or "Namaskar Meditation" use this gesture to cultivate mindfulness and awareness.

- **Universal Message**: While "Namaskar" is rooted in Indian culture and spirituality, its message of recognizing the divine in others and showing respect is universal. Many cultures around the world have similar gestures and greetings that convey similar sentiments of acknowledgment, respect, and unity.

In summary, "Namaskar" is much more than a simple greeting; it is a profound and heartfelt gesture that embodies the essence of Indian culture and spirituality. It encourages individuals to recognize the divinity within themselves and others, fostering a sense of connection, respect, and unity in a world where such qualities are deeply valued.

Chapter 6

Unlocking the Mind-Body Connection in Prayer Hands

Gesture, Seal or Mark

Both the **"Prayer Hands"** gesture and the **"Hakini Mudra,"** recognized as a "Gesture of Power," hold profound cultural significance and symbolism across various cultures, particularly in Sanskrit traditions. In Sanskrit, the term "mudra" translates to "gesture," "seal," or "mark." Let's explore each of these gestures in depth:

- **"Hakini Mudra"** is a hand gesture employed in yoga and meditation. It involves the union of the fingertips of both hands, forming a bridge between the left and right brain hemispheres. This gesture is believed to heighten concentration, enhance memory, and promote mental clarity. Practitioners adopt this specific hand position to harmonize and balance the functions of the brain, cultivating a sense of unity and focus within the mind. It is thought to activate the energy associated with the sixth chakra, commonly

known as the "third eye," which is linked to intuition
and inner insight.

- **The "Prayer Hands Gesture,"** often referred to as
  "Anjali Mudra," is a symbolic hand gesture involving
  the joining of the palms at the center of the chest, with
  fingers pointing upwards and thumbs touching the
  sternum. This gesture is widely observed in various
  cultures and spiritual practices, including Hinduism,
  Buddhism, and Christianity. It is a simple yet potent
  gesture that symbolizes the unity of opposites, such as the
  individual self and higher consciousness. It is commonly
  used as a sign of respect, gratitude, and connection in
  diverse spiritual and cultural traditions, promoting inner
  harmony and equilibrium in practices like meditation,
  yoga, and prayer.

Meaning and Symbolism

- **Unity and Respect**: The act of bringing the palms
  together symbolizes the union of opposites, such as the
  individual self and the divine, or two individuals coming
  together in respect and unity.
- **Balance:** The gesture is thought to help balance the left
  and right hemispheres of the brain, fostering harmony
  between the analytical and intuitive aspects of the mind.
- **Gratitude and Humility:** Bringing the hands
  together is often used as a gesture of thankfulness and
  humility, acknowledging something greater than oneself.
- **Connection to the Heart:** The hands are brought to
  the heart center, representing a connection to one's inner
  self, emotions, and compassion.
- **Hakini Mudra:** "Hakini Mudra" is a specific hand
  gesture used in yoga and meditation. It is believed to

stimulate and balance the brain's hemispheres, promoting mental clarity and concentration. The word "Hakini" refers to the sixth chakra, also known as the "Ajna" or "Third Eye" chakra, which is associated with intuition and higher awareness.

The Technique

- **Position:** Sit in a comfortable posture for meditation or pranayama (breathing exercises).
- **Gesture:** Place both hands in front of you, at chest level. The fingertips of each hand touch their corresponding fingers on the opposite hand, forming a network of connections between the fingers.
- **Visualize:** As you hold the mudra, visualize energy flowing freely between the fingertips, creating a harmonious connection between the left and right sides of your brain.
- **Breathing:** As you focus on your breath, inhale deeply through your nose and exhale slowly through your mouth. Maintain the mudra throughout the practice.

Symbolism and Benefits

- **Brain Balance**: The Hakini Mudra is believed to enhance the coordination and communication between the brain's hemispheres, leading to improved mental clarity, focus, and memory.
- **Intuition and Insight**: This mudra is associated with the third eye chakra, which governs intuition, insight, and inner wisdom. Practicing the Hakini Mudra is said to stimulate this chakra and enhance one's connection to higher consciousness.

In conclusion, this chapter illuminates the profound meanings inherent in both the Prayer Hands gesture (Anjali Mudra) and the Hakini Mudra. These gestures are not simply physical postures; they carry spiritual and mental significance. The chapter underscores their capacity to symbolize and nurture a profound connection between the physical body, mind, and spirit. It ultimately highlights their integral role in various spiritual and wellness practices, emphasizing the intricate interconnectedness of these fundamental aspects of human existence.

Chapter 7

Exploring the Art of Mindfulness

T hroughout this book, we will delve into the concept of mindfulness, and to lay the foundation, we aim to introduce its fundamental principles early on. **Mindfulness** is the practice of being fully present in the moment without judgment. It involves paying attention to your thoughts, emotions, physical sensations, and surroundings without getting attached to them. You can cultivate mindfulness through practices like meditation, yoga, and various techniques.

Think of mindfulness as training your attention. It means focusing on the present moment, even if it's uncomfortable, and learning not to react impulsively to your thoughts and feelings. Mindfulness also encourages compassion by making you more aware of your own suffering and the suffering of others, fostering empathy.

The benefits of mindfulness are numerous. It reduces stress, anxiety, and depression, while enhancing sleep, focus, and concentration. It also improves relationships and overall well-being.

Practical Ways to Practice Mindfulness

Let's explore some practical ways to incorporate mindfulness into your daily life:

- **Pay Attention to Your Breath:** Find a comfortable spot, close your eyes, and take slow, deep breaths. Pay attention to the sensation of your breath entering and leaving your body.
- **Body Scan:** Sit or lie down comfortably, close your eyes, and start with your feet, gradually moving your attention up through your body, noticing sensations in each part.
- **Mindful Walking:** Practice mindfulness on the go. Pay attention to the feeling of your feet on the ground, your body's sensations, and the sights, sounds, and smells around you.
- **Mindful Eating:** Savor your food by paying attention to its taste, texture, and smell. Notice how your body feels as you eat.

There are many other ways to practice mindfulness, and we'll cover some in this book. The key is to find what works for you and stick with it.

The Art of Mindfulness: Exploring Its Influence on Perception

"**The Art of Mindfulness**" explores the concept of mindfulness and delves into various mindfulness practices, examining their profound effects on the brain and mental health. Let's take a deeper look at various aspects of mindfulness:

- **Understanding Mindfulness:** Mindfulness is being fully present without judgment. It means paying attention to thoughts, emotions, and sensations, fostering non-reactivity and compassion.
- **Mindfulness Meditation:** Learn about different meditation techniques and their potential benefits.
- **The Brain and Mindfulness:** Delve into the neuroscience behind mindfulness, how it affects brain structure and function.
- **Mindfulness and Emotional Regulation:** Discover how mindfulness reduces emotional reactivity and feelings of anxiety and depression.
- **Stress Reduction and Resilience:** Understand how mindfulness activates the body's relaxation response, counteracting chronic stress.
- **Enhancing Focus and Attention:** Explore how mindfulness improves focus and concentration.
- **Mindful Living:** Learn to practice mindfulness in daily life, including mindful eating, walking, and communication.
- **Cultivating Compassion:** Understand how mindfulness fosters empathy and enhances relationships.
- **Mindfulness-Based Interventions:** Discover mindfulness-based approaches to address mental health issues.
- **Mindfulness for Well-being:** Explore the overall well-being benefits of mindfulness.

Practical Tips for Mindful Exercise

- **Start with Intention:** Set clear intentions for your exercise session.

- **Mindful Breathing:** Begin with deep, conscious breathing to connect with the present moment.
- **Body Awareness:** Pay attention to your body's sensations as you move.
- **Sensory Engagement:** Fully engage your senses to stay in the present.
- **Stay Present:** Focus on the sensations and alignment of each movement.
- **Let Go of Distractions:** Gently guide your focus back to your exercise if your mind wanders.
- **Mindful Walking or Running:** Pay attention to the rhythm of your steps.
- **Body Scan:** After exercise, do a body scan to check for tension or relaxation.
- **Gratitude:** Be grateful for your body's ability to move.
- **Cool Down with Mindfulness:** Stay present during the cool-down.
- **Reflect:** After exercise, reflect on how you feel.
- **Consistency:** Make mindful exercise a routine.

Remember, mindful exercise is about being fully engaged in the present moment and cultivating a deeper connection between your mind and body. With time and practice, you'll find that mindful exercise enhances not only your physical well-being but also your mental and emotional health.

The Practice of Mindfulness

Mindfulness involves focused awareness and non-judgmental presence in the present moment.

How It Helps:

- **Stress Reduction:** Observe thoughts and feelings without immediate reactions, reducing stress.
- **Emotional Regulation:** Understand emotions without becoming overwhelmed, promoting emotional well-being.
- **Improved Focus:** Enhance the ability to focus on tasks.
- **Self-Awareness:** Deepen self-understanding.
- **Better Relationships:** Improve communication and empathy.
- **Reduced Rumination:** Break negative thought patterns.
- **Coping with Challenges:** Accept discomfort and challenges.
- **Enhanced Creativity:** Foster creativity and innovative thinking.
- **Better Decision-Making:** Make more deliberate decisions.
- **Quality of Life:** Increase gratitude and life satisfaction.
- **Mindful Eating:** Promote healthier eating habits.
- **Better Sleep:** Improve sleep quality.

Develop this skill through practices like meditation, breath awareness, and body scan, experiencing increased resilience and inner peace.

Conclusion

In conclusion, mastering the art of mindfulness provides a powerful tool for a happier and healthier life. Through regular practice, such as meditation, breath awareness, body scans, and mindful movement, this skill gradually develops. Even fleeting moments of mindfulness in your daily routine can profoundly impact your well-being. By integrating mindfulness into your life, you're likely to experience increased resilience, inner peace, and a more intentional and fulfilling existence. This exploration of mindfulness and its transformative effects on the brain and mental health equips you with valuable tools for enhanced awareness, resilience, and inner peace.

If you're interested in learning how to master laser-sharp focus and want to discover the proprietary Focus Method created by Dr. Shawn Christian, you can check out the Mastering Laser-Sharp Focus (Book & Course) out at https://confidenceiatry.com/product/mastering-laser-sharp-focus/.

As we conclude Part I, we embark on an exhilarating journey in Part II: "Unlocking the Secret Code." Brace yourself for a series of chapters that delve into enigmatic puzzles, each one echoing within the uncharted corridors of your mind. Get ready to uncover hidden truths and confront the mysteries that lie ahead. See you shortly in the next part.

Part Two

Unlocking the Secret Code

Ever pondered if there's a secret code woven into the very fabric of your consciousness? Dive into the intrigue of "Unlocking the Secret Code," where each chapter poses questions that echo in the unexplored chambers of your mind. Imagine a journey not just through pages, but through the uncharted recesses of your own understanding. From the subtle alchemy of breath and neurons to the transformative power of love, smiles, and kindness, this section acts as your guide to a world where symbols hold the keys to universal comprehension. If you're prepared to decode the concealed secrets that bind humanity and reveal the profound meaning intricately threaded into your life, the journey begins with a simple act—turn the page and let the exploration unfold.

Chapter 8

Exploring

The Sign of the Cross

Catholics make the sign of the cross while praying as a gesture of reverence and a reminder of their faith in the Holy Trinity (Father, Son, and Holy Spirit). Here's how it's typically done:

1. **Start with your right hand:** Begin by placing your right hand (fingers together) on your forehead, just above your eyebrows. This gesture is accompanied by the words, *"In the name of the Father."*
2. **Move down to your chest:** Bring your hand from your forehead down to your chest, touching it lightly. This is done while saying, *"And of the Son."*
3. **Move to the left shoulder:** From your chest, move your hand to your left shoulder. This movement is accompanied by the phrase, *"And of the Holy Spirit."*

4. **Move to the right shoulder:** Finally, bring your hand to your right shoulder while concluding with "*Amen.*"

The motion of the sign of the cross is typically done in a smooth, continuous manner, from the forehead to the chest and then from the left shoulder to the right shoulder. The sign of the cross is an important part of Catholic prayers and is often made at the beginning and end of prayers, during the Gospel reading at Mass, and in various other liturgical contexts as an expression of faith and devotion.

This religious ritual with spiritual significance has some indirect connections between religious practices and their potential benefits, including the Eastern Chakra system.

How The Sign of the Cross Connects to The Eastern Chakra System

Step 1: Touching the Forehead (Ajna Chakra)

With your Right Hand, touch your forehead, just above the eyebrows. As you do this, say, "In the name of the Father..."

- **Location:** The Ajna Chakra, often referred to as the "Third Eye," is at the forehead, slightly above and between the eyebrows.
- **Benefit:** In the Chakra system, the Ajna Chakra is associated with intuition, insight, and higher perception. Touching or focusing on this area is believed to stimulate these qualities. It is also associated with inner peace and clarity of thought.
- **Mystical Significance:** The act of touching or focusing on the Ajna Chakra is a way to awaken one's inner wisdom and intuition. It is often practiced during

meditation to enhance concentration and access deeper levels of awareness.

Step 2: Touching the Heart' of "Anahata chakra"

Move your right hand down and place it at the center of your chest, usually over the Heart. This represents the **"Touching the Heart," or "Anahata Chakra,"** in the Eastern Philosophy. This represents the heart and symbolizes the Son. While touching your heart say, "... and of the Son."

- **Location:** The Anahata Chakra is at the center of the chest, near the heart.
- **Benefit:** This Chakra is associated with love, compassion, and emotional well-being. Touching or meditating on this area is believed to open the heart to love, empathy, and self-acceptance. It can promote emotional healing and balance.
- **Mystical Significance**: Touching the Anahata Chakra is a way to connect with the divine love within and around us. It encourages feelings of unity, forgiveness, and unconditional love. It can be a powerful practice for cultivating compassion and healing emotional wounds.

Step 3: Touch the Left Shoulder, then Touch the Right Shoulder

Make the first part of the Cross by touching the left shoulder. As you do this, say, "... of the Holy spirit..."

Finally, to complete the cross, move the right hand and touch the right shoulder and conclude by saying "Amen." This step symbolizes the Holy Spirit and the unity of the Trinity.

- **Benefit**: This gesture, which resembles the Sign of the Cross in Christianity, is not directly related to the Chakra system but has its own significance. In some spiritual traditions, it symbolizes the union of opposites or the harmonizing of **dualities**, such as the divine and the earthly, or the masculine and feminine aspects of existence.
- **Mystical Significance**: The act of making the cross can be seen to invoke divine blessings and protection. It represents a connection with the sacred and a reminder of one's faith.

Step 4: Bring the Hands Together

Following the sign of the Cross, numerous Catholics join their hands in a reverent manner, commonly either folding them in prayer hand position or gently placing them against their chest. This symbolizes their receptivity to God's grace and their surrender to the Holy Trinity.

In Eastern mysticism and spiritual practices, the act of bringing the palms of the hands together, known as "palms together" or "anjali mudra," is often associated with specific rituals or gestures that carry symbolic significance. While the exact meaning can vary among different Eastern traditions, here are a few common interpretations:

- **Unity and Balance**: Palms together symbolize the coming together of opposites, such as the left and right sides of the body. This gesture represents the harmonization of duality, bringing balance and unity to the practitioner's mind, body, and spirit.

- **Respect and Greeting**: In many Eastern cultures, placing the palms together is a sign of respect and a traditional way to greet others. It signifies humility and the acknowledgment of the divine spark within each person, fostering a sense of equality and reverence.

- **Connection to the Divine**: Palms together can also be a way to connect with the divine, expressing devotion and surrender. In some practices, it is used as a form of prayer or meditation, with the hands brought to the heart or forehead to signify different levels of spiritual connection.

- **Sealing Intentions**: The gesture is often used to seal one's intentions, prayers, or affirmations. By bringing the palms together, practitioners can concentrate their thoughts and energies, focusing them on a specific purpose or intention.

- **Centering and Grounding**: Palms together can serve as a centering and grounding practice, helping individuals to anchor themselves in the present moment and find inner peace. It is commonly used in yoga and meditation to enhance concentration and mindfulness.

- **Balance of Masculine and Feminine Energies**: Some Eastern traditions associate the right hand (masculine) and left hand (feminine) with specific energies. Bringing the palms together can symbolize the union and balance of these energies within oneself.

- **Cultural Variations**: The specific meaning of the palms-together gesture can also vary among different Eastern cultures and belief systems. For example, in Hinduism, it is often associated with the "Namaste" greeting and is seen as a recognition of the divine in others.

Overall, the act of bringing the palms together is a versatile and powerful gesture in Eastern mysticism and spirituality. Its interpretation can be deeply personal and may carry different nuances depending on the context and tradition in which it is used.

The Principle of Unity and Compassion

Together with All, Development for All, Trust of All, and Efforts of All

The Indian saying "Sabka Saath, Sabka Vikas, Sabka Vishwas, and Sabka Prayas" can be translated into English as **"Together with All, Development for All, Trust of All, and Efforts of All."** This phrase emphasizes inclusivity, progress, trust, and collective efforts for the betterment of everyone in society. It emphasizes inclusive development and the idea of working together for the benefit of all.

While the Bible doesn't contain this exact phrase, there are teachings of Jesus and principles in the Bible that promote similar concepts of unity, compassion, and working for the well-being of all people. Here are a few examples:

- **Love Thy Neighbor**: In the Bible, Jesus teaches the importance of loving one's neighbor as oneself. This is often interpreted as a call for compassion and empathy towards others, regardless of their background or circumstances.

- **The Good Samaritan**: In the Parable of the Good Samaritan, Jesus tells a story about a compassionate Samaritan who helps a wounded man on the side of the road. This story illustrates the idea of helping others in need, regardless of their social or ethnic background.
- **Golden Rule**: The Bible contains **the "Golden Rule," which is a principle of treating others as you would like to be treated.** This concept aligns with working together for the common good.
- **Unity in the Body of Christ**: In the New Testament, there are teachings about the unity of believers in the body of Christ. Christians should work together in harmony, recognizing their interconnectedness.
- While the specific phrase **"Together with All, Development for All, Trust of All, and Efforts of All,"** is not found in the Bible, the principles of unity, compassion, and working for the well-being of all are consistent with some teachings and values found in Christian scripture. **It's important to note that interpretations of biblical teachings may vary among individuals and denominations**.

In summary, it is vital to underscore the significance of delving into the intricate relationship between the mind and body, particularly in the context of the topics explored in this section. By emphasizing the interconnectedness of various subjects, including neuroscience, meditation, breathing techniques, and spiritual practices, we gain a more profound insight into the reciprocal influence of the mind and body.

The Concept of Global Unity and the Promise of a Brighter Future

The concept of global unity and the promise of a brighter future can be found in various passages throughout the Bible, reflecting the idea that humanity is interconnected and has a shared destiny. Here are a few biblical verses and themes that convey this message:

> Matthew 7:12 (NIV): **"So in everything, do to others what you would have them do to you, for this sums up the Law and the Prophets."**

This verse is often referred to as the **"Golden Rule"** and is a fundamental principle of ethical behavior. It emphasizes **treating others as you would like to be treated**. This idea promotes kindness, empathy, and a sense of shared humanity.

> 1 John 4:7 (NIV): "Dear friends, <u>let us love one another, for love comes from God.</u> Everyone who loves has been born of God and knows God."

This verse is talks about **Brotherly Love.** The Bible encourages believers to love one another, not just within their own communities, but across borders and cultures.

> Isaiah 2:4 (NIV): "They will beat their swords into plowshares and their spears into pruning hooks. **The nation will not take up sword against nation, nor will they train for war anymore.**"

This verse is in reference to **Peace and Unity**. The Bible frequently speaks about the importance of peace and unity among nations and people. It envisions a world where conflicts cease, and people live in harmony. This idea represents one earth, one world, and one family.

> Revelation 21:4 (NIV): "He will wipe every tear from their eyes. There will be no more death or mourning or crying or pain, for the old order of things has passed away."

This verse is about **Hope for the Future.** Many passages in the Bible offer hope for a better future, where suffering and sorrow will be no more.

> Galatians 6:2 (NIV): "Carry each other's burdens, and in this way, you will fulfill the law of Christ."

This verse is about **Responsibility for One Another.** The Bible teaches that we have a responsibility to care for those in need, irrespective of their nationality or background.

These verses and themes from the Bible emphasize the importance of compassion, unity, and a shared vision for a better world. They encourage believers to work together for the well-being of all, promoting a sense of global community and shared responsibility.

The concept of global unity and the promise of a brighter future align with the mind-body connection by promoting positive mental states, reducing stress, and emphasizing the importance of social connections, empathy, and compassion—all of which contribute to overall well-being.

The term "**Christ**" holds both a mystical and modern meaning. In its mystical sense, it often refers to the concept of "**Christ Consciousness**," which signifies *an elevated state of spiritual awareness, unity with the divine, and a profound connection to the universal source of wisdom and love. This transcends regular human consciousness and points towards higher consciousness, including the realm of super consciousness.*

In modern times, "Christ" is predominantly associated with Jesus

Christ, the central figure of Christianity. However, even in this context, many individuals interpret it as a symbol of the highest human potential and a path to spiritual enlightenment. So, yes, there is a correlation between the term "Christ" and "Christ Consciousness," *representing the idea of ascending to a more profound level of awareness and understanding beyond the confines of ordinary human consciousness.*

The idea of religious figures, such as Krishna, Rama, Buddha, and Jesus, making statements like "I am God," "I am Buddha," "I am Shiva," or "**I and my father are one**," can be seen in their teachings and interpreting their followers. It's important to note that these statements have been subject to various interpretations and are deeply rooted in the religious and spiritual traditions in which these figures are revered.

- **Krishna:** In Hinduism, Lord Krishna is considered an incarnation of the divine. When Krishna states "I am God" or "I am the Supreme," it is often interpreted within the framework of Hindu philosophy, where the ultimate reality (Brahman) is believed to manifest in various forms, including divine incarnations like Krishna. The statement underscores the belief in the divine presence within him.

- **Rama:** Similarly, Lord Rama is revered as a divine incarnation in Hinduism. When Rama is described as "I am God" or "I am the Supreme," it reflects the belief in the divinity within him and his role as an exemplar of dharma (righteousness) and devotion.

- **Shiva:** "I am Shiva" is a statement often used in Hindu philosophy and spirituality. Shiva is one of the principal deities in Hinduism, representing the destroyer and transformer of the universe. Uttering "I am Shiva" can be a symbolic way of expressing a sense of oneness with the divine, suggesting that one sees themselves as a manifestation of the same universal energy and consciousness that Shiva represents. It can be a spiritual affirmation of one's connection to the divine and a reminder of the unity of all existence.

- **Buddha**: In Buddhism, Siddhartha Gautama, known as the Buddha, never claimed to be a God but claimed to be a fully awakened and enlightened being. His statements, such as "I am awake" or "I am the awakened one," emphasize his realization of enlightenment and his role as a teacher guiding others toward the path of awakening.
- **Jesus:** In Christianity, Jesus Christ is considered the Son of God and the Savior of humanity. His statement **"I am the way, the truth, and the life"** (John 14:6) reflects his central role in Christian theology. While Jesus' divinity is a core belief in Christianity, interpretations may vary regarding whether his statements should be taken metaphorically or literally. When the consciousness principle is realized, one finds the individual consciousness, and cosmic consciousness is one.

These remarkable individuals, including Christ, Krishna, Shiva, Rama, and Buddha, all emphasized universal values like love, kindness, goodness, and spiritual truth, despite their different backgrounds. They aimed to guide people toward better lives, happiness, and wisdom. Although their moral teachings exhibit similarities, these figures are distinct historical and religious figures with unique messages shaped by their cultural and spiritual contexts. Their enduring influence continues to inspire and guide followers within their respective faiths.

Exploring Deity Consciousness: Christ, Krishna, Shiva, Rama, Buddha, and More

Regarding the concept of "**Christ Consciousness**" and its correlation with these figures, it's important to understand that the term "Christ Consciousness" is not part of traditional Christian doctrine but is rather a concept associated with spiritual and New Age movements. **It signifies an elevated state of spiritual awareness and unity with the divine**, often inspired by the life and teachings of Jesus.

In the provided passage, the term "Christ Consciousness" is used to emphasize the idea of reaching a higher level of spiritual understanding, which can be found in various religious traditions. It suggests that individuals can aspire to attain a state of heightened consciousness and awareness akin to the spiritual figures mentioned.

The terms "Christ Consciousness," "Krishna Consciousness," "Rama Consciousness," "Shiva Consciousness," and "Buddha Consciousness" are often used in various spiritual and philosophical contexts to describe a state of elevated awareness, inner awakening, and spiritual realization that aligns with the teachings and example of these respective spiritual figures. While each term is associated with a specific religious or philosophical tradition, they share some common themes:

- **Christ Consciousness:** "Christ Consciousness" is a term used primarily within Christian mysticism and New Age spirituality. It refers to the state of awareness and spirituality that Jesus Christ exemplified. Those who seek Christ Consciousness aim to embody the qualities of love, compassion, forgiveness, and spiritual awakening that Jesus demonstrated in his life and teachings.
- **Krishna Consciousness:** "Krishna Consciousness" is central to the International Society for Krishna Consciousness (ISKCON), also known as the Hare

Krishna movement. It is the state of being aware of and devoted to Lord Krishna, considering him the Supreme Personality of Godhead. Practitioners of Krishna Consciousness seek to develop a deep and loving relationship with Krishna through devotion (bhakti) and the chanting of the Hare Krishna mantra.

- **Rama Consciousness:** "Rama Consciousness" is less commonly used compared to Krishna or Christ Consciousness. It refers to a state of spiritual awareness that aligns with Lord Rama's virtues, especially his adherence to dharma (duty) and righteousness. Practitioners may aim to cultivate qualities like courage, integrity, and devotion to dharma, as exemplified by Lord Rama.

- **Shiva Consciousness:** "I am Shiva" or "Shiva consciousness" refers to a spiritual concept rooted in Hinduism, particularly within the Shaivism tradition. It signifies the realization of one's essential identity with Shiva, who is one of the principal deities in Hinduism. Shiva is often regarded as the Supreme Being, representing aspects of creation, destruction, and transformation. Saying "I am Shiva" suggests the understanding that one's innermost self (Atman) is inseparable from the universal consciousness (Brahman), of which Shiva is a representation. This realization reflects a state of profound spiritual awakening and unity with the divine. It implies recognizing one's divine nature and transcending the ego, understanding that the individual self is interconnected with the greater cosmic consciousness embodied by Shiva. In essence, "I am Shiva" expresses the profound unity of the individual soul with the universal consciousness, signifying a state of enlightenment and self-realization in the context of Hindu spirituality and mysticism.

- **Buddha Consciousness:** "Buddha consciousness" is associated with Buddhism and refers to the state of awakening and enlightenment as realized by Siddhartha Gautama, the Buddha. It involves an awareness of the impermanence of all things, the nature of suffering, and the path to liberation from suffering through the Four Noble Truths and the Eightfold Path.

These terms are used to describe states of spiritual realization and awakening that align with the teachings and examples of these spiritual figures. They emphasize inner transformation, ethical conduct, and a deep connection with the divine or ultimate reality.

Regarding your comparison to "Higher Consciousness" or "Ultimate Cosmic Consciousness," these concepts typically transcend the specific religious and cultural contexts associated with figures like Christ, Krishna, Shiva, Rama, and Buddha. Higher consciousness often refers to a state of expanded awareness, spiritual insight, and connection to a greater, transcendent reality. It can be a goal in various spiritual traditions.

"Ultimate Cosmic Consciousness" suggests a universal or all-encompassing awareness of the interconnectedness of all existence and the ultimate source of creation. This concept can align with the idea of a divine or cosmic consciousness that underlies and sustains the entire universe, transcending individual religious traditions.

While Christ, Krishna, Shiva, Rama, and Buddha Consciousness are associated with specific spiritual traditions and figures, higher consciousness and ultimate cosmic consciousness are broader, trans-religious concepts that encompass a state of elevated awareness and connection with a deeper, universal reality.

In summary, the statements made by figures like Krishna, Shiva, Rama, Buddha, and Jesus about their divine nature are deeply rooted in their respective religious contexts and should be understood within those frameworks. The concept of "Christ Consciousness" is a more recent interpretation that seeks to capture the essence of spiritual enlightenment and unity with the divine across various traditions.

The Revelation of Truth: A Section on Understanding Its Power

Biblical teachings convey several aspects of truth and its significance, and they can indeed be connected to the mind-body connection.

- **Truth as freedom and healing:** In the Bible, truth is often associated with freedom and healing. When individuals are truthful with themselves and others, it can lead to a sense of inner peace and emotional well-being. The absence of deception or falsehood reduces the mental and emotional burden, promoting a healthier state of mind.
- **Mind-Body Connection:** Embracing truthfulness can reduce stress, anxiety, and inner conflicts. When the mind is at ease, it positively affects the body by reducing the release of stress hormones and promoting overall relaxation, which is beneficial for physical health.
- **Truth as a Path to Righteousness:** Biblical teachings often emphasize living a righteous life guided by truth. Being in alignment with moral and ethical truths can lead to a sense of purpose and contentment. It promotes mental clarity and emotional stability.
- **Mind-Body Connection:** Living under one's moral values and truths can reduce cognitive dissonance. When there is harmony between one's beliefs and actions, it leads to reduced mental stress and anxiety. The mind is more at peace, positively affecting physical health.

- **Truth as Liberation:** According to the Bible, when you come to know the truth, that truth will liberate you (John 8:32). This concept implies that acknowledging and accepting the truth, even when it's uncomfortable, can lead to personal growth and liberation from mental and emotional bondage.
- **Mind-Body Connection:** When individuals confront and accept hard truths, they often experience emotional release and relief. This emotional liberation can manifest in physical relaxation, reduced muscle tension, and an overall sense of well-being.
- **Truth as a Foundation for Trust:** Truth is foundational for trust in relationships, both with others and with oneself. Trust is essential for healthy social connections and emotional well-being.
- **Mind-Body Connection:** Trusting relationships and a sense of emotional security have been linked to reduced stress and improved mental health. When individuals feel trusted and can trust others, it positively affects their overall well-being.
- **Truth as a Guiding Light:** Truth is often portrayed as a guiding light, providing clarity and direction in life. It helps individuals make informed decisions and navigate challenges.
- **Mind-Body Connection:** Clarity of thought and purpose promotes mental well-being and reduces the mental fatigue associated with confusion and uncertainty. This mental clarity can lead to improved focus and decision-making, benefiting both the mind and the body.

In summary, biblical teachings about truth emphasize its profound impact on the mind and body. Living in alignment with truth promotes emotional well-being, reduces stress, enhances mental clarity, and fosters healthy relationships—all of which contribute to a positive mind-body connection. The concept of "Truth must win" aligns with these teachings, emphasizing that truth leads to liberation and well-being.

In biblical teachings on truth emphasize that living in alignment with truth is not only a personal virtue but also a family value that contributes to emotional well-being, reduced stress, mental clarity, healthy relationships, and a positive mind-body connection within the family unit.

The Mind-Body Harmony: Applied Wisdom in the Modern Age

Applied wisdom in the modern age refers to the practical and thoughtful application of knowledge, experience, and ethical principles to navigate the complexities and challenges of contemporary life. It involves using one's understanding of various fields, including science, philosophy, psychology, and ethics, to make informed decisions, solve problems, and lead a purposeful life. Here's a breakdown of what applied wisdom entails in the modern era:

- **Integration of knowledge:** Applied wisdom involves integrating knowledge from diverse sources. In today's information-rich world, individuals need to synthesize insights from various disciplines to address complex issues effectively. It's about connecting the dots between different areas of expertise to gain a holistic perspective.
- **Critical Thinking:** Applied wisdom emphasizes critical thinking. It encourages individuals to question assumptions, analyze information critically, and evaluate the validity of ideas. Critical thinking enables people to

make well-informed choices and avoid falling victim to misinformation or cognitive biases.

- **Ethical Decision-Making:** Wisdom in the modern age includes a strong ethical component. It's about making decisions that align with one's values and principles while considering the broader impact on society and the environment. Ethical decision-making is crucial in addressing global challenges such as climate change, social justice, and inequality.

- **Adaptability:** Applied wisdom recognizes the importance of adaptability in a transforming world. It involves the ability to learn from experience, adjust one's strategies when necessary, and remain open to new ideas and perspectives. Wisdom is not static but develops with changing circumstances.

- **Emotional Intelligence:** Understanding and managing emotions are integral to applied wisdom. Emotional intelligence enables individuals to build meaningful relationships, empathize with others, and handle conflicts constructively. It contributes to personal well-being and positive social interactions.

- **Practical Problem-Solving:** Wisdom is not just theoretical but practical. It involves using knowledge and experience to solve real-world problems. Applied wisdom helps individuals address everyday challenges, whether in their personal lives, careers, or communities.

- **Global Awareness:** In an interconnected world, applied wisdom extends beyond individual concerns to encompass global issues. It includes an awareness of international affairs, cultural diversity, and the interconnectedness of all people. Wisdom in the modern age encourages global citizenship and a sense of responsibility toward the well-being of humanity.

- **Lifelong Learning:** Applied wisdom acknowledges that learning is a lifelong journey. It encourages individuals to seek continuous self-improvement, stay curious, and remain open to new ideas. Lifelong learning is essential for personal growth and adapting to an ever-changing world.
- **Balanced Well-Being:** Wisdom seeks to achieve a balanced state of well-being. It includes physical health, mental well-being, emotional resilience, and a sense of purpose. It recognizes that true wisdom involves not only understanding the world, but that also living a fulfilling and meaningful life.
- **Community and Collaboration:** Applied wisdom recognizes the importance of collaboration and community engagement. It encourages individuals to work together to address common challenges and create positive change in society.

In the modern age, applied wisdom means using knowledge, ethics, critical thinking, and emotional intelligence to lead a purposeful life, make informed decisions, and contribute to the well-being of oneself and the community. This evolving concept adapts to our interconnected world while upholding timeless principles of wisdom and ethics.

This section on applied wisdom highlights the profound connection between the mind and body. It emphasizes how informed, ethical decisions, emotional intelligence, and maintaining well-being, as discussed in this section, foster a positive mind-body connection. Integrating critical thinking, adaptability, and global awareness helps boost mental clarity, reduce stress, and nurture healthy relationships, essential for a harmonious relationship between the mind and body.

Chapter 9

The Science of Breath

Mindful Breathing and Its Impact on Neurological Well-Being

The Science of Breath is a comprehensive field of study that delves into the intricate interaction between our breath and its multifaceted impact on human health and consciousness. Within this scientific domain, it explores how various breathing patterns can exert profound influence over our physical, mental, and emotional well-being. One particular area of focus is the practice of mindful breathing, which plays a pivotal role in enhancing mindfulness and inner serenity.

Mindful breathing, possesses remarkable effects on our neurological well-being. Regular practice can activate the parasympathetic nervous system, reducing stress and promoting relaxation. Concurrently, it can enhance the functioning of the prefrontal cortex, thereby improving cognitive abilities such as attention and decision-making. Furthermore, mindful breathing can elevate the production of neurochemicals associated with well-being, such as serotonin and endorphins. It also exerts a substantial influence on neurotransmitter levels associated with our overall sense of well-being, including gamma-aminobutyric acid (GABA). Let's now explore the intricate relationship between mindful breathing, neurotransmitters, and their connections to the mind-body and neuroscience in greater detail.

Mindful Breathing and Serotonin

Serotonin is a neurotransmitter known for its role in regulating mood and overall well-being. Imbalances in serotonin levels are associated with mood disorders like depression and anxiety. Mindful breathing techniques, such as deep, slow, and deliberate breaths, have been found to stimulate the production and release of serotonin.

The Connection: Mindful breathing induces a state of relaxation and activates the parasympathetic nervous system. This state is associated with improved mood and reduced stress. The release of serotonin during mindful breathing contributes to a sense of calm, happiness, and emotional well-being.

Mindful Breathing and Gamma-Aminobutric Acid (GABA)

Gamma-aminobutyric acid (GABA) is an inhibitory neurotransmitter that helps regulate brain activity. Higher GABA levels are associated with reduced anxiety and increased relaxation. Mindful breathing practices have been linked to increased GABA activity.

The Connection: Mindful breathing promotes relaxation, and this relaxation response is associated with an increase in GABA. GABA helps counter the effects of stress and anxiety in the brain. This increase in GABA contributes to a sense of calm and mental well-being.

Mindful Breathing and the Mind-Body Connection

Mindful breathing bridges the connection between the mind and body. It involves focused attention on the breath, which helps individuals become more aware of bodily sensations, thoughts, and emotions.

The Connection: By paying attention to the breath and observing the sensations in the body without judgment, mindfulness helps individuals develop a better understanding of their emotional and physical states. This self-awareness can lead to better emotional regulation and stress management.

Mindful Breathing and Neuroscience

Neuroscience studies have shown that mindfulness practices, including mindful breathing, can lead to structural and functional changes in the brain. Regular practice can increase the density of gray matter in brain regions associated with self-awareness, compassion, and emotional regulation.

The Connection: Mindful breathing is a fundamental component of mindfulness meditation. It engages the prefrontal cortex, which handles executive functions like attention, decision-making, and emotional regulation. Over time, mindfulness practices can enhance the functioning of this brain region, contributing to improved well-being.

In summary, the practice of mindful breathing has a profound impact on neurotransmitters associated with well-being, such as serotonin and GABA. It promotes relaxation, emotional balance, and self-awareness. The mind-body connection fostered by mindfulness practices, including mindful breathing, is closely tied to these positive neurological and emotional effects. The field of neuroscience continues to provide valuable insights into how mindfulness practices reshape the brain and contribute to overall mental and emotional health.

Exploring Mindful Breathing

The connection between the Prayer Hands gesture (Anjali Mudra) during prayer and the practice of mindful breathing is a fascinating aspect of this mind-body-spiritual interaction.

Here's how it relates to breathing and mindfulness:

- **Synchronized Breathing**: While performing the Anjali Mudra, individuals often synchronize their breath with the movement of their hands. This conscious alignment of breath and gesture encourages rhythmic and intentional breathing. In mindfulness and meditative practices, synchronous breathing and movement help create a sense of unity between the physical body and the breath. This synchronization promotes relaxation, focusing the mind on the present moment.
- **Breath as an Anchor:** Employing mindful breathing during prayer can serve as an anchor to the present moment. When you bring your hands together in the Anjali Mudra, you can also direct your focus towards your breath. Breath is a fundamental element of mindfulness and meditation, helping individuals remain centered and fully present. By incorporating deep, intentional breaths into your prayer, you enhance the mindfulness experience.
- **Emotional Regulation Through Breath:** Deep, intentional breaths during the Anjali Mudra can

stimulate the vagus nerve, promoting emotional regulation. The vagus nerve is closely associated with breath and plays a significant role in calming the body's stress response. When you combine the calming effect of deep breaths with the emotional depth of prayer, it enhances the overall experience.

- **Brain Function and Breath:** The rhythmic breathing associated with the Anjali Mudra may also positively affect brain function. Deep, slow breaths activate the body's relaxation response, reducing the production of stress hormones. This can improve cognitive functions, such as decision-making, problem-solving, and emotional processing.

- **Mind-Body Connection Through Breath:** Mindful breathing reinforces the connection between the mind and the body. When you consciously breathe during prayer, you are linking your cognitive and emotional experience with the physical action of the breath, strengthening the mind-body connection.

- **Mindfulness and Presence Through Breath:** In the Anjali Mudra, mindful breathing encourages deep presence. You realize each breath, each sensation, and each aspect of your prayer. This aligns with the central tenet of mindfulness: staying fully engaged in the present moment. As you focus on your breath during the Anjali Mudra, you enhance the depth of your prayer experience.

In summary, the Prayer Hands gesture (Anjali Mudra), when combined with mindful breathing, creates a profound interplay between the physical, mental, and spiritual aspects of prayer. The synchronization of breath and movement during the Anjali Mudra enhances the practice of mindfulness and emotional regulation. This connection strengthens the relationship between the mind and body, contributing to the depth and authenticity of the prayer experience. It beautifully exemplifies *the holistic nature of human existence, where breath serves as a bridge between the spiritual and the physical, connecting the mind, body, and spirit in prayer.*

Chapter 10

Neurological Alchemy

Emotions and Reality Shaping

Neurological alchemy, in a metaphorical sense, refers to the transformative processes within the brain and nervous system that leads to profound changes in one's cognitive, emotional, and perceptual experiences. It suggests that through various practices, such as meditation, mindfulness, or even deep contemplation, individuals can "transform" their neurological patterns and perceptions, leading to heightened consciousness, self-awareness, and, in some cases, spiritual insights. It's a symbolic way of describing the potential for personal growth and transformation through neurological processes.

In the world of spiritual wisdom, we discover something remarkable that words can't fully describe. It encourages us to explore how our thoughts and feelings are deeply connected. In this chapter, we explore ancient teachings that show us how to use our emotions to make our desires a reality.

Feeling is the Prayer

In a complex world where faith and intention come together, "Feeling is the Prayer" shines as a source of hope. The ancient teachings in the Gospel of Thomas remind us that when our thoughts and emotions work together, we have the ability to change our reality. Imagine telling a mountain to move, and it actually moves – this becomes possible when we understand how our thoughts and emotions can work in harmony.

Unveiling the Divine Matrix

As we commence this profound transformative journey, a passage from the Gospel of Thomas (Verse 48) offers profound wisdom: Jesus once spoke, "If two make peace with each other in this one house, they will say to the mountain, 'Move away,' and it will move away." This statement resonates deeply with the profound power intrinsic to each of us. The "two" in this statement signifies the realms of thought within the mind and the emotions residing in the heart. It conveys the idea that when a harmonious partnership is established between our thoughts and emotions, we unlock a formidable power capable of moving mountains, whether they exist within us or in the greater world. As the reader, you assume a sacred role, serving as the vessel through which this alchemical union unfurls. The mystical merging of thought and emotion within your heart kindles the flame of sentiment, unlocking the very key to unveiling the divine blueprint.

The Language of the Heart

How can we convey the unspoken connection between our thoughts and feelings, often referred to as the enigmatic "language of the heart"? Spiritual texts advise us to "Ask, and You Shall Receive," yet true asking transcends mere words. It unfolds as a heartfelt dialogue between our innermost feelings and the universe, a profound conversation where the heart's electromagnetic pulses transform into the eloquent expressions of a cosmic exchange.

The Art of Enveloping Desire

In the Gospel of Thomas, there's a powerful idea that's been brought to light through Aramaic translations. It encourages us to ask for things without any hidden agendas and to go beyond our judgments and ego. Instead, we're advised to fully feel and embrace our desires as if they've already come true. By immersing ourselves in the sensation of having our wishes fulfilled, we can make our desires real.

The Fusion of Thought and Emotion

Think of your thoughts and feelings like partners in a dance. They come together to create your emotions. Imagine your thoughts as the things you want, your feelings as the energy that gives them life, and your heart as the place where they mix, creating the power that attracts what you want in life.

Beyond the Threshold of Reality

Move ahead and dream beyond what you usually consider real. When you start to feel as if your wishes have already come true, you link the possibility to reality. Whether you want more money or your dream home, this idea explains how your emotions can assist you in getting what you desire.

The Quantum Resonance of Feeling

"The Quantum Resonance of Feeling" is like a story where you'll learn how your feelings are connected to making things happen. It's about the special and strong link between your emotions and what you want to do. As you read about how thoughts, emotions, and feelings work together, you'll discover how everything in the world is connected in a beautiful way.

Becoming the Architect of Your Reality

Imagine you have the power to create your own life. You can do this by understanding how your thoughts, feelings, and emotions work together. This knowledge gives you the ability to overcome challenges and change people's lives for the better.

Your heart holds the key to this power, using your feelings as a tool to shape your reality. This section is here to help you realize your natural talent for creating your world through your feelings. By combining your thoughts and emotions, you can unlock the sacred art of prayer and discover your amazing potential to achieve big things.

Empowering Prayers: A Guide to Self-Discovery, Healing, and Compassion

Effectively praying for oneself and others is a practice that can be deeply meaningful and transformative.

Here's how you can approach it:

<u>Praying for Yourself</u>

- **Clarity of Intention:** Start by deciding what you want to pray about. Think about what's important to you, like your health, how you feel, what you want to do in life, or anything else.

- **Heartfelt Connection**: Find a quiet space where you can connect with your inner self. Close your eyes, take a few deep breaths, and let go of distractions.
- **Positive Affirmations:** Frame your prayers as positive affirmations. Instead of focusing on what you lack, express gratitude for what you have and ask for guidance, strength, healing, or whatever you need.
- **Visualize and Feel:** Begin by choosing what you want to talk to a higher power about. Consider things that matter to you, like your body's well-being, your emotions, your life goals, or anything else that's on your mind.
- **Gratitude and surrender**: Express gratitude for the blessings in your life and surrender your prayers to a higher power, the universe, or your chosen source of divinity. Trust that your intentions are being heard and will be addressed in the best way possible.

Praying for Others

- **Empathy and Compassion**: Begin by empathizing with the person you're praying for. Try to understand their challenges, desires, and needs. Cultivate a genuine sense of compassion and care.
- **Specific Requests**: Just like praying for yourself, frame your prayers for others as positive requests. Ask for their well-being, healing, guidance, or whatever applies to their situation.
- **Visualization and Healing Energy:** As you pray, visualize the person surrounded by healing and positive

energy. Imagine them experiencing a positive change in their circumstances.

- **Sending Love and Light**: Send thoughts of love, light, and positivity towards the person you're praying for. Imagine these thoughts reaching them and uplifting their spirits.
- **Affirmation of Connection:** Affirm your connection to the person. Let them know that you're holding them in your thoughts and prayers, and that you're there to support them.

Praying Simultaneously for Yourself and Others

You can pray for both youself and others at the same time. The key is to maintain a focused intention and heart-centered approach. Some people find it helpful to dedicate a portion of their prayer time to themselves and another portion to others. Here is the recommended method:

- **Begin with Yourself:** Start your prayer session by focusing on yourself. Set your intentions, visualize your desired outcomes, and express gratitude.
- **Expand to Others:** After praying for yourself, transition to praying for others. Visualize them, their needs, and your wishes for their well-being.
- **Combine Both**: Towards the end of your prayer, combine your intentions. Imagine a circle of positive energy that encompasses both yourself and those you're praying for. See this energy radiating outwards, touching, and benefiting all.
- **Gratitude and Closure**: Close your prayer session by expressing gratitude for the opportunity to connect

and send positive intentions. Trust that your prayers have been heard and will have a positive impact.

Remember, the essence of prayer lies in sincerity, intention, and the heart's connection. Adapt your approach to what feels most authentic and meaningful to you.

Chapter 11

Illuminating Love: "I Love You" and Its Profound Impact

Saying "I love you" is not solely reserved for family members, spouses, children, girlfriends, or boyfriends. It is equally significant to love oneself and all other human beings. The profound impact of those three simple words, "I love you," transcends cultural boundaries and resonates deeply with human nature. When these words are spoken, they set in motion a complex interplay of emotions, psychological reactions, and even physiological responses within both the speaker and the listener. In this chapter, we will delve into the intricate world of neuroscience and science to unravel the profound effects of "I love you." We'll explore the release of neurotransmitters, stress reduction, mood enhancement, social connections, and various long-term benefits, as well as examine how love is emphasized in various religions and spiritual traditions, gaining a comprehensive understanding of the profound impact these words can have on our well-being.

- **Release of neurotransmitters:** Expressing and hearing "I love you" can trigger the release of several neurotransmitters in the brain, including:

- **Oxytocin:** Often referred to as the "love hormone" or "bonding hormone," oxytocin plays a crucial role in social bonding, trust, and attachment. When you hear or say, "I love you," it can lead to increased oxytocin levels, promoting emotional connection and bonding.
- **Dopamine:** This neurotransmitter is associated with feelings of pleasure and reward. Expressing love and hearing it can activate the brain's reward system, leading to feelings of happiness and joy.
- **Stress Reduction:** The expression of love and the knowledge that you are loved can significantly reduce stress. It can lead to a decrease in the production of stress hormones, such as cortisol. Lower stress levels are beneficial for overall well-being and can reduce the risk of stress-related health issues.
- **Improved Mood:** The release of dopamine and oxytocin in response to "I love you" contributes to an improved mood. These neurotransmitters are linked to feelings of happiness, contentment, and well-being. This can lead to a more positive outlook on life and increased life satisfaction.
- **Enhanced Social Connection:** "I love you" reinforces social bonds and connections. It signals that you are cared for and valued, which contributes to a sense of belonging and social support. Strong social connections are associated with better mental and physical health.
- **Pain Relief:** Expressing love and hearing it may have a pain-relieving effect. Studies have shown that feelings of love and social connection can reduce the perception of physical pain.
- **Strengthened Immune System:** The reduction in stress and the associated hormonal changes can enhance the functioning of the immune system. This means that

expressing and receiving love may contribute to better immune health.

- **Positive Long-Term Effects:** Consistently experiencing love, care, and social support can have long-term positive effects on overall well-being and mental health. It can lead to lower rates of depression, anxiety, and other mental health issues.

Love Across Religions: Unveiling Its Spiritual Significance

The concept of love and its profound impact on the human experience is a central theme in many religions and spiritual traditions. Let's explore how various religions emphasize the importance of love and its profound effect on the spiritual aspect of human life:

1. Christianity

- In Christianity, love is a core teaching, with Jesus emphasizing the importance of love in the commandment to "love your neighbor as yourself" (Matthew 22:39).
- The Apostle Paul's writings, particularly in 1 Corinthians 13, describe love as the greatest of all virtues, emphasizing its enduring nature and its role in spiritual growth.

2. Islam

- In Islam, love and compassion are central to the faith. The Quran frequently mentions Allah's love for humanity and encourages believers to show love and kindness to others.

- The Prophet Muhammad emphasized love, stating, "None of you has faith until he loves for his brother what he loves for himself."

3. Buddhism

- Buddhism teaches the importance of loving-kindness (Metta), compassion, and empathy. These qualities are seen as fundamental to spiritual development and enlightenment.
- The Dalai Lama, a prominent Buddhist figure, often speaks about the transformative power of love and compassion in fostering inner peace and happiness.

4. Hinduism

- Hinduism emphasizes the idea of divine love and devotion (Bhakti). Loving devotion to a deity is seen as a path to spiritual realization and oneness with the divine.
- The concept of "Ahimsa" or non-violence is rooted in love and compassion for all living beings.

5. Judaism

- In Judaism, the commandment to "Love your neighbor as yourself" (Leviticus 19:18) is a fundamental ethical principle found in the Hebrew Bible, which highlights the importance of love and compassion for one's fellow human beings. This principle is shared with Christianity, where it is also emphasized in the New Testament (Matthew 22:39), illustrating a common ethical thread between the two Abrahamic faiths. Love and compassion are considered key attributes of God in Jewish theology,

and this concept resonates with the teachings of the Bible
in both Jewish and Christian traditions.
- Love and compassion are considered key attributes of
  God in Jewish theology.

In conclusion, the expression "I love you" transcends the boundaries of a mere sentiment and holds the remarkable power to initiate a
complex interplay of neurobiological and psychological responses.
These three simple words stimulate the release of neurotransmitters,
fostering emotional connections, happiness, and a sense of reward.
Simultaneously, they serve as a shield against stress, reducing pain
perception and strengthening our immune systems, all of which
contribute to our overall well-being and mental health. Furthermore,
the enduring benefits of love extend to enhancing life satisfaction and
building psychological resilience over time. By comprehending the
profound neurological and scientific dimensions of love, we not only
enrich our understanding of human connections but also emphasize
the pivotal role love plays in promoting both mental and physical
health. As we navigate the intricate realm of human emotions and
relationships, "I love you" remains a powerful testament to the
enduring influence of love on shaping our well-being.

In the next chapter, we will delve into "The Magic of Smiles,
Kindness, and Good Deeds," exploring the transformative impact of
these positive actions on our lives.

Chapter 12

The Magic of Smiles, Kindness, and Good Deeds

When you share a smile during a meeting or extend a helping hand to someone, you're actually unveiling a remarkable interplay between your thoughts and your physical self. This connection showcases the incredible way our minds and bodies work together, and it's a testament to the deep-seated aspects of human nature.

What's happening here is a profound demonstration of empathy, our ability to understand and share the feelings of others. When you smile, it not only conveys friendliness and positivity, but it also sends signals to your brain. Your brain, in turn, releases chemicals that make you feel good. This is like a built-in reward system for being kind and connecting with others.

The Science Behind the Magic of Smiles, Kindness, and Good Deeds

To delve deeper into the fascinating science behind this connection, let's explore the intricate neurological processes that underlie the human capacity to care for one another, form bonds, and experience fulfillment through helping and connecting with fellow human beings. This multifaceted neurological connection involved in activities like smiling and offering assistance reveals the intricate mechanisms at play in our brains. By unraveling the complexities of these processes, we can gain a deeper understanding of how our inherent nature contributes to our overall sense of well-being and happiness.

- **Release of Neurotransmitters**: When you smile or engage in acts of kindness, your brain releases neurotransmitters such as dopamine, serotonin, and endorphins. These chemicals are often referred to as "feel-good" neurotransmitters because they contribute to feelings of happiness, pleasure, and overall well-being. Smiling and helping trigger the release of these neurotransmitters, creating a positive emotional response.

- **Mirror Neurons:** Mirror neurons are specialized brain cells that become active both when you engage in an action and when you observe someone else performing the same action. These neural elements play a crucial role in fostering empathy and interpersonal connections. For instance, when you smile at someone or assist them, your mirror neurons facilitate the understanding and sharing of their emotional state. This empathetic resonance strengthens social bonds and cultivates a sense of shared experience. The well-known phenomenon of smiles being contagious can be attributed to the workings of mirror neurons. In the context of smiling, witnessing another person's smile can trigger the activation of mirror neurons in our brains, leading us to unconsciously replicate the observed facial expression by breaking into a smile ourselves.

- **Stress Reduction**: Smiling and acts of kindness have been shown to reduce stress by lowering cortisol levels. Engaging in positive interactions triggers the "relaxation response," counteracting the body's stress response and promoting a state of calmness.

- **Positive Feedback Loop**: The act of smiling or helping can create a positive feedback loop. When you smile, not only do you experience positive emotions, but the recipient of your smile often responds with their own positive emotions. Similarly, when you help someone, the gratitude and connection you receive contribute to a sense of fulfillment and happiness.

- **Enhanced Immune Function**: The release of feel-good neurotransmitters and reduction in stress levels associated with smiling and helping can positively affect your immune system. A healthier immune system contributes to overall well-being and resilience against illness.

- **Social Bonding:** Both smiling and acts of kindness strengthen social bonds. When you smile, you create an inviting and friendly atmosphere that encourages positive interactions. Helping others fosters a sense of connection and reciprocity, reinforcing social relationships.

In conclusion, the profound neurological connection between smiling, kindness, and good deeds serves as a testament to the fascinating complexities of human nature and the powerful ways in which positivity is both experienced and shared within our society. It is a connection that goes beyond mere physiology; it exemplifies the beautiful harmony between our individual well-being and the well-being of those we encounter on our journey through life.

Our brains are wired in such a way that the simple act of smiling not only lights up our own emotional landscape but also extends its radiance to those in our vicinity. When we choose to wear a smile, we become a beacon of light in the lives of others, offering hope, comfort, and a glimpse of the inherent goodness in our shared humanity. This reciprocal dance of emotions, this unspoken language of kindness, binds us together in a web of positivity that stretches far beyond ourselves.

As human beings, we possess the extraordinary ability to leverage this neurological connection for our personal growth and the betterment of the world around us. By consciously embracing the act of smiling and engaging in acts of kindness and good deeds, we unlock the potential for a life that is not only more fulfilling but also profoundly interconnected. We become architects of a world where every smile and every kind gesture contributes to a tapestry of compassion, creating ripples of positivity that can touch the lives of countless others.

Chapter 13

Symbolism: Spiritual Dimensions and Universal Meaning

The profound symbiotic relationship between the mind and the body in the realm of symbolism transcends cultural and religious boundaries. Symbolism serves as a bridge between the conscious and subconscious, granting access to profound layers of meaning. This connection becomes evident through its ability to unite disparate religions, convey the various states of deities, and bear sacred messages. As we explore the interconnected nature of symbolism and its power to bridge human consciousness with deeper, universal themes, we can further appreciate its role in shaping our understanding of spirituality, emotions, and personal growth. Now, let's delve deeper into this profound connection, with a particular focus on its spiritual dimension and the uncovering of universal meanings that enrich our exploration of the human experience.

- **Interconnected Symbolism Across Religions**: Symbolism often conveys universal concepts that transcend specific religious contexts. For example, the symbol of light is found in various religions, representing enlightenment, truth, and divine presence. Similarly, water is often associated with purification and spiritual cleansing in different faiths. This interconnected symbolism highlights the shared aspects of the human spiritual experience.

- **States of Deities and the Mind:** States attributed to different gods and goddesses can be understood as reflections of various aspects of the human mind and psyche. Deities represent archetypal energies, emotions, virtues, and qualities. For instance, a deity associated with love might represent the capacity for compassion and empathy within the human mind. Connecting with these states through symbolism enables individuals to tap into those aspects of their own consciousness.

- **Beneficial Ideology and Modern Message**: The ideology of using symbolism has many benefits to personal growth and spiritual development. It allows individuals to explore and integrate different facets of their psyche, fostering self-awareness, emotional balance, and inner harmony. Symbolism can serve as a tool for meditation, introspection, and self-discovery, aiding in the quest for meaning and purpose in a complex world.

- **Modern Usage vs. Ancient Wisdom**: In the modern world, the utilization of symbolism remains prevalent, albeit often in different forms. While ancient wisdom relied heavily on intricate symbolic systems, modern society has adapted symbolism to technology, art, literature, and even social media. The universal nature of symbols allows them to transcend time and culture, making them a powerful means of communication and expression.

The profound interplay of symbolism in the mind-body connection serves as a powerful conduit between human consciousness and the expansive realms of spirituality, emotion, and psychology. This intricate tapestry unites various religious traditions by illuminating common themes and the resonance of archetypal energies within each of them. By immersing ourselves in the symbolism of deities and ancient narratives, we unlock the potential to delve into the depths of our own psyche, accessing hidden layers of self-awareness and understanding. Embracing this ideology in our modern world enables us to foster personal growth, strengthen our bonds of interconnectedness, and ultimately forge a profound connection with the enigmatic mysteries of existence, offering a universal path to transcendence and self-discovery.

This brings us to the end of Part II. In Part III we welcome you to the immersive world of "Inner Realms Explored." Within these revered pages lies an extraordinary journey—a voyage transcending the mundane into a realm where the enigmas of existence await discovery. Unfold the ancient scrolls of wisdom that reveal the secrets of life's mysteries, beckoning you to join this odyssey into the unknown. See you in Part III.

Part Three

Inner Realms Explored

In the hallowed pages of "Inner Realms Explored," prepare to embark on an extraordinary odyssey that transcends the ordinary, where the mysteries of existence unfold like ancient scrolls waiting to be unraveled. As the journey commences with Chapter 14, "Ancient Wisdom Unveiled," you'll find yourself standing at the threshold of secrets that time has carefully guarded, beckoning you to peer into the depths of knowledge as old as civilization itself. As you traverse through Chapter 15, be prepared to traverse the varied landscapes of spiritual realization, navigating across diverse traditions that converge on the common ground of enlightenment. Chapter 16 beckons with "Mysteries of Consciousness and Unity," where the very essence of existence unfolds before your eyes, challenging preconceived notions and inviting you to explore the profound interconnectedness of all things. This journey culminates in the pursuit of purpose and fulfillment in Chapter 17, offering a roadmap for those seeking meaning in a world filled with chaos. Brace yourself for an exploration of the intricate terrain of human emotions and the inner landscape in Chapter 18, before finding solace in the transformative journey from stress to tranquility in Chapter 19. "Inner Realms Explored" is not just a section in a book; it's an expedition into the depths of the self, an odyssey that will leave you yearning for more profound revelations with every turn of the page.

Chapter 14

Ancient Wisdom Unveiled

"Ancient Wisdom Unveiled" refers to the process of uncovering and exploring the profound insights, teachings, and philosophies that have been passed down through generations across various cultures, religions, and traditions. This ancient wisdom is often found in sacred texts, teachings of sages, and cultural practices that offer timeless guidance for understanding human experience, the nature of reality, and the path to spiritual awakening. The concept of unveiling ancient wisdom involves delving into these teachings to extract their deeper meanings and applying them to our modern lives. Now, let's dive into exploring this treasure trove of ancient wisdom to unlock its secrets and enrich our understanding of our existence and our spiritual journey.

To make it easy to understand, we have written this chapter in bullet point format, breaking down the key concepts and insights into concise and digestible points. This format will help you grasp the essence of these profound ideas and realizations with clarity and simplicity.

Exploring Ancient Wisdom

- **Sacred Texts and Traditions**: Ancient wisdom is often encoded in sacred texts, scriptures, myths, and stories that are handed down from generation to generation in different cultures. These texts contain timeless insights into human nature, morality, ethics, and the mysteries of existence.
- **Universal Principles:** Many ancient teachings emphasize universal principles, such as compassion, love, humility, and interconnectedness. These principles transcend cultural and religious boundaries, offering a common thread that unites humanity.
- **Spiritual Practices**: Ancient wisdom includes practices like meditation, mindfulness, prayer, and rituals that have been refined over centuries to connect individuals with deeper aspects of themselves and the universe.

Relevance in the Modern Age

- **Guidance in Complexity**: In today's fast-paced and complex world, ancient wisdom provides guidance for navigating challenges, making ethical choices, and finding inner peace.
- **Deeper Understanding**: Ancient wisdom offers insights into reality, the purpose of life, and the relationship between the individual and the cosmos.
- **Connection to Roots**: Exploring ancient wisdom connects individuals to their cultural and spiritual heritage, fostering a sense of belonging and continuity.

- **Holistic Well-Being:** Many ancient practices promote holistic well-being by addressing physical, emotional, mental, and spiritual aspects of human life.

Decoding and using Ancient Wisdom

- **Symbolism and Metaphor**: Ancient teachings often use symbolism and metaphor to convey deeper truths. Decoding these symbols helps reveal profound insights.
- **Contextual Understanding**: Understanding the historical, cultural, and societal context in which teachings emerged enhances their relevance and meaning.
- **Integration with Science**: Modern scientific discoveries often align with ancient wisdom, showing the compatibility between spiritual insights and empirical knowledge.
- **Personal Reflection**: Engage in contemplative practices to apply ancient wisdom to your life. Reflect on how these teachings resonate with your experiences.

Benefits of Unveiling Ancient Wisdom

- **Deep Self-Understanding**: Ancient wisdom provides tools for self-discovery, allowing individuals to understand their purpose, desires, and challenges.
- **Inner Peace:** The practices of mindfulness, meditation, and self-awareness promoted by ancient wisdom can lead to inner calm and tranquility.
- **Ethical Guidance**: Ancient teachings offer ethical frameworks that help individuals navigate moral dilemmas and make principled decisions.

- **Expanded Consciousness**: Exploring ancient wisdom expands one's perspective, encouraging a broader understanding of reality and human existence.
- **Cultural Appreciation**: Studying ancient wisdom fosters appreciation for diverse cultures and traditions, promoting tolerance and unity.
- **Integration of knowledge**: Ancient wisdom provides a holistic perspective that complements modern knowledge, creating a more comprehensive understanding of life.

Application in Daily Life

- **Mindfulness Practice**: Incorporate mindfulness practice into your daily life to cultivate a deeper sense of awareness and presence. By taking moments to meditate and focus on the here and now, you can reduce stress, improve concentration, and enhance your overall well-being. Embracing these ancient techniques helps you navigate life's challenges with greater clarity and inner peace.
- **Compassion and Empathy**: Embrace teachings on compassion and empathy to enhance your relationships and contribute to a more compassionate world.
- **Personal Growth:** Embrace the wisdom of self-improvement from ancient teachings in your daily life, prioritizing personal growth and self-awareness. By continuously striving to better yourself, you unlock your full potential and achieve a greater understanding of your own strengths and weaknesses. This ancient practice empowers you to lead a more fulfilling and purpose-driven life.

- **Gratitude Cultivation**: Use practices of gratitude from ancient teachings to cultivate appreciation for life's blessings.
- **Harmony with Nature**: Draw inspiration from indigenous traditions' reverence for nature, striving to establish a more harmonious connection with the environment in your everyday life. By adopting their respect for the natural world, you'll become a better steward of the planet, fostering a healthier and more sustainable existence for both yourself and future generations.
- **Wisdom in Decision-Making**: Draw upon ancient teachings to guide ethical decision-making and promote value-based choices.

In conclusion, in the modern age, delving into the wellspring of ancient wisdom provides a timeless bridge between our past and present, offering invaluable insights that have endured through the ages. As we integrate these enduring teachings into our daily lives, we gain a profound understanding of ourselves, our relationships, and our interconnectedness with the universe, enriching our journey through the complexities of the contemporary world.

Chapter 15

Exploring Spiritual Realization Across Traditions

I n this chapter, we cover the journey of seeking and understanding the core spiritual insights, experiences, and realizations that are shared among diverse religious and philosophical traditions. It involves delving into the common threads of wisdom that run through different belief systems, cultures, and practices to uncover the universal aspects of spiritual awakening and self-realization.

Similar to the previous chapter, we've structured this chapter in a bullet point format to facilitate easy comprehension. This format breaks down the key concepts and insights into concise and digestible points, making it easier for you to grasp the essence of these profound ideas and realizations with clarity and simplicity.

Exploring Spiritual Realization

- **Common Essence:** Numerous spiritual traditions stress the importance of uncovering profound truths that extend beyond the material realm, encompassing insights into reality, one's own self, and the link between individuals and the divine or cosmic consciousness.

- **Inner Transformation:** Spiritual realization often involves a transformative shift in perception and awareness, leading to a profound sense of unity, peace, and purpose.
- **Awakening to Truth:** Realization frequently entails the emergence of a truth that surpasses the constraints of the ego and personal identity, resulting in a more profound comprehension of existence.

Unity in Diversity

- **Shared Insights**: While spiritual traditions may have different rituals and practices, they often share common insights into consciousness, love, compassion, and the ultimate reality.
- **Paths to Oneness:** Different paths to spiritual realization, such as meditation, prayer, self-inquiry, and contemplation, lead seekers to a similar experience of unity with the divine or the universe.
- **Essence of Wisdom**: Exploring various traditions reveals that the essence of wisdom lies in the transformation of one's consciousness and the realization of the interconnectedness of all life.

Understanding Across Traditions

- **Interfaith Dialogue:** By studying and understanding the teachings of different traditions, individuals can engage in meaningful interfaith dialogues that foster respect, tolerance, and cooperation.

- **Comparative Spirituality:** Comparative studies of spiritual traditions highlight the similarities and differences in their approaches to realization, leading to a deeper appreciation of shared insights.
- **Universal Principles**: Exploring spiritual realization across traditions reveals universal principles that transcend religious boundaries and connect humanity at a deeper level.

Benefits of Exploring Spiritual Realization

- **Universal Wisdom:** By studying various traditions, individuals gain access to a wealth of timeless wisdom that can guide their personal journeys of self-discovery.
- **Broadened Perspective:** Exploring different traditions expands one's perspective, allowing for a more inclusive and holistic understanding of spirituality.
- **Personal Growth:** Insights from multiple traditions provide tools for personal growth, leading to inner peace, self-awareness, and emotional well-being.
- **Cultural Sensitivity:** Learning about different traditions promotes cultural sensitivity, encouraging a deeper respect for diverse worldviews.

Methods for Exploring Spiritual Realization Across Traditions

- **Comparative Study:** Study the core teachings and practices of various traditions to identify common themes and approaches to spiritual realization.
- **Dialogue and Discussion:** Engage in dialogues with practitioners from different traditions to learn about their experiences and insights.

- **Meditation and Contemplation:** Practice meditation and contemplative techniques from different traditions to experience firsthand the shared states of higher consciousness.
- **Reading Sacred Texts:** Explore the scriptures and sacred texts of different traditions to gain insights into their unique perspectives on spiritual realization.

Applying Insights

- **Synthesis of Wisdom:** Synthesize the insights gained from different traditions into your spiritual practice, creating a personalized path that resonates with your inner journey.
- **Embracing Unity:** Embrace the shared truths that emerge from exploring spiritual realization across traditions to cultivate a sense of unity with all beings.
- **Living the Teachings**: Apply the insights gained from different traditions to your daily life, practicing compassion, mindfulness, and self-awareness.

In conclusion, the journey of exploring spiritual realization across diverse traditions beckons us to transcend the boundaries of our individual belief systems and reach for the profound, universal truths that underpin all spiritual paths. This voyage goes beyond mere enrichment of personal spirituality; it is a gateway to fostering a profound sense of interconnectedness, compassion, and unity that carries the potential to catalyze transformation on both a personal and global scale. As we embark on this shared expedition of discovery, we unearth the timeless wisdom that unites us as fellow travelers on the spiritual path, nurturing not only our own souls but also planting the seeds of positive change in the world at large. The quest to find common ground amidst diversity is not just an individual endeavor; it is a collective odyssey with the power to illuminate the human experience and forge a more harmonious and compassionate world for all.

Chapter 16

Mysteries of Consciousness and Unity

Within the pages of this chapter, we embark on a journey to unravel the secrets of "The Mysteries of Consciousness and Unity." Here, we will dive into the profound world of consciousness and the way everything is connected. We seek to answer the questions about what consciousness truly is, how it comes to be, and how it binds all living creatures and the universe together. In these answers, we may discover valuable insights that can greatly benefit us in our current world. So, let's delve into it a bit deeper as we explore the mysteries of consciousness and unity.

The Significance of Consciousness and Unity for Humanity

- **Expanded Perspective**: Exploring the mysteries of consciousness and unity can broaden our perspective beyond the boundaries of individual identities, cultures, and beliefs. This expanded view promotes a sense of interconnectedness and shared humanity, fostering empathy and cooperation on a global scale.

- **Overcoming Division**: The world is often divided by various factors, such as nationality, religion, and ideology. Recognizing the unity at the level of consciousness can help break down these barriers and promote a sense of oneness that transcends superficial differences.

- **Cultivating Compassion**: Understanding that all beings are interconnected through consciousness can naturally lead to the cultivation of compassion and care for one another. When we see the common thread that runs through all living beings, it becomes easier to empathize with their joys and sorrows.

- **Resolving Conflicts**: Many conflicts arise from a sense of "us versus them." By realizing the unity of consciousness, we can shift our focus from differences to commonalities, creating a foundation for dialogue and conflict resolution.

- **Environmental Awareness**: Recognizing the interconnectedness of all life can foster a deeper respect for the environment and the planet. This understanding can encourage sustainable practices and efforts to protect and preserve our natural world.

- **Promoting Well-Being**: The mysteries of consciousness can shed light on human well-being. By understanding the factors that contribute to happiness, inner peace, and fulfillment, individuals and societies can make choices that enhance the overall quality of life.

- **Mindful Living:** Understanding the unity of consciousness can inspire people to live more mindfully, making choices that consider the well-being of others and the planet. This can lead to more ethical and responsible behavior.

- **Spiritual Growth**: Exploring the mysteries of consciousness is often a deeply spiritual journey. It can lead to personal growth, self-discovery, and a deeper understanding of one's purpose in life.
- **Scientific Advancements**: The exploration of consciousness carries profound implications for a range of scientific disciplines, including neuroscience, psychology, and philosophy. The insights derived from this endeavor stand to catalyze advancements in our understanding of human cognition and behavior.
- **Coping with Challenges**: The current world situation is marked by challenges such as the global pandemic, environmental crises, and social unrest. Understanding the unity of consciousness can provide a source of inner strength and resilience in facing these challenges.
- **Promoting Unity**: In a world that often emphasizes differences, recognizing the unity of consciousness can be a unifying force. It can bring people together on a shared journey of exploration and understanding.
- **Ethical Foundations**: The recognition of consciousness as a unifying force can provide a solid ethical foundation for decision-making and societal structures. It encourages actions that promote the well-being of all.

Exploring the Depths of Consciousness in Biblical Verses

Before we wrap up this chapter, it's essential to delve into the profound exploration of consciousness as portrayed in Biblical verses. The Bible, a revered and ancient text, is replete with references to consciousness and related themes. It's important to note that the verses to follow are merely a limited selection, providing a glimpse into the vast array of references available. Let's take a closer look at a selection of verses that shed light on this fascinating subject:

- **1 Corinthians 2:11:** *"For who knows a person's thoughts except their own spirit within them? In the same way, no one knows the thoughts of God except the Spirit of God."* This verse draws parallels between human consciousness and the divine, emphasizing the idea of an inner, personal awareness.
- **Psalm 139:14:** *"I praise you because I am fearfully and wonderfully made; your works are wonderful, I know that full well."* This verse in Psalms highlights the awe-inspiring creation of human beings and underscores the sense of self-awareness and wonder within our consciousness.
- **Proverbs 20:27:** *"The spirit of man is the lamp of the Lord, searching all his innermost parts."* This verse from Proverbs illustrates the idea that our inner consciousness is like a divine lamp, illuminating and understanding our innermost thoughts and intentions.
- **1 Thessalonians 5:23:** *"Now may the God of peace Himself sanctify you completely, and may your whole spirit and soul and body be kept blameless at the coming of our Lord Jesus Christ."* This verse emphasizes the holistic nature of human existence, acknowledging the interplay between our spiritual consciousness, soul, and physical body.
- **Job 32:8:** *"But it is the spirit in a man, the breath of the Almighty, that makes him understand."* In the Book of Job, this verse underscores the idea that human understanding and consciousness are deeply connected

to the divine, where it is the very breath of God that grants understanding.

- **Ecclesiastes 12:7:** *"And the dust returns to the earth as it was, and the spirit returns to God who gave it."* Ecclesiastes poetically reflects on the nature of life and death, highlighting the idea that our consciousness, often represented as the spirit, returns to the divine source at the end of our earthly journey.
- **Colossians 3:2** - *"Set your minds on things above, not on things on the earth."* This verse encourages individuals to elevate their consciousness and focus on higher, spiritual matters.
- **Romans 12:2** - *"Do not be conformed to this world, but be transformed by the renewal of your mind, that by testing you may discern what is the will of God, what is good and acceptable and perfect."* Here, the transformation of one's mind and consciousness is highlighted as a means to discern the divine will and a higher moral standard.

These verses intricately explore the concepts of the human spirit, inner understanding, the profound connection between God and our consciousness, and the notion of the spirit's ultimate return to its divine source. While the term "consciousness" may not be explicitly employed in these verses, they beautifully unveil the deeper layers of human awareness, understanding, and our profound relationship with the divine. It's important to note that interpretations of these verses can vary significantly among different denominations and theological perspectives.

The exploration of these verses not only unveils the Bible's perspective on human consciousness but also imparts profound insights into the spiritual and moral dimensions of our inner worlds. The Bible's teachings on consciousness form an intricate tapestry of wisdom that continues to shape and inspire individuals on their spiritual journeys, offering a rich source of guidance and contemplation.

In conclusion, the exploration of consciousness and unity holds profound significance for humanity, offering a myriad of benefits that extend far beyond individual boundaries and beliefs. As we delve into the mysteries of consciousness and unity, we unlock the potential to expand our perspectives, fostering a sense of interconnectedness and shared humanity that promotes empathy and cooperation on a global scale. By recognizing the unity at the level of consciousness, we can overcome divisions rooted in nationality, religion, and ideology, promoting a sense of oneness that transcends superficial differences.

This journey towards understanding the interconnectedness of all beings through consciousness naturally leads to the cultivation of compassion and care for one another, enabling us to empathize with the joys and sorrows of our fellow human beings. In a world often divided by a sense of "us versus them," this newfound awareness of unity can shift our focus from differences to commonalities, creating a foundation for dialogue and conflict resolution.

Furthermore, the recognition of the interconnectedness of all life fosters a deeper respect for the environment, encouraging sustainable practices and efforts to protect and preserve our natural world. It also sheds light on the factors that contribute to happiness, inner peace, and fulfillment, enabling individuals and societies to make choices that enhance overall well-being and promote ethical and responsible behavior.

The exploration of consciousness is not just a philosophical or spiritual journey; it also holds profound implications for various scientific disciplines, from neuroscience to psychology, catalyzing advancements in our understanding of human cognition and behavior. In a world faced with challenges such as the global pandemic, environmental crises, and social unrest, understanding the unity of consciousness can provide inner strength and resilience.

Moreover, in a world that often emphasizes differences, recognizing the unity of consciousness can serve as a unifying force, bringing people together on a shared journey of exploration and understanding. It provides a solid ethical foundation for decision-making and societal structures, encouraging actions that promote the well-being of all. In these ways, the significance of consciousness and unity for humanity cannot be overstated, as it has the potential to transform our world for the better and lead us toward a brighter and more interconnected future.

Chapter 17

The Path to Purpose and Fulfillment

The road to finding your purpose and feeling fulfilled is a journey of self-discovery and personal growth. It leads you to a sense of meaning, happiness, and satisfaction in your life. This journey involves understanding what's most important to you, what you love, what you're good at, and what makes you happy, and then doing things that give your life meaning and joy. In other words it involves understanding one's core values, passions, strengths, and desires, and aligning them with actions that bring a sense of purpose and joy. This path is beneficial for everyone because it helps people live a more meaningful and fulfilling life.

Here are various ways in which the journey toward finding purpose and fulfillment can benefit individuals:

- **Clarity of Direction**: Embarking on the path to purpose helps individuals gain clarity about their goals and aspirations. When you have a clear sense of purpose, you are more focused and motivated to work toward meaningful objectives.

- **Enhanced Well-Being**: Living a purpose-driven life is associated with higher levels of well-being and life satisfaction. Knowing that your actions contribute to something greater than yourself brings a deep sense of contentment.

- **Resilience:** People who live with purpose are more resilient in the face of challenges. When you have a strong sense of purpose, you are better equipped to overcome obstacles and setbacks.

- **Motivation and Passion**: Pursuing what aligns with your purpose ignites your passion and enthusiasm. This enthusiasm provides intrinsic motivation, which can drive you to excel in your endeavors.

- **Positive Impact**: Finding your purpose often involves making a positive impact on others or the world. This sense of contribution generates feelings of fulfillment and satisfaction.

- **Empowerment:** The path to purpose empowers individuals to take ownership of their lives and make intentional choices. This empowerment leads to greater self-confidence and self-efficacy.

- **Personal Growth:** The journey to purpose is a journey of self-discovery and growth. It encourages you to step outside your comfort zone, learn new skills, and overcome personal limitations.

- **Alignment with values**: Living in alignment with your values creates a sense of authenticity and integrity. When your actions reflect your core beliefs, you experience a deeper sense of harmony.

- **Healthy Relationships**: Pursuing your purpose can lead you to connect with like-minded individuals who share your values and passions. These connections contribute to meaningful and fulfilling relationships.

- **Mindful Living**: When you're attuned to your purpose, you become more mindful of your choices and actions. This mindfulness fosters a greater appreciation for the present moment.
- **Overcoming Aimlessness**: Without a sense of purpose, individuals may feel adrift or aimless. The path to purpose provides a sense of direction and a compass for navigating life's choices.
- **Inspiration for others**: By following your own path to purpose, you inspire others to do the same. Your journey can serve as a beacon of hope and motivation for those around you.
- **Legacy:** Discovering and living your purpose can lead to the creation of a meaningful legacy. Your impact on others and the world can continue to inspire future generations.
- **Cultivating Mind-Body Connection**: Living with purpose often involves engaging in activities that promote well-being, such as exercise, meditation, and self-care. This cultivates a positive mind-body connection.
- **Lifelong Learning**: The path to purpose is ongoing as individuals continue to learn, strengthen, and adapt. This commitment to growth keeps the mind engaged and curious.

In summary, this chapter emphasizes that discovering your purpose and achieving fulfillment is a profound voyage of self-exploration and personal development. This journey has the power to change lives and extend its positive impact beyond the individual. Throughout the chapter, we've delved into how recognizing and aligning your core values, passions, strengths, and desires with purposeful actions can lead to a deep sense of significance, joy, and contentment in life.

The chapter has highlighted numerous ways in which this

pursuit of purpose can bring benefits to individuals. From providing clear direction and improving well-being to nurturing resilience and igniting motivation and enthusiasm, the journey to purpose is not only deeply personal but also universally meaningful. It empowers individuals to take control of their lives, fosters personal growth, and fosters an authentic way of living.

Furthermore, this journey often leads to the creation of meaningful relationships and a positive impact on others and the world. It promotes mindful living, overcomes aimlessness, and serves as an inspiration to those around us, leaving a lasting legacy.

Living with purpose also entails a commitment to overall well-being, self-improvement, and lifelong learning. It brings harmony to the mind and body and encourages a profound appreciation for the present moment.

In a world that can often seem chaotic and overwhelming, the path to purpose acts as a guiding beacon. It urges individuals to slow down, reflect on their values, and make choices that resonate with their deepest desires. By following this path, individuals can unlock greater happiness, satisfaction, and a deeper connection with themselves and the world around them. Ultimately, the journey to purpose and fulfillment is a transformative and enriching process with the potential to enhance the quality of life for everyone, offering not just personal satisfaction but also a positive ripple effect on the broader community and the world.

Chapter 18

Mapping Human Emotions and Inner Landscape

Mapping human emotions and the inner landscape requires the ability to comprehend, recognize, and traverse the intricate terrain of your emotions, thoughts, and mental states. This journey can lead to a deeper understanding of your emotional well-being, a heightened sense of self-awareness, and the developing strategies to effectively managing your emotions. Below, we'll explore several methods for mapping human emotions and leveraging this insight to promote personal growth and well-being:

- **Emotional Awareness**: The first step is to cultivate emotional awareness by paying attention to your feelings and thoughts. Regularly check in with yourself to identify the emotions you're experiencing. Mindfulness meditation can be a valuable practice to increase emotional awareness.

- **Emotion Identification**: Develop a vocabulary for emotions. Learn to differentiate between various emotions beyond just basic categories like happy, sad, angry, etc. Recognize nuances in emotions like frustration, contentment, disappointment, etc.

- **Emotion Journaling**: Keep an emotion journal where you record your daily emotions, triggers, and situations that evoke certain feelings. This practice helps you identify patterns and gain deeper insights into your emotional responses.

- **Body Sensations**: Pay attention to how different emotions manifest in your body. For example, stress might lead to tension in your shoulders or a clenched jaw. Awareness of physical sensations can give you clues about your emotional state.

- **Visual Mapping:** Use visual aids like mind maps, color-coded charts, or diagrams to represent your emotions. This can help you visualize connections between different emotions and their triggers.

- **Emotion Wheel:** Use an emotion wheel, which categorizes emotions into primary and secondary levels. Some examples of primary emotions include happiness, sadness, anger, fear, surprise, and disgust. Secondary emotions are variations or nuances of the primary emotions. They provide a more detailed and specific description of how a person is feeling. For instance, under the primary emotion "anger," secondary emotions could include frustration, irritation, or rage. Similarly, under "happiness," you might find secondary emotions like contentment, joy, or elation. This tool helps you identify the core emotion you're experiencing and its related variations. The emotional wheel is usually presented as a circular diagram with the primary emotions in the center and the secondary emotions radiating outward from them. Each emotion is connected to the related primary emotion. By using this wheel, individuals can pinpoint the specific emotion they are feeling, which can be particularly useful when trying to communicate their feelings to others or when working on self-reflection and emotional regulation.

- **Guided Reflection**: Set aside time for reflective practices, such as journaling or deep contemplation. Ask yourself questions like, "What am I feeling right now?" and "Why might I be feeling this way?"
- **Emotion Tracking Apps**: There are several mobile apps designed to help you track and understand your emotions. These apps often provide prompts, mood tracking features, and data analysis to offer insights.
- **Therapy and Counseling**: Seeking professional support from therapists or counselors can provide you with guidance and techniques for exploring your emotions in a safe and supportive environment.
- **Emotion Regulation Strategies**: Once you've mapped your emotions, learn and practice strategies to regulate them. Techniques like deep breathing, mindfulness, progressive muscle relaxation, and cognitive reframing can help manage overwhelming emotions.
- **Emotion Expression:** Find healthy ways to express your emotions, such as through creative activities like art, writing, or music. Expressing emotions can provide relief and a better understanding of their origins.
- **Social Support**: Discuss your emotions with trusted friends or family members. Sharing your feelings with others can lead to a deeper understanding of your emotions and offer different perspectives.
- **Self-Compassion**: As you explore your emotions, practice self-compassion. Treat yourself with kindness and understanding, especially when facing difficult emotions.
- **Feedback from others:** Ask for feedback from people close to you about how they perceive your

emotions. This external perspective can provide insights you might not be aware of.

- **Continual Learning**: Recognize that the process of mapping your emotions is an ongoing journey. Emotions are intricate and multifaceted, and fresh insights can surface over time. This underscores the importance of continuous self-discovery and personal growth, as life itself is an everlasting voyage of self-improvement and self-awareness.

In the pursuit of mapping human emotions and exploring the intricate terrain of our inner landscape, we've uncovered a profound journey towards greater self-awareness and emotional mastery. By employing a range of strategies such as emotional awareness, identification, journaling, and visual aids like emotion wheels, we will gain a deeper understanding of our emotional responses and their triggers. This self-discovery is further enriched through practices like guided reflection, emotion tracking apps, and seeking professional support. It's a journey marked by self-compassion, expression, and valuable feedback from trusted individuals. Importantly, this process is ongoing, emphasizing that our emotions are multifaceted, and as we evolve, so does our understanding of them. Mapping our emotions is a transformative voyage towards self-improvement and self-awareness, an investment in our most precious resource – ourselves.

Chapter 19

Transitioning from Stress to Tranquility

Welcome to the "From Stress to Tranquility" chapter, a comprehensive exploration into the transformative power of mindfulness and spiritual practices. This chapter is structured into three distinct sections, each providing unique insights and strategies to help you cultivate inner peace and embrace serenity. In Section 1, "Understanding Stress," we delve into the physiological responses to stress, highlighting its impact on the body and the importance of stress management for overall well-being. Section 2, "The Power of Mindfulness," introduces the practice of mindfulness, emphasizing its role in reducing stress and fostering a calmer state of mind. Finally, Section 3, "Spiritual Practices for Inner Peace," guides you through the calming effects of ancient traditions, such as meditation, prayer, and rituals, and their role in grounding and connecting with a deeper sense of self. This chapter serves as a voyage of self-discovery, uncovering the invaluable role these practices play in guiding individuals from stressful states to a state of peaceful tranquility. Let us now embark on this enlightening journey, where the wisdom and potential of these practices are unveiled.

Section 1: Understanding Stress

In this first section, we delve into the impact of stress on our bodies and minds, emphasizing the cascade of physiological responses it triggers. Understanding the profound influence of stress is essential, as it serves as the foundation for what follows. This section aims to shed light on the physiological intricacies of stress, highlighting the critical role of managing and reducing stress for our overall well-being. It sets the stage for subsequent sections that explore practical approaches to cultivating inner peace.

1. **The Impact of Stress:** Stress triggers a cascade of physiological responses in the body. When we experience stress, the brain releases stress hormones, such as cortisol and adrenaline, which prepare the body for a "fight or flight" response. These hormonal changes lead to increased heart rate, elevated blood pressure, heightened alertness, and the redirection of energy away from non-essential functions like digestion and immunity. Over time, chronic stress can lead to the prolonged release of these hormones, resulting in a weakened immune system, inflammation, and an increased risk of health issues, including heart disease, gastrointestinal problems, and mental health disorders such as anxiety and depression. Understanding these physiological effects underscores the importance of managing and reducing stress for overall well-being and a peaceful existence.

2. **Mindfulness as Stress Reduction:** Mindfulness is the practice of being fully present in the moment without judgment. It allows individuals to become aware of their thoughts and feelings. When applied to stress, mindfulness can help individuals observe their stressors without becoming overwhelmed. It enables a more

constructive response to stress, leading to a calmer state of mind.

3. **The Calming Effects of Spiritual Practices:** Spiritual practices like meditation, prayer, and rituals have been used for centuries to find inner peace and solace. These practices often involve connecting with a higher power or a deeper sense of self, which can provide a profound sense of calm and a feeling of being grounded.

4. **The Role of Gratitude:** Gratitude, the practice of acknowledging and appreciating the positive aspects of life, has a profound impact on both the mind and body. Physiologically, expressing gratitude activates the brain's reward center, releasing "feel-good" neurotransmitters like dopamine. This boost in positive emotions can counteract the effects of stress hormones, reducing anxiety and depression. Gratitude is also associated with improved sleep quality, enhanced immune function, and lower blood pressure. Furthermore, the practice of gratitude fosters a more optimistic and positive outlook, which can lead to increased resilience and an overall sense of well-being. By focusing on the things we're thankful for, gratitude helps individuals shift their perspective away from stressors, ultimately contributing to a calmer and more peaceful existence.

5. **Compassion and Well-Being:** Compassion towards oneself and others is a core component of spiritual and mindfulness practices. Developing compassion can enhance well-being by promoting a sense of interconnectedness and reducing judgments and harsh self-criticism. This, in turn, contributes to inner peace and tranquility.

6. **The Mind-Body Connection:** Stress triggers a complex physiological response, with the release of stress

hormones like cortisol and adrenaline. This response increases heart rate, elevates blood pressure, and tenses muscles, often leading to physical symptoms such as headaches, muscle tension, and digestive problems. Chronic stress can weaken the immune system, making individuals more susceptible to illness, and can exacerbate conditions like skin disorders. Furthermore, the body's inflammatory response can be heightened, increasing the risk of chronic diseases. Understanding this mind-body connection is essential, as it underscores the significance of stress management for physical health and overall well-being. Mindfulness and spiritual practices offer effective means to restore balance and alleviate these physical symptoms, contributing to a healthier, more tranquil existence.

7. **The Importance of Self-Care:** Self-care is essential for managing stress and achieving tranquility. This includes setting boundaries, taking time for relaxation, and engaging in activities that bring joy and rejuvenation. Self-care is a proactive way to prevent stress from accumulating and maintain emotional balance.

8. **Building Resilience:** Resilience is the ability to bounce back from adversity and stress. Mindfulness and spiritual practices can strengthen resilience by teaching individuals how to adapt and cope with challenging situations. This resilience ultimately contributes to a greater sense of tranquility.

9. **Embracing Serenity:** To embrace serenity is to cultivate a state of inner peace, calm, and contentment amidst life's inevitable challenges and uncertainties. It involves acknowledging and accepting both the joys and difficulties of existence with equanimity. Embracing serenity entails living in the present moment, letting go of

ruminations about the past or anxieties about the future.
It's about finding solace in simple pleasures, nurturing a
sense of gratitude for what we have, and practicing self-
compassion. Through mindfulness, spiritual practices,
and self-care, individuals can develop the resilience
needed to navigate life's ups and downs with grace,
maintaining a serene and tranquil state of mind that
promotes overall well-being.

10. **The Healing Power of Nature:** Connecting with
the natural world has a profound impact on reducing
stress and enhancing tranquility. Spending time in
nature, whether it's through activities like forest bathing,
hiking, or simply relaxing in a green space, can lower
cortisol levels, boost mood, and promote a sense of calm.
This reconnection with nature fosters a deeper
appreciation for the world around us and can be a
powerful source of healing and serenity in our lives.

This exploration of mindfulness, spiritual practices, gratitude,
compassion, the mind-body connection, self-care, and the healing
power of nature underscores the profound impact these practices can
have on reducing stress, promoting emotional well-being, and
nurturing a serene existence. By embracing these practices, individuals can experience the calming effects of mindfulness, strengthen
resilience, and cultivate gratitude and self-compassion. This holistic
approach reconnects the mind and body, alleviates physical symptoms of stress, and encourages the importance of self-care. Moreover,
engaging with the natural world provides a powerful source of healing. Ultimately, the goal is to inspire you to incorporate these practices into your daily life, nurturing a calmer and more centered mind
and enabling you to navigate life's challenges with grace while experiencing the transformative power of serenity.

Section 2: The Power of Mindfulness

As we continue our exploration into the pursuit of tranquility, we transition to the world of mindfulness in this second section. Mindfulness is a practice that enables us to fully embrace the present moment without judgment. In contrast to the previous section's focus on the physiological aspects of stress, this section delves into the mental and emotional dimensions of our well-being. Here, we discover how mindfulness, much like treating the body as a temple of Christ, empowers us to observe and respond to stressors in a constructive manner, ultimately guiding us toward a calmer state of mind. It offers a distinctive perspective, shifting our attention from the impact of stress to the potential for inner transformation through mindfulness, just as the maintenance of a temple ensures that negativity and toxic elements are kept at bay, preserving its sanctity.

Serenity, a state of calm and inner peace, stands as our next destination on the path to tranquility. As we delve into this pursuit, it's worth noting that there are commonalities with the first section, which focused on the physiological aspects of stress. Achieving serenity requires consistent practice and a firm commitment to certain principles and habits, mirroring the approach taken in maintaining the sanctity of a temple. Let's now explore how this serene state can be attained through continuous effort:

1. **Mindfulness and Meditation**: Regular mindfulness meditation cultivates an awareness of the present moment and helps you detach from worries about the past or future. Consistent practice can lead to a calmer mind and a greater sense of serenity.

2. **Stress Management**: Developing effective stress management techniques, such as deep breathing, progressive muscle relaxation, or guided imagery, can help you handle challenges with composure and maintain serenity in the face of stressors.

3. **Positive Daily Rituals**: Establishing positive routines, such as starting your day with affirmations, journaling, or engaging in a calming activity like yoga, sets a serene tone for your day and reinforces a peaceful mindset.

4. **Self-Care**: Begin by recognizing your body as a sacred temple, a vessel for a higher power, such as the Temple of Christ. Just as one tends to a sacred temple by keeping it clean and free of defects, you must prioritize self-care. This includes ensuring you get enough rest, maintaining a balanced diet, staying hydrated, and engaging in activities like going to the gym, exercising, walking, running, and more. Consistently tending to your physical and emotional needs in this manner contributes to an overall sense of serenity.

5. **Healthy Boundaries**: Treating your body as a temple means establishing and maintaining sacred boundaries within yourself, akin to those you'd maintain in a sacred place of worship. By defining and upholding these personal boundaries, you ensure the tranquility and purity of your inner temple, creating an environment that promotes physical, mental, and spiritual well-being. Just as a temple may have rules of conduct and a serene atmosphere, setting boundaries within yourself can involve healthy lifestyle choices, emotional self-care, and maintaining a calm and balanced mindset. These boundaries are essential for nurturing a deeper connection with yourself and optimizing your overall health.

6. **Letting Go of Control**: Practice relinquishing the need to control every outcome. Accept that some things are beyond your control and focus on how you respond to situations rather than trying to dictate their outcome.

7. **Gratitude Practice**: Regularly expressing gratitude for the positives in your life can shift your focus away from stressors and create a sense of contentment, fostering serenity.

8. **Adopting a Balanced Perspective**: Train yourself to view challenges and setbacks as opportunities for growth, rather than as insurmountable obstacles. This mindset shift can contribute to a more serene approach to life's ups and downs.

9. **Limiting Negative Influences**: Just as in a sacred temple where negativity is kept at bay, maintaining serenity within your body-as-temple involves limiting negative influences. Reduce your exposure to negative news, toxic relationships, and environments that disrupt your inner peace. In the same way that a temple strives to keep out negativity, surround yourself with positivity and intentionally choose relationships that contribute to the peace and sanctity of your inner sanctuary. This connection between limiting negative influences and safeguarding your body as a temple is fundamental to preserving its tranquility and well-being.

10. **Resilience Building**: Cultivate resilience by learning from setbacks and bouncing back stronger. The ability to adapt and persevere enhances your inner strength and contributes to a tranquil mindset.

11. **Embracing Imperfection**: Just as a temple may have age-old imperfections that add to its character and history, accept that perfection is not attainable within your body-as-temple. Realize that, like in the natural course of life, mistakes are a common and inevitable part of the journey. Embracing these imperfections empowers you to release self-criticism and instead, view your path towards serenity as a natural process filled with opportunities for growth. Understand that mistakes are a

part of life, offering you the chance to learn and do things better the next time, contributing to your overall well-being and inner tranquility.

12. **Seeking Support**: Just as people within a temple come together to support one another, it's crucial to have your support system in place within your body-as-temple. Reach out for support when needed, whether through therapy, counseling, or by confiding in a trusted friend. Sharing your challenges not only allows you to gain perspective but also fosters emotional serenity. Remember that just as a temple's community provides strength and solace, your support system can be a source of comfort and guidance on your journey toward inner well-being.

13. **Mindful Breathing**: Practice mindful breathing techniques throughout the day to anchor yourself in the present moment and reduce anxiety, ultimately fostering serenity.

14. **Consistent Reflection**: Engage in regular introspection and self-reflection to understand your emotions, triggers, and patterns. This self-awareness empowers you to respond to situations in a more serene manner.

15. **Patience and persistence**: Achieving serenity is a journey that requires patience and persistence. Consistently practicing these techniques and committing to your well-being will gradually lead to a greater sense of calm and inner peace.

In our exploration of tranquility, we've embarked on a journey to discover the pathways that lead to inner serenity. Throughout this section, we've delved into the profound art of mindfulness and the principles of serenity, with a central focus on treating our body as a temple. By mirroring the care and vigilance shown in safeguarding a sacred place, we've learned to establish boundaries, limit negativity, and embrace imperfection, fostering a serene environment within ourselves. Just as a temple is a space for spiritual reflection, so too can our bodies serve as a sanctuary for emotional well-being and connection with our inner selves.

As we continue our quest for tranquility, we're equipped with a toolbox of practices, from mindfulness and meditation to stress management and self-care, each contributing to a sense of inner peace. We've explored the power of positive daily rituals, the transformational potential of gratitude and balanced perspectives, and the importance of resilience and support. The journey to serenity is a path of patience and persistence, one that unfolds gradually as we commit to nurturing our emotional well-being. As we move forward, these principles and practices will serve as guiding lights, leading us further along the path to the tranquil and serene state we seek.

Section 3: Spiritual Practices for Inner Peace

As we begin this third section of our journey towards serenity and tranquility, our path takes a new direction, guided by the calming effects of spiritual practices. While the preceding sections delved into the realms of stress and mindfulness, here, we venture into the profound traditions of meditation, prayer, and sacred rituals. These centuries-old practices have served as beacons of inner peace and solace, offering a unique connection with a higher power or a deeper sense of self.

In the sections that follow, we'll explore the richness of these ancient traditions, delving into the ways they have been harnessed to nurture inner tranquility. We'll also discover how these spiritual practices may overlap with and complement some of the concepts we've discussed earlier in this chapter, such as reducing stress and mindfulness. Our focus shifts from the individual's physiological and mental responses to stress to a broader, spiritual approach that acknowledges the interconnectedness of inner peace and spirituality. We will delve deep into the timeless wisdom of these practices, discussing how they help us cultivate and maintain states of calm and inner peace, and the profound and far-reaching benefits they bring to our overall well-being, mentally and physically. Our journey now leads us to explore the power of calmness and inner peace in enhancing our response to life's challenges and experiences.

1. **Reduced Stress:** Calmness and inner peace act as buffers against stress. When we are calm, our body's stress response is minimized, leading to lower levels of stress hormones like cortisol. This helps protect our physical and mental health, reducing the negative impact of chronic stress.

2. **Emotional Regulation:** Inner peace fosters emotional resilience. When we are internally peaceful, we can respond to emotions with greater clarity and balance, rather than being swept away by powerful reactions. This leads to healthier emotional expression and fewer mood swings.

3. **Improved Mental Clarity:** Calmness of mind allows us to think more clearly and make sound decisions. Inner peace enhances cognitive function, concentration, and problem-solving abilities, leading to better outcomes in various areas of life.

4. **Enhanced Relationships**: Inner peace helps us interact with others from a place of stability and emotional balance. We can engage in conversations with greater presence, active listening, and empathy, fostering healthier and more meaningful relationships.

5. **Better Sleep:** A calm and peaceful mind contributes to improved sleep quality. Inner peace reduces racing thoughts and worries that can interfere with falling

asleep and staying asleep, leading to a more restful night's rest.

6. **Physical Health**: Inner peace positively affects physical health by promoting relaxation, which supports cardiovascular health, immune function, and digestion. Chronic stress is associated with a range of health issues.

7. **Resilience and Coping**: Calmness and inner peace empower us to face challenges with greater resilience. When we are internally grounded, we can navigate difficulties with a clearer perspective and find constructive solutions.

8. **Mindfulness and Present Moment Awareness**: Inner peace encourages mindfulness, which involves being fully present in each moment. This mindfulness enhances our experience of life, deepening our connection with the present and reducing rumination about the past or worries about the future.

9. **Positive Well-Being**: Experiencing calm and inner peace contributes to an overall sense of well-being and contentment. When we are at peace within ourselves, we are more likely to experience joy, gratitude, and a positive outlook on life.

10. **Personal Growth and Self-Discovery**: Inner peace allows us the mental space to explore our thoughts, beliefs, and aspirations. It supports self-awareness, personal growth, and persuading our life's purpose.

11. **Reduced Anxiety:** Inner peace serves as an antidote to anxiety. When we are calm, we are less likely to be consumed by anxious thoughts, and we can manage anxiety more effectively when it arises.

12. **Spiritual Connection**: Many people experience a deeper connection to their spiritual beliefs and practices when they cultivate inner peace. It creates a conducive

environment for contemplation, meditation, and a sense of oneness with something greater than themselves.

In this section, we explored the calming effects of meditation, prayer, and sacred rituals—centuries-old practices offering a unique connection to a higher power or a deeper sense of self. These spiritual practices not only help us nurture inner tranquility but also intersect with and complement concepts discussed earlier in this chapter, such as stress reduction and mindfulness.

Embracing calmness and inner peace through these practices extends their benefits beyond the spiritual realm. They act as buffers against stress, foster emotional resilience, and improve mental clarity. These states of being contribute to healthier relationships, enhanced sleep quality, and better physical health. They also provide fertile ground for personal growth, self-awareness, and the cultivation of a positive outlook on life. As we continue our journey, we carry with us the wisdom of these spiritual practices, understanding their role in helping us respond to life's challenges with greater resilience, mindfulness, and inner strength, ultimately leading us closer to the serenity we seek.

With this, we bring to a close the extensive journey through Part III, where we ventured deep into the inner realms.

Part Four

Transformation and Growth

Immerse yourself in the captivating realm of "Transformation and Growth," where the odyssey of self-discovery unfolds across three compelling chapters poised to revolutionize your outlook on personal development and spirituality. Prepare to push the limits of your mind as you delve into Chapter 20, "Unleashing Neuroplasticity for Advancement," where the mysteries of tapping into your brain's remarkable adaptability are revealed. Brace for a soul-stirring journey through Chapter 21, "The Inward Expedition," a narrative beckoning you to peel away the layers of your identity in a quest for profound self-discovery. The saga continues with Chapter 22, "Nurturing Gratitude and Compassion," a magnetic force that will tug at your emotions and reshape your worldview. These chapters transcend mere words on a page; they serve as keys to unlock your true potential. The adventure beckons—are you prepared to take the plunge?

Chapter 20

Harnessing Neuroplasticity for Development

The human brain is a remarkable organ, capable of constant adaptation and improvement. Harnessing the power of neuroplasticity allows us to intentionally sculpt and reconfigure the intricate network of neural pathways within our brains. This transformational process not only empowers us to boost our cognitive abilities and acquire new skills but also enables us to navigate life's evolving challenges with greater resilience and agility. Neuroplasticity, the brain's innate capacity to restructure itself through the formation of new neuronal connections in response to learning, experience, and environmental shifts, holds the key to unlocking our untapped potential. In this chapter, we will explore how you can leverage neuroplasticity for your transformation and growth journey.

- **Lifelong Learning:** Promoting lifelong learning actively boosts the brain's neuroplasticity by fostering the creation of new neural connections. When we engage in continuous learning and expose ourselves to new experiences, challenges, and knowledge, our brain's neurons create and strengthen connections. This process, known as synaptic plasticity, allows for the efficient transmission of information between neurons. Learning new skills, languages, or instruments triggers the brain's adaptability, as it must rewire and reorganize itself to accommodate the new information and skills. As a result, this ongoing stimulation of the brain through learning not only helps to maintain cognitive function but also supports the brain's ability to adapt and reconfigure itself, thus enhancing neuroplasticity.

- **Mindfulness and Meditation**: Regular mindfulness and meditation practices can enhance neuroplasticity by increasing the density of gray matter in brain regions associated with attention, emotional regulation, and self-awareness.

- **Physical Exercise:** Regular physical exercise positively influences neuroplasticity by improving blood flow to the brain. This increased blood circulation fosters the growth of new neurons and the formation of synapses, which are crucial for learning and memory. Activities like aerobic exercises, yoga, and even something as simple as walking have been demonstrated to enhance neuroplasticity. These exercises not only contribute to overall brain health but also facilitate the brain's ability to adapt, change, and rewire itself, ultimately supporting cognitive functions and learning.

- **Healthy Diet:** A healthy diet contributes to neuroplasticity through its impact on brain structure and function. Nutrients like antioxidants, omega-3 fatty acids, and various vitamins promote neuronal growth and synaptic connections. Omega-3 fatty acids, for example, play a role in maintaining the integrity of cell membranes and supporting the communication between neurons. Antioxidants protect neurons from oxidative stress, which can otherwise impair neuroplasticity. Foods such as fruits, vegetables, whole grains, and fish are rich in these beneficial nutrients, providing essential building blocks for a healthy and adaptable brain.

- **Brain Training Activities**: Engaging in cognitive challenges like puzzles and memory games is a prime example of how synaptic plasticity works. These activities stimulate the strengthening or formation of synapses (connections between neurons) that underlie cognitive improvements.

- **Social Interaction:** Meaningful social interactions can also involve synaptic plasticity. When we engage in conversations, listen, and empathize with others, synaptic connections are formed or reinforced in areas related to communication, empathy, and social bonding.

- **Novel Experiences:** Exposure to novel experiences leads to the formation of new synaptic connections as the brain adapts to process and remember unfamiliar stimuli.

- **Positive Mindset**: Maintaining a positive attitude triggers the release of neurotransmitters like dopamine and serotonin, which create a favorable environment for neuroplasticity. These chemicals act as messengers in the brain, affecting mood and motivation. When dopamine is released, it strengthens synapses by reinforcing the connections between neurons. Additionally, serotonin plays a role in mood regulation, and higher levels of serotonin are associated with a more positive and less anxious state of mind. The activation of these neurotransmitter systems encourages the growth and strengthening of neural connections, facilitating memory, learning, and overall cognitive function.

- **Challenge Yourself**: Push your boundaries by tackling challenges that demand problem-solving and creativity, and welcome failure as a chance for personal growth and adaptation. When you venture outside your comfort zone, the brain's synaptic plasticity is engaged, leading to the formation of new neural connections that support problem-solving and adaptability.

- **Visualization**: Mental rehearsal and visualization often involve strengthening existing synaptic connections or forming new ones as you mentally practice specific tasks or skills.

- **Multisensory Learning**: Multisensory learning involves engaging multiple senses, such as sight, sound, and touch, during the learning process. This approach enhances synaptic plasticity by stimulating various brain regions responsible for processing sensory information. For instance, when you combine visual and auditory stimuli, multiple areas of the brain are activated, including the occipital cortex for vision and the auditory cortex for hearing. These diverse sensory inputs converge, reinforcing connections between these regions and the areas responsible for memory and understanding, like the hippocampus and prefrontal cortex. As a result, the information is processed more comprehensively and efficiently, leading to improved memory and understanding.

- **Sleep and Rest**: Quality sleep and rest contribute to synaptic plasticity by allowing the brain to consolidate memories and reorganize neural connections.

- **Limit Stress**: Managing stress to promote synaptic plasticity is crucial, as chronic stress can lead to the weakening or pruning of synapses, negatively affecting brain function.

- **Music and Art**: Engaging in artistic activities can lead to synaptic plasticity by creating and reinforcing connections in regions responsible for creativity, emotion, and motor skills.
- **Adaptation to Change**: Embracing change and challenges stimulates synaptic plasticity as the brain forms new connections to adapt to evolving situations.
- **Structured Practice**: Deliberate and focused practice promotes synaptic plasticity by strengthening or forming connections relevant to skill acquisition.
- **Feedback and Reflection**: Seeking feedback and reflecting on your performance can influence synaptic plasticity by encouraging the reinforcement of connections associated with learning and self-improvement.
- **Consistency**: Consistent engagement in challenging activities supports synaptic plasticity by maintaining and strengthening neural connections over time.

In conclusion, the human brain's incredible capacity for neuroplasticity is an invaluable gift that empowers us to continually adapt, learn, and grow. This chapter has explored the multifaceted ways in which we can leverage this natural phenomenon to enhance our cognitive abilities, acquire new skills, and navigate life's challenges with resilience and agility. From lifelong learning and mindfulness practices to physical exercise and a healthy diet, the chapter has provided a comprehensive roadmap for fostering brain plasticity.

By integrating these strategies into your daily life, you can actively create an environment that promotes synaptic plasticity, strengthening neural connections and facilitating personal development. The importance of a positive mindset, social interaction, and exposure to novel experiences cannot be overstated, as these elements contribute to the formation of new synaptic connections and the release of mood-enhancing neurotransmitters. Embracing change, structured practice, feedback, reflection, and consistency are the cornerstones of this transformative journey. In the end, it is through intentional effort and dedication that you can unlock your brain's untapped potential, allowing it to adapt, learn, and grow throughout your life, ultimately leading to improved cognitive function, enhanced skills, and a greater capacity for personal development.

Chapter 21

The Journey Inward

In "The Journey Inwards," we embark on an exploration of the profound practice of meditation, a journey that leads to heightened consciousness and profound inner awareness. The chapter delves into the timeless connection between the biblical verse "Be still and know" and meditation, encouraging the quieting of the mind and uncovering self-awareness. This chapter reveals meditation's transformative potential, from stress reduction and emotional well-being to enhanced concentration, spiritual growth, and a holistic impact on mind, body, and spirit. As we traverse these pages, you'll discover how meditation unlocks the serenity, wisdom, and connection that lie within, offering a transformative path to self-discovery and spiritual enlightenment.

Power of Meditation

In the practice of meditation, we must cultivate a delicate balance between intensity and attentiveness. It's crucial to sustain our alertness, for it is in this state that the realm of God consciousness becomes accessible. When graced by divine presence, our focus naturally sharpens, offering a subtle technique for achieving this balance.

The biblical verse **"Be still and know"** resonates with the essence of meditation, urging us to find inner tranquility and engage in deep introspection. This principle harmonizes with the meditative process, which entails calming the mind, discovering inner serenity, and gaining profound self-awareness.

Through meditation, individuals embark on an inward journey, delving into the realms of their thoughts, emotions, and consciousness. This inner exploration can yield a deeper self-understanding, a heightened spiritual connection, and a profound sense of inner peace and enlightenment. *Both the biblical verse and the practice of meditation underscore the significance of inner stillness and self-discovery as pathways to wisdom and spiritual insight.*

Meditation's power resides in its transformative impact on the mind, body, and spirit, bestowing a plethora of physical, mental, emotional, and spiritual benefits. Meditation, as a contemplative discipline, entails the focused redirection of attention, effectively quieting the incessant stream of thoughts that typically occupy the mind. Here, we present a brief overview of the profound impact that meditation offers. It's important to acknowledge that some of these points may recapitulate ideas mentioned in previous chapters. Hence, you may find that several aspects are briefly mentioned, with a primary focus on emphasizing their relevance to the practice of meditation.

- **Stress Reduction**: One of the most well-known benefits of meditation is its ability to reduce stress. Meditation activates the relaxation response, which counteracts the body's stress response, **leading to a decrease in stress hormones and a sense of calm.**
- **Emotional Well-being:** Meditation helps regulate emotions by increasing awareness of emotional patterns

and reactions. Regular practice can lead to emotional resilience, reduced anxiety, and improved mood.

- **Enhanced Concentration**: Meditation cultivates focused attention and concentration, which can improve productivity, decision-making, and overall cognitive function.

- **Mindfulness and Present-Moment Awareness**: Mindfulness meditation teaches you to be fully present in the moment, enhancing your ability to engage with your surroundings and experiences without judgment.

- **Brain Health**: Meditation has been shown to increase the thickness of the prefrontal cortex, the brain region responsible for decision-making, attention, and self-awareness. It also promotes neuroplasticity, the brain's ability to reorganize itself.

- **Improved Sleep:** Through meditation, the mind experiences a soothing effect that helps reduce racing thoughts and promote relaxation, which, in turn, enhances sleep quality. This practice can positively influence the physiology of the sleep cycle, fostering more restful and rejuvenating slumber.

- **Pain Management**: Mindfulness meditation influences the brain's response to pain signals by engaging various brain regions associated with pain perception. This practice activates the prefrontal cortex, which regulates emotional responses, including pain-related distress. Additionally, meditation prompts the release of endorphins, the body's natural painkillers, reducing the sensation of pain. It also modulates the amygdala, responsible for emotional processing, leading to a decreased perception of pain and an improved pain tolerance. These physiological changes collectively contribute to the effectiveness of mindfulness meditation in managing pain.

- **Anxiety and Depression**: Meditation can ease symptoms of anxiety and depression by promoting relaxation, reducing negative thought patterns, and increasing feelings of well-being.
- **Self-Awareness:** Meditation encourages self-reflection and self-awareness, allowing you to gain insights into your thoughts, behaviors, and reactions.
- **Cultivation of Compassion**: Loving-kindness meditation (Metta) fosters feelings of compassion and empathy, promoting positive relationships and reducing feelings of hostility.
- **Reduced Blood Pressure**: Regular meditation elicits changes in the autonomic nervous system, specifically, an increase in parasympathetic activity and a decrease in sympathetic nervous system activity. This shift promotes relaxation and reduces stress, leading to vasodilation (widening or relaxation of blood vessels) and decreased peripheral resistance in blood vessels. As a result, there is a reduction in overall blood pressure, which supports cardiovascular health. Meditation's influence on the autonomic nervous system and vascular responses contributes to its positive impact on blood pressure regulation.
- **Boosted Immune System**: Meditation mitigates the release of stress hormones, such as cortisol, by activating the parasympathetic nervous system and reducing sympathetic activity. Lower stress hormone levels result in less suppression of the immune system. Additionally, relaxation induced by meditation fosters the production of immune-enhancing substances like interleukin-2 and antibodies, strengthening immune function. These combined effects contribute to an overall improvement in immune system performance.

- **Enhanced Creativity**: Meditation can enhance creative thinking by quieting the mind's constant chatter, allowing space for new ideas to emerge.
- **Spiritual Growth:** Meditation serves as a central practice in numerous spiritual traditions by guiding individuals to delve into their inner selves, facilitating introspection, and contemplation. It allows individuals to explore profound existential questions, connect with their spiritual essence, and reach heightened states of consciousness. This inward journey, often accompanied by focused attention and mindfulness, helps individuals align with their spiritual path, fostering a sense of purpose and enlightenment.
- **Self-Regulation**: Meditation cultivates the ability to observe one's thoughts and emotional responses in a non-judgmental manner, fostering a heightened awareness of inner processes. This skill, developed during meditation, extends beyond the practice itself. It allows individuals to better regulate their reactions and behaviors in everyday life. By detaching from impulsive responses, individuals can make more deliberate, balanced choices in various aspects of their lives, including managing stress, maintaining emotional composure, and enhancing decision-making. This improved self-regulation can contribute to overall well-being and more harmonious relationships, as it minimizes reactivity and encourages thoughtful responses.
- **Positive Mindset**: Meditation shapes a positive mindset by emphasizing gratitude, contentment, and self-acceptance. Practicing gratitude encourages individuals to appreciate life's blessings, fostering a more positive outlook. Meditation also promotes contentment by emphasizing the value of finding satisfaction in the present moment, reducing the constant pursuit of

external sources of happiness. Furthermore, self-acceptance is nurtured through meditation, as it encourages self-compassion and diminishes self-criticism, leading to a more positive self-image and an overall constructive mindset.

- **Relationship Improvement**: Meditation plays a significant role in relationship improvement by fostering mindful communication and empathy. When individuals engage in meditation, they enhance their ability to be present in conversations, actively listening and responding with clarity and compassion. This mindful communication contributes to more effective and harmonious interactions. From an anatomical perspective, meditation can stimulate areas in the brain associated with empathy, such as the anterior insula and the anterior cingulate cortex. These neural changes can lead to heightened emotional intelligence, allowing individuals to better understand and connect with others on an emotional level. Consequently, these improved communication and empathetic skills help **build stronger relationships and deeper emotional connections.**

- **A Sense of Connection**: Meditation can create a sense of interconnectedness with others, nature, and the universe, fostering a deeper sense of purpose and belonging.

- **Enhanced Intuition:** Regular meditation can improve your ability to tap into your inner wisdom and intuition.

- **Personal Growth**: Meditation fosters personal growth by encouraging self-discovery, self-improvement, and the development of inner strengths.

- **Well-being**: Ultimately, the power of meditation lies in its holistic impact on overall well-being, balancing mind, body, and spirit.

In our exploration of "The Journey Inwards," we've ventured into the profound practice of meditation, uncovering its profound impact on our inner worlds. This chapter has beautifully connected the timeless wisdom of "Be still and know" with the art of meditation, emphasizing the need for inner tranquility and self-discovery. Through meditation, we embark on a journey within ourselves, where we unravel our thoughts, emotions, and consciousness to gain a deeper understanding of our true selves. This journey leads us to profound self-awareness and heightened spiritual enlightenment, transcending the boundaries of mere stress reduction and emotional well-being.

Meditation's transformative potential is nothing short of remarkable. It enhances our overall well-being by reducing stress, promoting emotional resilience, and improving concentration. It also fosters brain health, enhances sleep quality, and helps manage pain. This practice facilitates personal growth, strengthens relationships, and even instills a sense of interconnectedness with the world. To harness the full power of meditation, a regular practice is essential. Various techniques, such as mindfulness meditation, loving-kindness meditation, guided visualization, and more, are available for exploration. Consistent practice over time leads to cumulative benefits, and there are numerous resources, including classes, apps, books, and online guides, to assist you in initiating and deepening your meditation journey. May your meditation practice continue to bring peace, wisdom, and profound transformation into your life, leading to a harmonious and well-balanced existence.

Chapter 22

Cultivating Gratitude and Compassion

C ultivating gratitude and compassion are transformative practices that can significantly enhance emotional well-being, improve relationships, and contribute to a more positive and fulfilling life. Here's how to cultivate these qualities and how they can benefit everyone:

Cultivating Gratitude

- **Practice Mindfulness**: Pay attention to the present moment and notice the surrounding things you are grateful for. This can be as simple as the warmth of the sun, the taste of your food, or a kind gesture from someone.
- **Keep a Gratitude Journal**: Regularly write three things you're grateful for each day. This practice shifts your focus from what's lacking to what you have, fostering a positive mindset.

- **Express Gratitude**: Let people know when you appreciate them. Send a thank-you note, express your gratitude verbally, or perform acts of kindness to show your appreciation.
- **Count Your Blessings**: Reflect on the positive aspects of your life, acknowledging the good things that you might take for granted.
- **Shift Perspective**: When faced with challenges, try to find the silver lining or lesson within them. This reframing can help you see difficulties in a more positive light.
- **Practice Gratitude Meditation**: Set aside time to meditate on gratitude. Focus on the things you're thankful for and allow those feelings to fill your heart and mind.

Benefits of Cultivating Gratitude

- **Improved Mood**: Regular gratitude practice is linked to increased feelings of happiness and decreased symptoms of depression.
- **Stress Reduction**: Gratitude helps shift your focus from worries and stressors to positive aspects of your life, reducing stress and anxiety.
- **Enhanced Relationships**: Expressing gratitude strengthens relationships by fostering positive feelings and showing appreciation to others.
- **Resilience**: Grateful individuals cope better with challenges and adversity as they focus on their strengths and resources.
- **Better Physical Health**: Gratitude is associated with lower blood pressure, improved sleep quality, and a stronger immune system.

Cultivating Compassion

- **Practice Loving-Kindness Meditation**: This meditation involves sending positive thoughts and wishes to yourself and others. Start with yourself, then extend to loved ones, acquaintances, and even those you might have conflicts with.
- **Empathetic Listening**: Listen deeply when someone shares their feelings or experiences. Try to understand their perspective without judgment.
- **Acts of Kindness**: Engage in minor acts of kindness toward others, whether it's offering help, a smile, or a kind word.
- **Shift Focus from Self to Others**: Practice selflessness by putting the needs and feelings of others before your own.
- **Develop Empathy**: Put yourself in others' shoes and imagine their feelings and experiences. This helps you connect on a deeper level.

Benefits of Cultivating Compassion

- **Enhanced Relationships**: Compassion improves communication and connection, leading to healthier and more fulfilling relationships.
- **Reduced Conflict**: Compassion helps to minimize misunderstandings and conflicts by fostering understanding and empathy.
- **Inner Peace:** Engaging in compassionate acts brings a sense of fulfillment and inner peace as you contribute positively to others' lives.

- **Positive Self-Image**: Being compassionate toward others often translates into self-compassion, allowing you to treat yourself with kindness and understanding.
- **Increased Well-Being**: Compassion generates positive emotions, which contribute to overall well-being and a more optimistic outlook on life.

Both gratitude and compassion have the power to transform your mindset, enhance your relationships, and promote a sense of connectedness with others. By practicing these qualities, you contribute to a more positive and harmonious environment for yourself and those around you.

This brings us to the close of Part IV. Part V, Synthesis of Wisdom, invites you on an immersive and transformative journey through the profound realms of human consciousness, unraveling ancient philosophies and modern discoveries to illuminate new perspectives and unlock the secrets of self-awareness. See you in the next part.

Part Five

Synthesis of Wisdom

In today's information-saturated world, navigating the constant influx of data can be challenging. Part five, Synthesis of Wisdom, takes you on a transformative journey into the profound realms of human consciousness. The chapters offer a unique blend of ancient wisdom and contemporary insights, each serving as a key to unlocking personal development and enlightenment. Chapter 23, "Sharper Mind: 'Eyebrow' Center Concentration Techniques," explores the untapped potential of your mind through focused concentration techniques. Chapter 24 reveals "The Unity of Science and Spirituality," showcasing the harmonious interplay between two seemingly disparate realms. Chapter 25 provides insight into "The Influence of First Instinct and Thought," offering a compass for decision-making. Finally, Chapter 26, "Transforming Dreams and Desires into Reality," guides you through the alchemical process of turning aspirations into tangible achievements. Synthesis of Wisdom is not just a compilation; it is a guide to unlocking your potential and understanding the intricate tapestry of existence. Turn the page, and let the journey begin.

Chapter 23

Sharper Mind: "Eyebrow" Center Concentration Techniques

In everything you do, concentrate your mind on the spot between your eyebrows. When you do this regularly, you'll experience a fresh start or renewal. This timeless wisdom echoes through the ages, and its roots can be traced back to ancient scriptures. In the Bible, Exodus 13:16 instructs, "This observance will be for you like a sign on your hand and a reminder on your forehead that this law of the Lord is to be on your lips. For the Lord brought you out of Egypt with his mighty hand." Similarly, Deuteronomy 11:18 emphasizes, "Fix these words of mine in your hearts and minds; tie them as symbols on your hands and bind them on your foreheads."

The practice of directing our focus to the point between our eyebrows carries deep and meaningful importance, and here are a few compelling reasons why.

1. **Focus Point:** The point between the eyebrows is believed to be a center of energy and consciousness in many spiritual traditions. Concentrating there helps direct our awareness inward.

2. **Mind's Center:** In this context, "mind" refers to our thoughts, feelings, and awareness. By centering our attention on this spot, we are directing the mind's energy to a single point, reducing mental distractions.

3. **Renewal:** A "fresh start" suggests a new beginning or a revitalization of our inner state. By focusing our mind, we can let go of cluttered thoughts and achieve mental clarity, like hitting a mental reset button.

4. **Concentration's Role:** Concentration means focusing all our attention on one thing. In this practice, concentration helps quiet the mind, which is often scattered with various thoughts. By concentrating on a specific point, we bring our scattered mental energy to a singular focus.

Ultimately, this practice aims to quiet the mind's chatter, redirecting it to a specific point of focus. This can lead to a sense of inner calm, clarity, and renewal, enabling us to approach life with a clearer perspective.

In modern medical and neurological understanding, *concentrating between the eyebrows aligns with the concept of mindfulness and its effects on the brain's structure and function.* While this practice may not be explicitly mentioned in medical literature, there are correlations with existing scientific concepts:

1. **Prefrontal Cortex Activation:** Concentrating on a specific point can activate the prefrontal cortex, a part of the brain responsible for executive functions like decision-making, attention, and awareness. This activation can enhance cognitive control and emotional regulation.

2. **Mindfulness and Neuroplasticity:** Mindfulness practices, including focused attention on a specific point, have been shown to induce neuroplasticity. Repeatedly

concentrating on a particular spot could lead to structural and functional changes in the brain over time.

3. **Reduced Default Mode Network Activity:** The default mode network (DMN) is associated with mind-wandering and self-referential thinking. Mindfulness practices, such as focusing on a single point, can reduce DMN activity, leading to increased present-moment awareness and decreased rumination.

4. **Stress Reduction and Neural Regulation:** Concentration practices have been linked to reduced stress levels and enhanced neural regulation. By focusing on a specific point, individuals may activate the parasympathetic nervous system, which promotes relaxation and a sense of calm.

5. **Neurotransmitter Balance:** Concentration practices may influence neurotransmitter levels, particularly those associated with mood and focus. Dopamine and serotonin, for example, play roles in attention and emotional well-being. Regular practice might affect these neurotransmitter levels.

While the scientific community continues to explore the specific effects of concentration practices, the alignment with concepts like mindfulness, neuroplasticity, and neural regulation suggests that focusing between the eyebrows could have a positive impact on mental well-being and cognitive function. It's important to note that individual experiences may vary, and further research is needed to fully understand the mechanisms at play.

The specific mention of the "brow" or "eyebrow" in the Bible is relatively limited, but there are passages that refer to the forehead, which are closely related anatomically.

<u>Here are a couple of examples from Bible verses:</u>

- Ezekiel 3:8-9 (ESV): "Behold, I have made your face as hard as their faces, and your forehead as hard as their foreheads. Like emery harder than flint. Have I made your forehead? Fear them not, nor be dismayed at their looks, for they are a rebellious house."
- Exodus 13:9 (ESV): "And it shall be to you as a sign on your hand and as a memorial between your eyes, that the law of the LORD may be in your mouth. For with a firm hand the LORD has brought you out of Egypt."

These passages mention the forehead, which is a symbolic location for various ideas in the Bible, such as strength, obedience, and adherence to God's law. While the term "eyebrow" may not be explicitly mentioned, the symbolism associated with the forehead is significant in biblical teachings.

Reference from the Bible

The Revelation of Saint Thomas, The Divine: Ch7:10 is a copyrighted version of the Bible derived from the Ancient Eastern Text, specifically the Aramaic of The Peshitta, as translated by George M. Lamsa. It reads, "Do not harm the earth, neither the sea nor the trees, until we have sealed the servants of our God on their foreheads." This version is a direct translation from the Aramaic of The Peshitta. The terms "forehead" and "brows" both pertain to parts of the human head, but they have slightly different meanings:

- **Forehead**: The forehead is the area of the face above the eyes and below the hairline. It is a flat, smooth surface on the front of the head. In many cultures and religious texts, the forehead is associated with various symbolic meanings, including wisdom, spirituality, and divine connection.
- **Brows**: The brows, also known as eyebrows, are the two strips of hair-covered skin that lie above the eyes. Brows play a role in facial expressions and can help prevent

sweat and debris from entering the eyes. They also have cultural and symbolic significance in various traditions.

In religious or symbolic contexts, the mention of "forehead" or "brows" might hold different meanings. The forehead can be seen as a more general reference to the front of the head, while "brows" specifically refer to the eyebrow area above the eyes. Both terms can carry spiritual and cultural connotations, depending on the context in which they are used.

Decoding the Significance of "Forehead," "Brows," "Eyebrows," and "Human Frontal Lobe"

Nestled behind the forehead just above the eyebrows and encompassing various regions, the frontal lobe is a critical component of the brain. It is often likened to the brain's "executive center" due to its pivotal role in governing complex cognitive functions and behaviors. This section will delve into the multifaceted functions and importance of the frontal lobe in areas such as decision-making, personality, problem-solving, and more.

The frontal lobe is intricately involved in an array of tasks, including planning, reasoning, problem-solving, attention, working memory, motor control, language processing, emotional regulation, and social behavior. It is home to the primary motor cortex, which directs voluntary muscle movements, and the prefrontal cortex, associated with facets like personality, inhibitory control, and social awareness.

The Third Eye and Frontal Lobe: Ancient Wisdom and Modern Science

Ancient Wisdom: The Third Eye

In Eastern spiritual traditions, such as Hinduism and Buddhism, the "third eye" or Ajna chakra is thought to reside in the area between the eyebrows. It serves as the center of intuition, perception, and spiritual insight. Activating and harmonizing this chakra is believed to enhance one's ability to perceive beyond the physical world and gain deeper insights into reality.

Modern Science: The Frontal Lobe

From a contemporary scientific perspective, the anatomical counterpart to the area between the eyebrows is the frontal lobe of the brain. This vital part of the brain is responsible for a range of cognitive functions, including decision-making, problem-solving, intuition, and self-awareness. The prefrontal cortex, a specific region within the frontal lobe, plays a key role in executive functions and higher-order thinking.

Connecting the Dots

Although the language and terminology may differ, the parallels between these two concepts are intriguing. Both underscore the significance of the region between the eyebrows or the forehead in terms of perception, insight, and understanding. It's important to note that while ancient traditions attribute spiritual significance to the third eye, modern science focuses on the neuroanatomy and cognitive functions associated with the frontal lobe.

The practices and techniques linked to the activation or balancing of the third eye in ancient wisdom, such as meditation or mindfulness, can be viewed as methods to enhance the functioning of the frontal lobe in modern science. These practices can assist individuals in cultivating greater self-awareness, emotional regulation, and intuitive insights.

By integrating practices from both traditions, we can adopt a holistic approach to personal development. Ancient wisdom and modern science can complement each other, offering a deeper under-standing of consciousness and the mind.

Comparative Spirituality: The Solar Plexus Chakra and Biblical References

In Eastern philosophy, the solar plexus chakra, often called the Manipura, is associated with personal power, confidence, and trans-formation. It is situated in the upper abdomen area.

While the Bible does not specifically mention chakras, there are parallels to the concept of inner spiritual insight or perception. For instance, Matthew 6:22-23 (NIV) can be interpreted allegorically as a reference to inner vision and understanding, emphasizing the importance of spiritual perception and its profound impact on one's entire being.

Despite differences in terminology, both the biblical verses and Eastern chakra concepts focus on inner perception, understanding, and spiritual insight.

To summarize the chapter, we explored the practice of concen-trating the mind between the eyebrows, which provides mental clarity and renewal. Symbolic references to the forehead and brows in the Bible were found, paralleling the concept of the "third eye" in ancient wisdom and the modern understanding of the frontal lobe. This convergence encourages a holistic approach to personal develop-ment, offering a deeper understanding of consciousness and the mind.

Chapter 24

The Unity of Science and Spirituality

In a world where science and spirituality are often perceived as distinct and separate realms of human understanding, this chapter embarks on a journey to bridge the gap and explore their profound interconnectedness. "The Unity of Science and Spirituality" refers to the recognition and harmonious integration of scientific knowledge with spiritual insights, unveiling a more comprehensive and holistic understanding of the universe, human existence, and the quest for meaning. In light of this exploration, let us move forward and delve into the key aspects of this unity, discussing the shared pursuit of truth, the complementary perspectives of science and spirituality, and the promotion of a holistic approach to knowledge.

Key Aspects of Unity of Science and Spirituality

- **Shared Quest for Truth:** Both science and spirituality share a fundamental desire to understand the nature of reality, the origins of existence, and the deeper meaning of life.

- **Complementary Perspectives**: Science seeks to understand the physical and material aspects of the universe, while spirituality delves into the metaphysical and experiential dimensions. These perspectives can complement each other rather than conflicting.
- **Holistic Understanding**: The unity of science and spirituality encourages a holistic approach to knowledge, recognizing that reality is multi-dimensional and that different disciplines offer unique insights.
- **Integration of Wisdom**: The unity of science and spirituality encourages the integration of scientific discoveries with timeless spiritual wisdom, providing a more complete understanding of human existence.

Exploring the Confluence of Science and Spirituality

In the quest to bridge the seemingly disparate realms of science and spirituality, there exist areas of convergence that offer profound insights into the nature of human consciousness. This exploration delves into the fascinating intersections between these domains, highlighting how they mutually seek to decipher the enigmatic facets of awareness, selfhood, and subjective experience.

- **Consciousness Studies**: At the crossroads of science and spirituality, Consciousness Studies takes center stage. It serves as the crucible where the profound inquiries of both disciplines converge. Scientists and spiritual seekers alike are drawn to this field as they probe the depths of human awareness, aiming to unravel the mysteries that lie within. This shared objective underscores the common ground where science and spirituality can harmonize, as they seek to understand the essence of consciousness itself.

- **Quantum Physics**: The world of quantum physics, with its intricate dance of particles and waves, challenges conventional notions of reality. Astonishingly, some of its foundational principles align with age-old spiritual teachings, blurring the boundaries between science and mysticism. Concepts like interconnectedness, non-locality, and the profound influence of consciousness take center stage in the realm of quantum mechanics. Here, science and spirituality find a fascinating overlap, offering a glimpse into the potential unity of all existence.

- **The Mind-Body Connection**: Within the realm of scientific research, the investigation of the mind-body connection stands as a testament to the interplay between mental states and physical well-being. Studies in neuroscience have illuminated the profound ways in which our thoughts and emotions impact our physiological health. This empirical evidence lends credence to spiritual practices such as meditation and mindfulness, which have long posited that the mind wields a transformative power over the body. The resonance between scientific findings and spiritual beliefs in this domain underscores the synergy that can be achieved when the two realms collaborate.

- **Neuroscience and Meditation**: In the pursuit of understanding meditation's effects on the human brain, neuroscience has unveiled compelling evidence. Research in this field not only sheds light on the structural and functional changes that meditation induces in the brain but also validates spiritual assertions about the profound impact of meditative practices. This convergence of scientific inquiry and spiritual wisdom provides a solid foundation for the transformative potential of meditation and its contribution to the holistic understanding of human existence.

The journey to harmonize science and spirituality brings us to a place where consciousness studies, quantum physics, the mind-body connection, and the science of meditation converge. It is in these intersections that we discover a shared quest to fathom the nature of awareness, selfhood, and subjective experience. The enigmatic world of consciousness serves as a unifying arena, drawing both scientific and spiritual seekers into its depths. Quantum physics challenges our fundamental notions of reality and resonates with spiritual teachings about interconnectedness and the profound influence of consciousness. The mind-body connection underscores the impact of mental states on physical well-being, offering empirical support to the spiritual practices of meditation and mindfulness. Neuroscience, in turn, validates spiritual claims about the transformative power of meditation. As we traverse these realms of shared exploration, we are presented with the tantalizing prospect of a more unified understanding of existence, one that bridges the chasm between science and spirituality and offers a holistic perspective on the intricate tapestry of human consciousness.

Benefits of Unity of Science and Spirituality

In the unique convergence of science and spirituality, we unearth a wealth of transformative advantages. This powerful union not only reshapes our worldview but also enhances the very essence of our lives. Now, let's delve into the specific benefits that this unity offers:

- **Holistic Well-Being:** The fusion of scientific and spiritual insights paves the way for a more comprehensive sense of well-being, addressing not only the physical but also the emotional and spiritual dimensions of our lives.

This unity empowers individuals to achieve a state of holistic health and balance.

- **Deeper Understanding:** The unity of science and spirituality opens doors to a profound comprehension of the world and ourselves. It provides answers to questions that may remain elusive when viewed from either perspective in isolation. This holistic approach helps us uncover the deeper truths that underlie our existence.

- **Enhanced Problem-Solving:** The amalgamation of scientific analytical thinking and spiritual intuition equips us with a powerful tool for tackling complex challenges. It fosters innovative solutions by harnessing the strengths of both realms, pushing the boundaries of conventional problem-solving.

- **Promotion of Compassion:** Through the lenses of both science and spirituality, we come to recognize the interconnectedness of all life. This realization naturally fosters a sense of compassion and responsibility toward our planet and all its inhabitants. We are inspired to care for and protect the fragile web of life that binds us all together.

In summary, the unity of science and spirituality offers a transformative blend that enhances holistic well-being, deepens understanding, sparks innovative problem-solving, and fosters compassion. By harmoniously integrating scientific and spiritual insights, individuals can find balance across physical, emotional, and spiritual dimensions, uncover profound truths about the world, approach complex challenges with creativity, and cultivate a sense of interconnected responsibility toward all life on our planet. This synergy of knowledge and wisdom promises a brighter and more enlightened future for humanity.

Methods for Integrating Science and Spirituality

As we delve into the intricate dance between science and spirituality, it becomes evident that both domains offer unique insights into the nature of our existence. This synthesis brings to light the shared facets and opportunities for a more comprehensive comprehension of the world. Now, let's explore practical methods for weaving these diverse threads together, paving the way for a more enriched perspective:

- **Interdisciplinary Exploration:** Embrace interdisciplinary studies that facilitate the seamless integration of scientific theories and spiritual doctrines, unearthing the harmonious elements shared between the two realms.
- **Mindful Scientific Observation:** Apply mindfulness practices to your scientific observations, granting you a profound and intuitive comprehension of the intricacies of natural phenomena, thereby promoting a more holistic perspective.
- **Scientific Inquiry into Spirituality:** Approach spiritual tenets with the curiosity and rigor of scientific inquiry, aiming to substantiate their assertions through personal experiences and empirical evidence, fostering a synergistic relationship between these domains.
- **Comprehensive Holistic Education:** Seek out educational resources that offer a well-rounded perspective on the interplay between science and spirituality. This approach nurtures a more profound comprehension of the universe, acknowledging the interconnectedness of these fundamental aspects of human understanding.

In this section, we've discussed methods for integrating science and spirituality, promoting interdisciplinary studies, mindful observation, scientific inquiry into spirituality, and holistic education. These approaches encourage a more comprehensive understanding of the convergence between these two realms.

Now, let's explore how this integration impacts personal growth and contributes to global well-being. It offers transformative potential that extends beyond intellectual pursuits, influencing the very essence of our existence. By understanding the symbiotic relationship between these domains, we can appreciate how it nurtures individual development and contributes to a more harmonious and enlightened world.

Impact on Personal Growth and Global Well-Being

- **Inward Balance:** Discovering the convergence of science and spirituality forges a path to inner balance, guiding individuals as they navigate their personal growth journey, gaining deeper insight into their role in the vast cosmos.
- **Global Synergy:** As more individuals embrace the fusion of science and spirituality, a shift in collective awareness may unfold, promoting a more harmonious and sustainable world.
- **Embracing Diversity:** Recognizing the value in both scientific and spiritual perspectives fosters respect for diverse viewpoints and beliefs, nurturing tolerance and understanding.

The fusion of science and spirituality beckons individuals to transcend perceived divides, instead recognizing them as complementary facets of human comprehension. By embracing this union, individuals can access a profound sense of purpose, significance, and interconnectedness in their lives, contributing to personal growth and global well-being.

Harmonizing Ancient Wisdom with Modern Insight entails integrating ageless teachings, philosophies, and practices from various spiritual, philosophical, and cultural traditions with contemporary knowledge from modern science, psychology, and other disciplines. This integration strives to bridge the gap between traditional wisdom and present-day understanding, creating a harmonious and enriched perspective that adeptly navigates the complexities of the modern world. This synthesis enables individuals to draw upon the collective wisdom of the past while adapting it to the challenges and opportunities of today.

In this chapter, we bridge the gap between science and spirituality, highlighting their shared quest for truth, complementary perspectives, and the pursuit of a holistic understanding. We delve into Consciousness Studies, Quantum Physics, the Mind-Body Connection, and meditation's scientific underpinnings, finding common ground. This exploration offers the promise of a more unified understanding of existence.

The unity of science and spirituality yields transformative benefits, enhancing well-being, deepening understanding, fostering innovation, and promoting compassion. Methods for integration and their impact on personal growth and global well-being are discussed. This chapter is a journey toward the interconnectedness of science and spirituality, offering a symphony of possibilities for self-discovery and a harmonious world.

Chapter 25

The Influence of First Instinct and Thought

The influence of our first instincts and initial thoughts is a powerful force in shaping our perceptions, decisions, behaviors, and ultimately, our lives. This concept underscores the significance of our spontaneous, intuitive responses and how they can play a pivotal role in defining our reality and the outcomes we encounter. It's akin to having a vast reservoir of knowledge tucked away in the depths of our minds, waiting to be accessed by our unconscious, whether it's knowledge we've consciously acquired through learning or honed through extensive practice, or perhaps even a cosmic connection that brings forth the right answers at the right moment.

Key Aspects of the Influence of First Instinct and Thought

1. **Influence on Perception:** Our initial thoughts and instincts significantly shape how we perceive situations,

people, and events. They act as the lens through which we view the world.

2. **Decision-Making:** These initial responses play a substantial role in the decisions we make. They often guide us toward certain choices based on subconscious evaluations and biases.

3. **Behavioral Patterns:** Consistently following our first instincts and thoughts can lead to the development of behavioral patterns, influencing how we respond to recurring situations.

4. **Cognitive Biases:** First instincts and thoughts can sometimes be influenced by cognitive biases, which are mental shortcuts that unconsciously affect our thoughts and actions.

Utilizing First Instinct and Thought for Positive Outcomes

1. **Self-Awareness:** Cultivating self-awareness enables us to recognize our first instincts and thoughts. By understanding their sources, we can make more informed decisions.

2. **Mindful Reflection:** Taking a moment to pause and reflect on our initial reactions helps us assess whether they align with our values and goals.

3. **Balanced Decision-Making:** While quick decisions based on instincts can be valuable, taking the time to analyze options and consequences can lead to more balanced and thoughtful choices.

4. **Intuition and Creativity:** Trusting our intuition can enhance creativity and innovative thinking, allowing us to explore unconventional solutions.

Cautionary Considerations

1. **Biases:** First instincts may be influenced by biases of which we are not consciously aware. It's essential to critically examine our initial reactions to ensure they are fair and rational.

2. **Emotional Influence:** Strong emotions can color our initial responses. When emotions are heightened, it's beneficial to take a step back before deciding.

3. **Changing Circumstances:** While first instincts can provide valuable insights, circumstances can evolve. Reevaluating decisions based on developing information is essential.

Conclusion

Understanding and harnessing the influence of first instincts and thoughts involves a combination of mindfulness, self-awareness, and conscious decision-making. By observing our reactions, examining their underlying causes, and allowing space for rational evaluation, we can make more informed choices that align with our values, aspirations, and long-term well-being.

In summary, the influence of first instincts and thoughts underscores the power of these initial reactions in shaping our experiences and decisions. It emphasizes the importance of approaching them with awareness, mindfulness, and a willingness to adapt based on changing circumstances and broader perspectives.

Chapter 26

Transforming Dreams and Desires into Reality

Transforming dreams and desires into reality involves a process of turning your aspirations, goals, and visions into tangible outcomes and accomplishments. It requires setting clear intentions, taking proactive steps, and maintaining a focused mindset to bring your dreams to life. This process combines elements of goal setting, determination, action, and perseverance to create positive change and manifest the things you desire in your life.

The biblical statement **"Ask and you shall receive"** originates from the **New Testament, specifically from the teachings of Jesus in the Gospel of Matthew 7:7.** The full verse reads: "Ask, and it will be given to you; seek, and you will find, knock, and it will be opened to you." It's easy to remember as **ASK: "A"** for Asking, **"S"** for Seeking, and **"K"** for Knocking.

In Indian spiritual and Vedic teachings, similar concepts emphasize the power of asking, seeking, and receiving. **The Law of Karma**, rooted in Hinduism and other Indian spiritual traditions, suggests that one's actions and intentions have consequences. Performing *good deeds* and harboring *positive intentions* increase the likelihood of receiving *positive outcomes in return*.

It's important to note that the neurological processes associated with asking and seeking can vary from person to person and are influenced by individual beliefs, emotions, and experiences. The context in which asking occurs, whether it's spiritual, personal, or professional, can shape specific neurological responses and outcomes.

Key Elements for Transforming Dreams and Desires into Reality include

- **Clarity of vision:** When defining your dreams, utilize the **SMART** approach, which stands for **S**pecific, **M**easurable, **A**chievable, **R**elevant, and **T**ime-bound. This means that you should outline your aspirations in a way that is precise, quantifiable, attainable, pertinent, and set within a specific timeframe.
- **Positive Mindset:** Cultivate a positive and optimistic attitude, maintaining confidence even in the face of challenges.
- **Goal setting:** Apply the **SMART** format to your goal setting, which involves breaking down your dreams into smaller, more actionable and achievable objectives. Unlike the broader clarity of vision, this approach centers on creating smaller, more attainable and focused goals.
- **Action Planning:** Create a roadmap detailing the actions and resources needed to achieve your goals.
- **Commitment:** Stay committed to your goals and consistently work toward them, even when faced with setbacks or obstacles.
- **Visualization:** Visualize your desired outcomes as if they have already been achieved to align your thoughts and actions with your goals.
- **Positive Affirmations:** Use empowering statements to replace negative self-talk.

- **Adaptability:** Be open to adjusting your approach as needed.
- **Consistent Action:** Small, consistent actions accumulate over time.
- **Persistence:** Staying determined when faced with obstacles is crucial.

Steps to Transform Dreams and Desires into Reality

- **Define Your Dreams:** Clearly articulate what you want to achieve in writing.
- **Set Goals:** Break down your dreams into smaller, specific, measurable, and achievable goals within a defined timeframe.
- **Create a Plan:** Develop a detailed action plan outlining the steps required to achieve each goal.
- **Act:** Start taking steps toward your goals, no matter how small.
- **Stay Persistent:** Persistence is essential, even when progress seems slow.
- **Visualize Success:** Regularly visualize yourself achieving your dreams and feeling the success.
- **Overcome Challenges:** Expect challenges and setbacks and develop strategies to overcome them.
- **Celebrate Milestones:** Acknowledging progress boosts motivation.
- **Adapt and adjust:** Be willing to adjust your plan based on changing circumstances or new opportunities.

Benefits of Transforming Dreams and Desires into Reality include a sense of accomplishment, personal growth, increased confidence, a positive impact on others, motivation, and a deep sense of fulfillment and happiness.

Challenges and Considerations include the need for patience, perseverance, adaptability, and focusing on what you can control.

To turn your dreams into reality, remember three things: keep your focus on your goals, stay positive, and keep working. Challenges are part of the journey, but your determination and resilience will help you reach your dreams.

In the context of transforming dreams and desires into reality, a biblical verse worth considering is **Mark 11:24 (NIV):** *"Therefore I tell you, whatever you ask for in prayer, believe that you have received it, and it will be yours."* This verse underscores the power of belief and faith in fulfilling your desires through prayer and positive action.

In the following section, we will shift our focus slightly to provide you with a broader perspective and assist you in making connections between various elements.

The Connection Between Martial Arts and Realizing Dreams

Dr. Shawn Christian holds a Second-Degree Black Belt in Tang Soo Do a form of Korean martial arts. Some of the famous renowned martial arts champions amoung various martial arts disciplines include Jean-Claude Van Damme, Jackie Chan, Jet Li, Bruce Lee, Chuck Norris, Jason Statham, Steven Seagal. In the world of martial arts, such as Tang Soo Do, a remarkable bridge exists between physical discipline and the transformation of dreams into reality. Beyond the physical feats, martial arts offer a profound link to the realm of neuroscience and the power of visualization in making one's aspirations come to life. Practices like board breaking emphasize a unique connection to the transformative potential of dreams through the art of visualization and controlled breathing.

Simultaneously, in the world of martial arts, there's a profound connection to spiritual and philosophical dimensions that echo time-less wisdom found in various religious texts, including the Bible. The biblical statement "Ask and you shall receive," originating from the New Testament and the teachings of Jesus in the Gospel of Matthew 7:7, resonates with the core principles of martial arts. It underlines the transformative power of asking, seeking, and believing. In martial arts, individuals ask for guidance, set goals, visualize success, and have faith that dedication and hard work will grant them the wisdom and abilities needed to overcome challenges and attain their goals.

This dual connection within martial arts showcases that the pursuit of dreams and aspirations encompasses physical and spiritual dimensions, united by the common threads of determination, visual-ization, and belief in one's potential. Now, let's take a look at how martial arts teaches us about transforming dreams and desires into reality.

- **Motor Skills and Coordination:** Board breaking, an essential aspect of martial arts, demands precise motor skills and coordination. These capabilities find their roots in neuroscience's exploration of motor control, showcasing how the brain's adaptability plays a pivotal role in mastering skills that bridge the gap between dreams and reality.
- **Muscle Memory:** Through rigorous training, martial artists cultivate muscle memory, reinforcing neural connections between the brain and muscles. In this process, neuroscience teaches us how the brain adapts to repeated actions, a fundamental concept when striving for dreams that necessitate mastery.
- **Pain Tolerance and Endorphins:** In martial arts, particularly board breaking, individuals encounter physical discomfort and pain. Neuroscience provides insights into the body's response to pain and the release of endorphins, acting as natural painkillers. This

knowledge is essential for those seeking to overcome obstacles on their journey to achieving their dreams.

- **Visualization and Mental Practice:** In the realm of cognitive neuroscience, the art of visualization and mental preparation takes center stage. *Visualization involves the powerful act of seeing oneself as having already achieved the goal* – in the case of board breaking, visualizing the board breaking effortlessly and going through it. This mental rehearsal is a key that unlocks the door to transforming dreams into reality.

- **Controlled Breathing:** Much like meditation, martial arts involve the practice of controlled breathing. This controlled respiration aligns with the principles of centeredness and mindfulness, contributing to a calm, focused state that complements the act of visualization.

- **Stress and Performance:** Neuroscience studies how stress impacts neural function. Understanding and managing stress are crucial when individuals face anxiety or pressure in their pursuit of challenging objectives. Controlled breathing becomes an indispensable tool in maintaining composure and enhancing performance under stress.

- **Focus and Attention:** The demanding focus and attention required for successful board breaking align with neuroscience's exploration of attention and concentration mechanisms in the brain. Visualization, when coupled with controlled breathing, becomes a cornerstone in enhancing one's ability to concentrate by picturing the desired outcome and maintaining a calm, centered mindset.

- **Motivation and Goal Setting:** Neuroscience delves into motivation and goal setting, unraveling the brain's reward processing and objective setting. This aligns perfectly with the goals and motivations of martial artists, highlighting the importance of visualizing the end result – the realization of dreams and desires.

In board breaking, mental preparation, visualization, and controlled breathing coalesce into a holistic approach. Students set clear intentions, engage in positive self-talk, and control their breathing to optimize their mental and physical states for the challenge. The spectrum of sensations experienced, from focused concentration to the physical impact and the satisfaction of achievement, parallels the emotional journey of transforming dreams into reality.

Visualization, along with controlled breathing, stands as a linchpin in this process, allowing individuals to picture themselves as already having achieved their dreams while maintaining a calm and centered presence. By seeing the end goal as a reality and utilizing controlled breathing to manage stress and enhance focus, martial artists leverage the power of their minds to manifest their dreams.

This connection between martial arts and spiritual wisdom, echoing the biblical statement "Ask and you shall receive" from the teachings of Jesus, underlines the transformative power of asking, seeking, and believing. In the world of martial arts, individuals ask for guidance, set goals, visualize success, and have faith that dedication and hard work will grant them the wisdom and abilities needed to overcome challenges and attain their goals. This connection underscores that the pursuit of dreams, whether on the physical or spiritual plane, shares a common thread – the power of visualization, belief, and determination.

This is the end of Part V. In Part VI, we'll start an exciting journey that unlock the mysteries of human perception and consciousness. Looking forward to seeing you in Part VI!

Part Six

Awakening the Senses

In the enchanting realm of "Awakening the Senses," embark on a transformative journey through the chapters that unlock the mysteries of human perception and consciousness. Chapter 27, "The Creative Power of Sound Vibration," invites you to explore the profound influence of sound on the tapestry of existence, unraveling the threads that connect vibration to creation. In Chapter 28, "Breath: Gateway to Spiritual and Neurological Awakening," discover the pivotal role of breath as the conduit between the physical and the metaphysical, guiding you toward spiritual enlightenment and neurological harmony. As you delve into Chapter 29, "Illumination: Light's Profound Role in Spirituality," witness the ethereal dance of light and shadow that shapes the spiritual landscape. Concluding this enlightening journey, Chapter 30, "Mind-Conscious Synergy," uncovers the intricate dance between mind and consciousness, revealing the synergistic forces that propel us towards a higher state of being. Prepare to be captivated by the symphony of senses and the cosmic melodies that resonate through the pages, beckoning you to explore the boundless possibilities that lie within the awakening of your senses.

Chapter 27

The Creative Power of Sound Vibration

I n this chapter, we'll explore the intriguing world of sound vibrations and their connection to both spirituality and science. We'll also delve into their potential effects on our physical and emotional well-being.

Biblical Perspectives

In the Bible, specifically in the Book of Genesis, there is a verse that is often interpreted in relation to sound vibration and creation. The verse is:

"And God said, **'Let there be light,' and there was light."** - Genesis 1:3 (NIV),

This verse is often seen as an example of the power of the divine word or sound vibration that brought creation into existence. *The spoken word, representing sound or vibration, was the creative force behind the formation of light and, subsequently, the entire universe.*

While this interpretation is more symbolic and metaphorical, it reflects the concept of sound vibration as a creative force, a notion that is found in various spiritual and philosophical traditions.

As previously noted, the renowned biblical passage "Let there be light, and there was light" originates from the Book of Genesis within the Bible, specifically in the account of creation found in Genesis 1:3. It offers a profound and symbolic portrayal of God's creative action. While traditionally understood within religious and theological frameworks, certain people and spiritual traditions have explored the relationship between God's spoken word and the concept of sound vibrations.

Within the Rigveda, one of the most ancient Vedic texts, you can find hymns that poetically depict the universe's creation and the emergence of various natural elements. Though these hymns are replete with metaphorical and symbolic language, they serve to convey the profound notion of a divine cosmic order and the origins of life and light from the cosmic wellspring.

Across diverse spiritual and philosophical traditions, the significance of sound as a potent creative force is acknowledged. To shed light on the possible connection between the biblical declaration and the concept of God's sound vibrations, consider the following perspective:

- **Vibrational Creation:** Some spiritual and metaphysical beliefs suggest that sound or vibration is at the core of creation. In this view, the universe was formed through the vibration of divine energy or consciousness. The spoken word is seen as a manifestation of this divine vibration.

- **Sound as a Creative Force:** Sound is considered a fundamental creative force in many spiritual traditions. The idea is that when God spoke, the vibrations of His words initiated the creation of the universe, including the light.

- **Divine Utterance:** The act of God uttering, "Let there be light," is seen as a divine command that set the creative process into motion. It represents the power of God's word to bring things into existence.

- **Metaphorical Interpretation**: Some interpret this passage metaphorically, suggesting that it symbolizes the idea that God's will and intention are the driving forces behind creation. The "let there be light" statement signifies the divine intention for order and illumination in the cosmos.
- **Unity of Sound and Light:** In some mystical traditions, there is a belief in the interconnectedness of sound and light. Sound is seen as a precursor to light, and they are both considered expressions of the divine.

It's important to note that these interpretations are not universally accepted within all religious traditions, and they are often influenced by specific spiritual beliefs and practices. The connection between the spoken word of God and the concept of sound vibration is a matter of theological and philosophical interpretation and can vary among individuals and religious groups.

Exploring the Positive Effects of Vibrational Frequency on the Body and Health

The First Law of Thermodynamics

The First Law of Thermodynamics, also known as the law of conservation of energy, forms the foundation of our understanding of energy in the universe. This law states that the total energy in an isolated system remains constant; it is conserved over time. Energy can change from one form to another, but it cannot be created or destroyed.

Intriguingly, this principle of energy conservation is closely connected to the concept that everything in the universe, from the smallest atom to inanimate objects, living creatures, plants, and even celestial bodies like planets and the universe itself, possesses a fundamental attribute - vibration. Each entity in the cosmos resonates with a unique set of vibrational frequencies.

The universe is not a silent void; it is a symphony of energy and vibrations. Countless energy particles dance and vibrate incessantly, creating an ever-present sound that may not be audible to the human ear or visible to the naked eye. This omnipresent vibration is often metaphorically referred to as a "hum" – a subtle, underlying resonance that underlies the entire fabric of existence. Some even draw parallels between this cosmic hum and the concept of God's energy, suggesting that this pervasive vibration is a manifestation of the divine force that permeates all of creation. While this idea resides in the realm of philosophy and spirituality, it serves as a reminder that the universe is far from silent; it hums with the unseen energy that connects all things, from the tiniest subatomic particles to the grandest galaxies.

Chanting "AUM" or "AMEN" and Vibrational Resonance

The practice of chanting "AUM" (also spelled as "OM") holds a significant place in various spiritual and meditative traditions, particularly those associated with the chakra system. Chanting "AUM" is believed to induce a calming and centering effect on both the mind and body, resonating with the vibrations of the universe.

Notably, the sound "AUM" shares a similarity with the word "AMEN." Both "AUM" and "AMEN" are sacred sounds that are used in various religious and spiritual practices to invoke a sense of connection with the divine or the cosmos. They both have a commonality in that they carry sound vibrations that hold special significance in these practices.

While scientific research on the specific effects of chanting "AUM" on chakra balance and overall health remains limited, there are potential mechanisms through which this practice could be beneficial:

- **Vibration and Resonance:** Chanting "AUM" or "AMEN" generates specific vibrational frequencies that might influence the body's energy centers. Each chakra is linked to a particular frequency, and the vibrations from chanting "AUM" or "AMEN" could resonate with and stimulate these frequencies, fostering balance and energy flow.
- **Mind-Body Connection:** Chanting "AUM" or "AMEN" can deepen the connection between the mind and body. The heightened awareness and focus on each chakra during chanting can lead to a greater sense of balance and well-being.
- **Breath and Relaxation:** Chanting "AUM" or "AMEN"often involves slow, deliberate breathing. Mindful breathing activates the parasympathetic nervous system, promoting relaxation and stress reduction. This relaxation response can contribute to overall health and well-being.
- **Psychological Effects:** Chanting "AUM" or "AMEN" can have a meditative and calming effect on the mind, helping to reduce anxiety, enhance mental clarity, and improve emotional balance, potentially positively impacting overall health.
- **Intention and Focus:** Chanting "AUM" or "AMEN" with the intention to balance and harmonize each chakra may create a positive mental framework for healing and wellness.

While chanting "AUM" or "AMEN" can be a valuable practice for individuals seeking spiritual growth and well-being, it's crucial to approach it with an open mind and an understanding of its potential effects.

Here are some key considerations:

- **Individual Variation**: People may experience different responses to chanting "AUM" or "AMEN" based on their beliefs, experiences, and physiological factors.
- **Complementary Practice**: Chanting "AUM" or "AMEN"can be used alongside other well-established wellness techniques, such as meditation, mindfulness, yoga, and conventional medical treatments.
- **Personal Comfort**: If you resonate with the practice and find it beneficial, incorporating chanting "AUM" or "AMEN" into your routine may contribute to your overall health and well-being.
- **Cultural and Spiritual Considerations**: Chanting "AUM" or "AMEN" has specific spiritual and cultural roots. It's essential to approach the practice with respect and an understanding of its origins, even if you're adopting it for its potential health benefits.

Like any wellness practice, the effects of chanting "AUM" or "AMEN" on chakra balance and overall health can vary from person to person. If you're intrigued by this practice, consider starting slowly, paying close attention to how your body responds, and don't hesitate to seek guidance from experienced practitioners or teachers if you have questions or need assistance.

Exploring the Influence of Vibrations on the Human Body: Positive and Negative Outcomes

Let's explore the intriguing interplay between science and spirituality as it revolves around the concept of vibrations. These vibrations are ubiquitous, resonating in various forms, from the soothing strains of a violin to the depths of our emotions and the vibrations from words, such as AUM (OM) and AMEN. Their influence extends far beyond the boundaries of conventional measurement and perception, reaching into the realms of both the tangible and the ethereal.

These vibrations help us see the link between science, spirituality, and our lives. They connect what we can touch and what's beyond our senses. They make us think about things we can measure, like physical vibrations, and things we can't, like our emotions and hidden energies.

This expedition highlights the profound link between vibrations, an integral component of both ancient wisdom and contemporary science. It unveils the intricate interconnection between the visible and the unseen. This concept is exemplified by a passage from the Bible, Proverbs 17:22 (NIV), which asserts, "A cheerful heart is good medicine, but a crushed spirit dries up the bones." This encapsulates the idea that our emotions and thoughts wield a significant influence on our physical well-being.

As we explore vibrations, we'll find that science and spirituality are deeply connected through them. Vibrations have many effects on our bodies, depending on factors like how often they happen, how strong they are, and how we react to them. This journey shows that vibrations help us understand the link between science and spirituality.

Vibrations come in different forms, from peaceful meditation to the jarring sensations in our everyday lives. Our goal is to understand the spiritual side of vibrations, how they relate to things beyond the physical world. We want to see how vibrations connect our bodies with the spiritual and metaphysical parts of our lives.

Let's now examine various effects of vibrations. It's essential to emphasize that the following list encompasses a wide spectrum of vibrations, encompassing not only spiritual but also occupational and therapeutic vibrations.

Positive Vibrational Influences

- **Therapeutic Applications:** Within the realm of vibrations, we find an array of therapeutic applications. Controlled vibrations, emanating from massage devices or therapeutic equipment, hold the power to induce profound relaxation, enhance the flow of life force within us, and untangle the knots of muscle tension. Vibrational therapy is a well-recognized method for easing pain and expediting the recovery process, offering a glimpse into the healing potential of vibratory energy.

- **Exercise and Fitness:** Vibrations extend their positive touch into the world of fitness training. Whole-body vibration (WBV) platforms, when skillfully utilized, prove instrumental in augmenting muscle strength, enhancing flexibility, and fortifying bone density. These platforms serve as conduits for vibrations that mimic the effects of physical exercise, unveiling the potential for vibrations to amplify our physical vitality.

Negative Vibrational Impacts

- **Occupational Hazards:** Vibrations, when encountered in the occupational sphere, bring forth their own set of challenges. Extended exposure to vibrations stemming from tools or machinery can culminate in conditions such as hand-arm vibration syndrome (HAVS) or whole-body vibration syndrome (WBVS). These maladies unfurl as vascular, neurological, and musculoskeletal issues, offering a stark reminder of the dual nature of vibratory energy.

- **Noise-Induced Vibration:** Vibrations linked to noisy equipment or environments usher in a different kind of discord. Here, vibrations kindle stress, fatigue, and discomfort, often evolving into a symphony of adverse health outcomes. Prolonged exposure to the cacophony of excessive noise and vibrations can orchestrate a crescendo of hearing loss and other health complications, painting a somber portrait of the detrimental aspects of vibrational energy.

- **Motion Sickness:** Within the cacophony of vibrations, we encounter instances where the human body's equilibrium is disrupted. Repetitive or irregular vibrations, as experienced in vehicles or boats, have the power to induce the unsettling symphony of motion sickness, characterized by the discord of nausea, dizziness, and discomfort. This phenomenon sheds light on the intrinsic connection between vibrations and our inner balance.

- **Resonance Effects:** Vibrations possess a resonating power that, when harnessed at specific frequencies, can lead to resonance in bodily tissues, potentially causing discomfort, pain, or even injury. This phenomenon takes center stage in situations like prolonged journeys on rugged terrain, serving as a testament to the delicate harmony between vibratory frequencies and the human body.

Health Considerations

- **Individual Variability:** People exhibit wide-ranging sensitivity to vibrations. While some individuals may be more susceptible to negative effects, others may remain unaffected by any discomfort or harm.

- **Frequency and Intensity:** The frequency and intensity of vibrations play a pivotal role in determining their impact on the body. High-frequency vibrations can affect nerves and blood vessels, whereas low-frequency

vibrations are more likely to influence muscles and
bones.

It is important to recognize that the effects of vibrations on the
human body are multifaceted and influenced by multiple factors.
Should you have concerns about the potential repercussions of vibrations in your environment or activities, consulting relevant experts
such as medical professionals, occupational health specialists, or
ergonomics experts is advisable.

In closing, our exploration of vibrations reveals them as the
binding thread between science and spirituality. Vibrations bridge
the gap between the tangible and the metaphysical, unveiling a
profound unity. We've witnessed their dual nature, capable of both
positive and negative effects, and recognized the diverse individual
responses they elicit. The frequency and intensity of vibrations offer
a glimpse into their subtle yet powerful influence. This journey
affirms that the unity of science and spirituality is not a distant dream
but a reality, grounded in the vibrations that harmonize our understanding of the universe and our place within it.

How Different Frequencies Can Benefit You

Many people believe that various frequencies and sound vibrations
have the potential to promote healing and well-being. While scientific research in this area continues, proponents suggest that certain
frequencies can influence the body, mind, and energy systems,
including the chakras. Here are a few examples of frequencies and
their potential benefits:

- **Binaural Beats:** Binaural beats involve playing two
  slightly different frequencies in each ear, creating the
  perception of a third frequency. These beats are thought
  to influence brainwave patterns and may have various
  effects, including relaxation, stress reduction, improved

focus, and better sleep. They could complement chakra balancing practices by affecting brainwave activity linked to different states of consciousness.

- **Solfeggio Frequencies:** Solfeggio frequencies are specific tones derived from ancient musical scales, each associated with different effects, such as healing, spiritual awakening, and transformation. For example, the 528 Hz frequency is often referred to as the "Love Frequency" and is believed to promote healing and positive transformation.

Here are the Solfeggio Frequencies and their associated effects:

1. UT – 396 Hz – transforms grief into joy and guilt into forgiveness.
2. RE – 417 Hz – clears negativity and removes subconscious blockages.
3. MI – 528 Hz – stimulates love, restores equilibrium, and repairs DNA.
4. FA – 639 Hz – strengthens relationships, family, and community unity.
5. SOL – 741 Hz – physically cleanses the body from many toxins.
6. LA – 852 Hz – awakens intuition and helps you return to spiritual balance.
7. 888 Hz – attracts healing and abundance and is known as a powerful angelic frequency.

- **Schumann Resonance:** The Schumann Resonance is a natural electromagnetic frequency generated by the Earth's electromagnetic field, typically around 7.83 Hz. Some proponents suggest that aligning with the Schumann Resonance can promote a sense of grounding, well-being, and harmony with nature.

- **Chakra Frequencies:** Each chakra is associated with a specific frequency. Chanting, toning, or listening to these frequencies is believed to resonate with the energy centers, potentially promoting balance and well-being.

It's important to note that while these frequency-based practices have gained popularity in alternative and holistic health communities, their effects are still under study, and scientific evidence is limited. Individual experiences may vary widely. If you're interested in exploring sound frequencies for potential benefits, consider the following:

- **Seek Guidance:** Consult experienced practitioners or teachers with a deep understanding of these practices for proper instruction.
- **Approach with Openness:** Understand that the effects may be subtle and may take time to notice.
- **Integrate with Other Practices:** Use frequency-based practices alongside other wellness approaches like meditation, yoga, mindfulness, and conventional medical treatments.
- **Personalize Your Approach:** Recognize that everyone responds differently to sound frequencies, so pay attention to your body's responses and adjust your practices accordingly.
- **Respect Cultural Context:** Many of these practices have cultural and spiritual origins, so approach them with respect and an understanding of their context.

It is worth mentioning here that before making substantial alterations to your health or wellness routine, particularly if you have preexisting health issues or concerns, it is recommended to seek guidance from healthcare professionals.

In conclusion, our exploration of sound vibrations reveals their significance in both spirituality and science. Vibrations bridge the gap between the tangible and the metaphysical, influencing our physical and emotional well-being. The frequency and intensity of vibrations offer a glimpse into their subtle yet powerful influence. This journey highlights the unity of science and spirituality, grounded in the vibrations that harmonize our understanding of the universe and our place within it.

Chapter 28

Breath: Gateway to Spiritual and Neurological Awakening

Breathing, a fundamental physiological process central to sustaining life, intricately links the realms of anatomy, physiology, spirituality, and neurology. The anatomy and physiology of breathing involve the respiratory system, which encompasses the lungs and diaphragm. This complex system orchestrates the journey of air, beginning with inhalation through the nose or mouth, passing through the pharynx and larynx, and finally entering the trachea. The trachea subsequently branches into bronchi and then bronchioles, leading to the alveoli, where vital gas exchange takes place. The diaphragm, a muscular powerhouse, contracts and relaxes in harmonious cadence, facilitating the inhalation and exhalation cycles. This symphony of respiratory mechanics allows oxygen to infiltrate the bloodstream and ushers carbon dioxide out.

Throughout this book, we've consistently emphasized the significance of breathing. This orchestration of breath extends beyond the confines of mere biology. In the realms of mindfulness and meditation practices, a profound connection between breath and spiritual or neurological awakening emerges. Breath serves as a conduit to heightened physical and mental awareness. The deliberate manipulation of breath in practices such as yoga, meditation, and pranayama opens a gateway to self-awareness, and for some, it paves the way to spiritual awakening. On a neurological level, controlled breathing techniques actively engage the parasympathetic nervous system, reducing stress and anxiety while nurturing a sense of tranquility and presence. This, in turn, can amplify one's receptivity to profound spiritual and introspective experiences.

This overarching connection between breath and the realms of spirituality, neurology, and the body's harmony sets the stage for further exploration. Let's delve deeper into this concept:

- **Breath as a Gateway:** The concept posits that breathing transcends the physical; it serves as a bridge between body, mind, and spirit. By embracing conscious breathing, individuals can unearth profound layers of consciousness and understanding.
- **Spiritual Awakening:** Delving into intentional breathing implies accessing altered states of consciousness, mystical experiences, and a profound connection to the divine. Breath, when focused upon, can lead to spiritual revelations.
- **Neurological Awakening:** The term signifies that mindful breathing has the power to transform brain activity, neural pathways, and neurotransmitter release. It can amplify cognitive functions, sharpen awareness, and even open the door to altered states of consciousness.

These key themes and implications paint a vivid picture:

- **Breath and Presence:** Focusing on the breath anchors individuals in the present moment, a core practice in mindfulness and spiritual traditions. It fosters self-awareness and deep connection with reality.

- **Alignment of Mind and Body:** When breath aligns with intention, harmony and balance manifest within.
- **Integration of Spiritual Practices:** Incorporating specific breathing techniques into meditation, prayer, or yoga enhances the effectiveness of these practices, deepening one's connection with their inner self and higher consciousness.
- **Neuroplasticity and Neural Pathways:** Purposeful breathing is suggested to stimulate the creation of new neural pathways in the brain, potentially leading to expanded cognitive abilities and profound perceptual experiences.

The benefits and applications are manifold:

- **Stress Reduction:** Conscious breathing triggers the body's relaxation response, reducing stress and promoting a sense of calm.
- **Enhanced Focus:** Breath-focused concentration enhances the ability to stay present and maintain focus.
- **Heightened Spiritual Experiences:** Mindful breathing nurtures spiritual experiences, forging deeper connections with higher powers, inner wisdom, or universal consciousness.
- **Neurological Enhancement:** Intentional breathing practices may activate brain regions linked to higher cognitive functions, creativity, and insight.
- **Mind-Body Connection:** Consciously breathing deepens the awareness of the interplay between mind and body, fostering overall well-being.

By practicing deep and extended breaths, humans can foster longer and healthier lives through improved oxygen efficiency, reduced stress, enhanced lung function, better heart health, heightened mental clarity, and reduced inflammation. This approach is closely associated with the equilibrium and circulation of life force energy, often known as Prana. While various cultures and systems may hold distinct beliefs and practices regarding life force, they all share a fundamental recognition of an underlying energy that upholds and nurtures life.

In summary, "Breath: Gateway to Spiritual and Neurological Awakening" underscores the profound potential of conscious breathing to unlock spiritual insights and neurological enhancements. This transformative power of breath resonates through philosophical, spiritual, and scientific traditions, exemplifying the interconnectedness of life through breath and sound. It symbolizes a shared vitality, an unifying experience transcending species, race, and borders, and influences the autonomic nervous system, brain function, and overall well-being through rhythmic conscious breathing practices.

Chapter 29

Illumination: Light's Profound Role in Spirituality

B efore we get into Light's Profound Role in Spirituality, we should understand what light is. Light is a form of electromagnetic radiation that is visible to the human eye. It is a fundamental natural phenomenon characterized by the emission of photons, which are tiny particles or packets of energy. Light travels in waves and is often associated with the sensation of brightness or the absence of darkness. It can originate from various sources, including the sun, artificial lighting, or bioluminescent organisms, and it plays a crucial role in our perception of the world, enabling us to see objects and the colors that surround us.

Now that we understand what light is, let's delve into Light's Profound Role in Spirituality. This exploration delves into the profound symbolic significance of light in various spiritual traditions. It investigates how light transcends its physical nature to become a metaphor for spiritual awakening, enlightenment, and the presence of the divine. The underlying concept underscores that light carries deep spiritual meaning, symbolizing clarity, knowledge, purity, and the illumination of one's inner self.

Understanding the Concept

- **Metaphor of Light:** This concept introduces the metaphorical use of light in spiritual contexts, emphasizing that light isn't merely a physical phenomenon but a symbol that transcends the material world. In spirituality, light serves as a symbol of profound significance, representing the eternal presence of the divine and the inherent luminosity within the human soul. Just as physical light pierces through the darkness, spiritual light penetrates the veil of ignorance and materialism, illuminating the path to spiritual awakening and profound insights.

- **Spiritual Illumination:** The concept of spiritual illumination implies that light symbolizes spiritual awakening and enlightenment. Just as physical light dispels darkness, spiritual light banishes ignorance and the veils of illusion. This metaphorical use of light in spirituality emphasizes its role as a guiding force, casting a metaphorical beacon of wisdom and clarity along the path of the spiritual journey. It signifies the transformative journey from spiritual obscurity to the radiant awakening of one's inner self, wherein seekers gain profound insights into the nature of existence and attain a heightened state of consciousness. Across many spiritual traditions, the pursuit of this inner light is synonymous with the quest for spiritual enlightenment and self-realization, representing the ultimate goal of the spiritual voyage.

Key Themes and Implications

- **Inner Transformation:** The concept of light representing inner transformation and the journey from spiritual darkness to awakened consciousness suggests a fundamental spiritual truth. It signifies that, in the realm of spirituality, light serves as a powerful symbol for the profound changes that can occur within a person. This inner transformation, facilitated by the metaphorical light, leads individuals from a state of spiritual obscurity to a place of awakened awareness.

- **Divine Presence:** Delving into the belief that light symbolizes the divine or higher consciousness reveals a connection between the inner and outer realms. Just as physical light illuminates the external world, spiritual light is seen as the manifestation of the divine within. This connection sets the stage for exploring light's profound role in spirituality, where it represents not only an abstract concept but a tangible bridge to the divine presence experienced in various spiritual practices.

- **Guidance and Wisdom:** The metaphor of light is often linked to guidance, wisdom, and clarity, suggesting that spiritual insight can navigate life's complexities. This notion provides an essential foundation for understanding the multifaceted role of light in spirituality. Light serves as a beacon, guiding individuals on their spiritual quests and bestowing the wisdom necessary to navigate the intricate pathways of existence.

- **Purity and Cleansing:** In spiritual contexts, light is commonly associated with purity and cleansing, symbolizing the removal of impurities, negativity, and ignorance from the soul. This theme sets the context for exploring how light's transformative power purifies and

cleanses the inner self, preparing it for spiritual growth
and enlightenment.

- **Universal Symbol:** The idea that the symbolism of
  light transcends specific religious or cultural boundaries
  establishes a common thread among diverse spiritual
  traditions. This universality creates a solid foundation for
  comprehending how light plays a profound and unifying
  role in spirituality across various cultures and belief
  systems.

Benefits and Applications

- **Spiritual Awakening:** Contemplating the symbolism
  of light can lead to spiritual awakening and a deeper
  understanding of one's true nature.
- **Positive Mindset:** Engaging with the concept of
  spiritual light can foster a positive mindset, promoting
  inner peace and resilience.
- **Mindfulness and Presence:** Reflecting on the
  symbolism of light encourages mindfulness and being
  present in the moment, fostering a deeper connection to
  the here and now.
- **Transformation:** The metaphor of light inspires
  personal growth and transformation, encouraging
  individuals to shed limiting beliefs and embrace their full
  potential.
- **Connection to the Divine:** Contemplating the
  significance of light can deepen one's connection to the
  divine or a higher source of consciousness.
- **Harmony and Unity:** Understanding the spiritual
  significance of light fosters a sense of unity and
  interconnectedness with all living beings.

- **Cultivation of Virtues:** Exploring the symbolism of light encourages the cultivation of virtues such as compassion, kindness, and humility.
- **Meditative Practices:** Engaging in meditation or visualization practices involving light enhances relaxation, focus, and a sense of inner peace.

Unveiling the Mystical Encounters of Near-Death Experiences

Light's Profound Role in Spirituality extends to various mystical experiences, including those reported during near-death experiences (NDEs). Many individuals who have gone through NDEs describe encountering a bright, white light. This connection highlights the universality of light as a symbol of divine presence and spiritual awakening.

During near-death experiences, people often report encountering a radiant, white light. This phenomenon resonates deeply with the spiritual symbolism of light as a metaphor for enlightenment, divinity, and purity. It suggests that the light experienced during NDEs transcends the physical realm, becoming a powerful symbol of spiritual awakening. This connection underscores that the profound role of light in spirituality is not limited to religious texts or practices but extends to extraordinary, firsthand accounts of individuals who have ventured to the edge of existence and returned with stories of encountering a divine radiance.

Furthermore, some NDE reports involve encounters with beings they interpret as angels, often surrounded by this same white light. This interpretation aligns with the idea that light symbolizes divine presence. In these experiences, the white light can be seen as an aura or a celestial glow that envelops these angelic figures, signifying their connection to the divine. This reinforces the concept that light, particularly in the form of a radiant, white glow, is perceived as a tangible manifestation of the divine or God.

The convergence of these experiences with the spiritual symbolism of light not only offers a profound link between mystical occurrences and religious or spiritual beliefs but also invites further contemplation of the metaphysical and transformative power of light in guiding individuals towards greater awareness, spiritual enlightenment, and the perception of the divine. These accounts affirm that light, whether encountered in moments of crisis or during deep meditation, carries deep spiritual meaning and serves as a bridge between the material and the metaphysical realms, leading people toward a more profound understanding of existence and their own spirituality.

Intuitive Understanding of Good and Evil

In various cultures and spiritual traditions, there's a shared belief that young children possess a special sensitivity to the spiritual realm, displaying an exceptional ability to distinguish between good and evil. It's fascinating how these little ones often describe seeing a radiant white light enveloping those they instinctively identify as having a pure and good heart. This connection mirrors the spiritual symbolism found in Matthew 18:3 (NIV): "And he said: Truly, I tell you, unless you change and become like little children, you will never enter the kingdom of heaven." The verse suggests a profound truth—that, like children, embracing innocence and heightened awareness allows us to discern and embody the qualities that lead to the kingdom of heaven.

It's important to note that the symbolism of white light, as seen around virtuous individuals, generally represents purity, goodness, and spiritual clarity. This white light is often associated with a sense of divine presence and inner purity. However, in contrast, when discussing the perception of evil, it is not typically associated with light but rather with darkness. Evil or malevolence is often symbolized by darkness, shadows, or a lack of light. The fundamental difference lies in the symbolism itself, with light representing goodness and darkness signifying the absence of light, which can be associated with malevolence or spiritual obscurity.

Therefore, children's accounts of seeing a white light around those they consider virtuous emphasize the positive connotations of light and its role as a symbol of goodness and spiritual purity. This innate perception reinforces the idea that light carries profound spiritual significance and serves as an intuitive bridge between the material and spiritual worlds, enabling children to express their understanding of good and evil through this powerful symbolism.

Conclusion

In conclusion, this exploration reveals the profound and versatile role of light in spirituality. It serves as a powerful metaphor for spiritual awakening, divine presence, and inner transformation. As we've seen in the previous sections, this symbolism extends beyond the confines of religious texts and practices, touching various aspects of human experience.

The experiences of individuals encountering radiant, white light during near-death experiences resonate deeply with the spiritual symbolism of light. This light, transcending the physical realm, acts as a potent symbol of spiritual awakening, enlightenment, and the presence of the divine. These firsthand accounts, shared by those who ventured to the edge of existence, provide an authentic link between mystical occurrences and spiritual beliefs, illustrating the transformative power of light on the journey to greater awareness.

Furthermore, the intuitive perception of children, who describe seeing a white light around individuals they perceive as virtuous, offers a unique perspective. This phenomenon connects their innocence and heightened spiritual awareness to the symbolic power of light, revealing its significance in distinguishing goodness and spiritual purity. It reminds us that the role of light in spirituality isn't limited to the adult world, as children, unburdened by skepticism, seamlessly bridge the material and the spiritual through their intuitive understanding.

Chapter 30

Mind-Conscious Synergy

M ind-Conscious Synergy is the idea that mindfulness, consciousness, and cognitive enhancement are closely linked and have a big impact on shaping how we experience life, our awareness, and mental well-being. Exploring these connections can provide valuable insights into improving cognitive function and overall well-being. Mindfulness, Consciousness, and Cognitive Enhancement play interconnected roles in awakening the senses for the spiritual journey:

- **Mindfulness** awakens the senses by promoting present-moment awareness and non-judgmental observation, which is crucial for spiritual exploration. This heightened awareness allows individuals to connect deeply with their inner selves and surroundings, fostering a more profound spiritual experience. In line with these principles, the Biblical verse is Matthew 7:1, and in the New International Version (NIV), it reads: *"Do not judge, or you too will be judged."* This biblical injunction seamlessly aligns with the essence of mindfulness, emphasizing the importance of non-judgmental awareness in the journey of spiritual discovery.

- **Consciousness** is the foundation of the spiritual journey. It encompasses sensory perception, self-awareness, and the stream of thoughts and emotions. In various religious and spiritual practices, expanding one's consciousness through meditation, prayer, or contemplation is a common goal. This expanded consciousness leads to a deeper understanding of the self and the divine.
- **Cognitive Enhancement**, particularly in terms of improved focus, memory, creativity, and emotional regulation, can facilitate the spiritual journey. Clearer thinking and emotional balance provide individuals with the mental tools necessary to explore their spirituality more deeply.

Mindfulness: The Art of Being Present

Throughout the pages of this book, we've consistently emphasized the significance of mindfulness. This underscores the crucial nature of being mindful. At its core, mindfulness is the practice of immersing oneself in the here and now without passing judgment. It involves developing a heightened awareness of our thoughts, emotions, physical sensations, and the environment that envelops us. It encourages us to calmly observe our experiences, refrain from impulsive reactions, and resist the allure of distractions.

Benefits of Mindfulness

- **Stress Reduction**: Mindfulness acts as a refuge for individuals dealing with stress, providing a sanctuary of tranquility in the midst of life's chaos. By encouraging the practice of being fully present without judgment, it disrupts the cycle of rumination, reducing the tendency to dwell on past regrets or future anxieties and ultimately diminishing overall stress levels.

- **Emotional Regulation**: Mindfulness serves as a guiding light in the unpredictable realm of emotions, instilling a non-reactive approach. This non-reactive attitude enables individuals to observe their feelings without being carried away by them, fostering emotional resilience and the ability to choose healthier responses to their emotions.
- **Improved Focus**: Mindfulness practice enhances focus and concentration as individuals learn to anchor their attention to the present moment, whether through techniques like focusing on their breath or bodily sensations. This honed focus can be applied to various aspects of life, improving performance in work, studies, and relationships.
- **Enhanced Well-Being**: Mindfulness establishes the groundwork for mental well-being and life satisfaction. By promoting self-acceptance and self-compassion through present-moment awareness, individuals develop healthier relationships with themselves, reducing self-criticism and nurturing self-love.
- **Cultivation of Self-Awareness:** Mindfulness acts as a reflective mirror through which individuals gain profound insights into their thoughts, emotions, and behaviors. By observing their inner processes without judgment, individuals cultivate a deeper understanding of themselves, enabling personal growth, the identification of limiting thought patterns, and the opportunity for positive behavioral change.
- **Consciousness**: Consciousness, ranging from sensory perception to self-awareness, forms the core of human

experience. Mindfulness, by promoting intentional awareness without judgment, utilizes this consciousness as the foundation for observing thoughts and emotions in the present moment. This deepened consciousness aids in recognizing thought patterns and reactions, fostering greater self-awareness and the capacity to respond consciously to life's stimuli. In essence, mindfulness harnesses consciousness to enhance our connection with our inner world, allowing us to navigate life with increased clarity and presence.

Facets of Consciousness

- **States of Consciousness:** States of consciousness encompass the range of our waking experiences, from the vibrancy of alert wakefulness where we engage with our surroundings to the depths of altered states, like the surreal and often emotionally charged world of dreams that occur during REM sleep, as well as the focused tranquility of meditation, where we can enter altered states of perception, often marked by heightened awareness and relaxation.
- **Self-Consciousness:** Self-consciousness is the fundamental awareness of oneself as an individual with unique thoughts, emotions, and experiences. It's our ability to recognize our own existence and differentiate it from others, which includes not only introspection about our own thoughts, feelings, and actions but also understanding that others possess their own distinct perspectives and motivations, forming the foundation for empathy and complex social interactions, and influencing our personal identity and sense of self.

- **Stream of Consciousness**: The stream of consciousness represents the continuous and ever-flowing sequence of thoughts, emotions, and sensory perceptions that occupy our minds. Our thoughts range from the mundane and practical aspects of daily life to profound and abstract musings, while emotions often arise in response to our thoughts, external stimuli, or memories, affecting our decision-making and behavior. Our sensory perceptions, encompassing what we see, hear, touch, taste, and smell, continuously provide information about the external world, shaping our ongoing understanding of reality and playing a vital role in our subjective experience of the world.

Implications of Consciousness

- **Subjective Experience:** Consciousness serves as the portal through which we traverse our subjective experiences and engage in introspection, giving rise to our unique perspectives and interpretations of the world. It is the lens through which we perceive and make sense of our reality, profoundly shaping our individual narratives.
- **Higher Cognitive Functions**: Consciousness is the cornerstone of higher cognitive functions, enabling the complex art of thinking, decision-making, and problem-solving. It provides the canvas upon which the intricate tapestry of human intellect is woven, allowing us to analyze, reason, and innovate
- **Sense of identity**: Within the vast landscape of consciousness, the sense of identity emerges, weaving the fabric of self and personal identity. It is our consciousness that connects our past, present, and future, providing the

narrative continuity that defines who we are as individuals.

- **Cognitive Enhancement**: Cognitive enhancement encompasses an array of strategies and practices aimed at refining cognitive functions, including memory, attention, creativity, and problem-solving. In this quest for cognitive empowerment, mindfulness practices shine as a holistic and effective method.

Mindfulness as Cognitive Enhancement

- **Attention and Focus:** Mindfulness meditation acts as a beacon, sharpening attention control and shielding against the temptations of distraction, helping us maintain a clear and focused mind.
- **Working Memory**: As we voyage deeper into mindfulness training, the capacity of our working memory expands, allowing us to juggle multiple pieces of information and process them more efficiently. This deepening of working memory enhances our knowledge retention and problem-solving abilities.
- **Creativity:** Flexible thinking blossoms within the garden of mindfulness, fostering ingenious problem-solving. By breaking free from rigid thought patterns, mindfulness promotes creative ideation and innovative solutions to complex challenges.
- **Emotional Regulation**: Emotional regulation becomes the cornerstone of clarity, nurturing sound decision-making. Through mindfulness, we gain greater control over our emotional responses, reducing impulsivity and facilitating more thoughtful and informed choices.

- **Interconnectedness**: Mindfulness practices intricately involve the cultivation of conscious awareness of our inner landscape. Engaging in mindfulness meditation transcends mere self-reflection and ushers in cognitive enhancement through heightened attentional control, a shield against mind-wandering, and a newfound ability to orchestrate cognitive processes.

Benefits of Integrating Mindfulness, Consciousness, and Cognitive Enhancement

- **Holistic Well-Being**: The fusion of mindfulness and cognitive enhancement strategies is the foundation of holistic well-being, tending to the cognitive, emotional, and awareness-related dimensions of our lives. It aligns these dimensions, resulting in a more balanced and fulfilling existence.
- **Stress Reduction**: Mindfulness serves as a bastion against stress and anxiety, clearing the path to improved cognitive function. By allowing us to better manage stressors and maintain mental clarity, mindfulness contributes to overall cognitive enhancement.
- **Better Decision-Making:** Enhanced self-awareness and emotional regulation pave the way for thoughtful, informed decisions. The integration of mindfulness and consciousness empowers us to make choices that align with our values and long-term goals.
- **Improved Learning**: Mindfulness practices become our allies in the quest for effective learning, enhancing our focus and memory retention. By nurturing attention and memory, mindfulness optimizes the learning process, making it more efficient and rewarding.

References to Religions

- **Buddhism**: Buddhism places significant emphasis on mindfulness through practices like Vipassana meditation. Mindfulness is considered a path to enlightenment and awakening, where individuals can deepen their understanding of reality and their own nature.
- **Hinduism**: In Hinduism, practices like yoga and meditation are employed to expand consciousness and achieve spiritual enlightenment. Through these practices, individuals aim to transcend the ordinary, ego-bound state of consciousness and connect with a higher, universal consciousness.
- **Sufism (Islamic Mysticism)**: Sufism often employs conscious awareness and mindfulness to deepen the connection with God. Sufi practices include meditation and the remembrance of God (Dhikr), which enhance consciousness and spirituality.
- **Christian Mysticism**: Christian mysticism encourages practices such as contemplative prayer and mindfulness of God's presence. These practices aim to deepen one's consciousness of the divine and foster a more profound spiritual connection.
- **Native American Spirituality**: Various Native American spiritual traditions involve rituals and ceremonies that utilize mindfulness and heightened consciousness to connect with nature and the spiritual world. These practices aim to awaken the senses and gain deeper insights into the mysteries of life.

Conclusion

The intricate interplay between mindfulness, consciousness, and cognitive enhancement unfolds a profound narrative of their interconnection. Together, these elements shape not only our cognitive prowess but also our self-awareness and overall well-being. Embarking on the path of mindfulness serves as the key to unlocking a heightened conscious awareness, enabling us to harness its transformative potential, thus propelling us towards a more enriched and meaningful existence. This dynamic synergy extends beyond the realm of personal growth, deeply resonating within various religious and spiritual traditions. Through the practice of mindfulness, the expansion of consciousness, and the cultivation of cognitive capabilities, individuals embark on a profound exploration of the spiritual dimensions of life. These practices awaken the senses and facilitate a deeper connection with the mysteries of existence.

We've reached the end of Part VI. Moving on to Part VII, we'll explore Inner Practices and Reflections, a section dedicated to delving into the fundamental elements of personal well-being and spirituality.

Part Seven

Inner Practices and Reflections

Step into the heart of "Inner Practices and Reflections," a section of our book that delves into the core aspects of personal well-being and spirituality. In Chapter 31, explore the dynamics of Inner Joy, Well-Being, Prosperity, and Contentment, decoding the essentials for a rich and meaningful life. Chapter 32, titled "Illuminating Unity," sheds light on the interconnected threads that bind us all. Chapter 33 reveals the Harmonic Nexus of Love, Health, and Spirituality, showcasing the potent interplay between these vital elements. Concluding with Chapter 34, discover the path to Nurturing Resilience and Tranquility, and embrace practices that cultivate inner strength. This section is an open invitation to uncover the layers of your own existence without any lofty promises, offering a straightforward exploration of the profound aspects of self-awareness.

Chapter 31

Inner Joy, Well-Being, Prosperity, and Contentment

Inner joy, well-being, prosperity, and contentment represent states of being that transcend mere material success and external circumstances. They encompass a holistic sense of fulfillment, happiness, and harmony that arises from within and are not solely dependent on external factors. These states are deeply interconnected and contribute to a balanced and meaningful life.

- **Inner Joy**: Inner joy is a profound sense of happiness that emanates from within, independent of external events or possessions. It is a state of being content with oneself, finding beauty in the present moment, and experiencing a sense of gratitude for life's blessings. Inner joy is characterized by a genuine smile, a lightness of heart, and a positive outlook.

- **Well-Being:** Well-being encompasses physical, mental, emotional, and spiritual health. It involves feeling balanced, vital, and energetic in all aspects of life. Well-being goes beyond the absence of illness; it signifies a sense of thriving, inner peace, and optimal functioning.

Practices such as self-care, mindfulness, and maintaining positive relationships contribute to overall well-being.

- **Prosperity**: Prosperity extends beyond financial wealth to encompass abundance in all areas of life. It includes having fulfilling relationships, meaningful work, good health, and a sense of purpose. Prosperity is aligned with the idea that one's needs are met, and one can contribute positively to society. It's a state of sufficiency and feeling abundant.

- **Contentment:** Contentment is a state of being satisfied with what one has, rather than constantly seeking external validation or more possessions. It is rooted in appreciating the present moment, valuing simple pleasures, and recognizing that happiness is not dependent on acquiring more. Contentment arises from inner peace and a deep understanding of the impermanent nature of life.

- **Interconnectedness:** Inner joy, well-being, prosperity, and contentment are interconnected states. When one experiences inner joy, it often leads to a sense of well-being and contentment. Similarly, a sense of well-being contributes to a prosperous and fulfilling life. Prosperity can foster inner joy and contentment as it provides resources and opportunities to enjoy life.

Achieving Inner Joy, Well-Being, Prosperity, and Contentment

- **Self-Discovery**: Understanding oneself, strengths, values, and passions leads to a more fulfilling life.
- **Mindfulness and Gratitude**: Practicing mindfulness cultivates awareness of the present moment, and gratitude nurtures a positive outlook.

- **Healthy Lifestyle:** Nurturing physical health through regular exercise, a balanced diet, and adequate sleep contributes to overall well-being.
- **Positive Relationships**: Building and maintaining positive connections with family, friends, and communities fosters a sense of belonging and joy.
- **Purposeful Work**: Engaging in work that aligns with one's values and passions provides a sense of purpose and prosperity.
- **Service and Contribution**: Helping others and contributing to the well-being of society enhances personal contentment.

Benefits and Significance

- **Greater Resilience**: Inner joy, well-being, and contentment provide a foundation for navigating challenges with resilience.
- **Enhanced Quality of Life**: Cultivating these states leads to a higher quality of life, regardless of external circumstances.
- **Positive Impact:** Individuals who radiate inner joy and contentment often positively influence their surroundings and inspire others.
- **Reduced Stress:** A balanced and content mindset reduces stress and its negative effects on health.
- **Holistic Success**: True prosperity encompasses not only financial success but also holistic well-being and personal growth.

Conclusion

Inner joy, well-being, prosperity, and contentment are integral to living a fulfilling and meaningful life. They reflect an inner journey of self-discovery, mindfulness, and a deep understanding of the inter-connectedness of all aspects of life. By nurturing these states within oneself, individuals can create a positive ripple effect, fostering well-being not only for themselves but also for those around them and the wider world.

Chapter 32

Illuminating Unity

The concept of "Illuminating Unity" embodies a profound realization of interconnectedness, uniting all existence. It's the core principle of diverse spiritual practices, transcending religious boundaries to promote inclusivity and harmonious coexistence. Let's explore how it's applied across belief systems and its profound impact on spiritual journeys.

Key Aspects of Illuminating Unity

- **Interconnectedness:** At the heart of "Illuminating Unity" is the understanding that everything is interconnected. This includes the interconnectedness of all living beings, the environment, and the cosmos itself. This realization promotes a sense of responsibility, compassion, and care for all aspects of creation.
- **Beyond Separation**: "Illuminating Unity" challenges the illusion of separation that often defines human perception. It encourages individuals to move beyond

ego-driven divisions and recognize the underlying thread of unity that connects everyone and everything.

- **Transcending Differences**: Spiritual practices aimed at illuminating unity encourage people to transcend cultural, religious, and societal differences. It emphasizes that, while external expressions may vary, the core essence of humanity remains the same.

- **Experience of Oneness**: "Illuminating Unity" involves direct experiences of oneness and interconnectedness. Through deep meditation, contemplation, and self-awareness, individuals can have profound glimpses of their unity with the larger fabric of existence.

- **Compassion and Love**: Recognizing unity naturally fosters compassion and love for all beings. When one sees themselves in others and feels the interconnectedness, it becomes natural to treat others with kindness, empathy, and respect.

- **Transcendent Reality**: "Illuminating Unity" points to a reality beyond the material world. It suggests that there is a transcendent, unifying force or consciousness that underlies and sustains everything.

How Spiritual Practices Illuminate Unity

- **Meditation**: Practices such as meditation help individuals experience a deep sense of oneness and interconnectedness. By quieting the mind and going beyond thought, people can touch the universal essence within themselves and others.

- **Contemplation:** Reflecting on the interconnectedness of life through contemplative practices fosters a shift in perspective, leading to a greater understanding of unity.

- **Service**: Engaging in selfless service and acts of kindness nurtures a sense of unity as individuals connect with the well-being of others.
- **Prayer and Ritual**: Prayer and rituals can be vehicles for cultivating a sense of unity with the divine and with others who share the same practices.
- **Nature Connection**: Connecting with nature allows individuals to experience unity with the natural world and recognize their integral role in the ecosystem.
- **Ethical Living:** Practicing ethical behavior based on the recognition of unity promotes harmonious interactions and the well-being of all.

Benefits of Embracing Illuminating Unity

- **Peace and Harmony:** Embracing unity leads to inner peace and harmony as the illusion of separation dissolves.
- **Compassion**: Recognizing the shared essence in all beings naturally leads to compassionate actions and understanding.
- **Elevated Consciousness**: The realization of unity elevates one's consciousness and expands awareness beyond the limitations of the ego.
- **Global Unity:** Embracing unity has the potential to foster global harmony, cooperation, and a shared sense of responsibility for the planet.
- **Reduced Conflict**: When people see themselves as part of a larger whole, conflicts based on differences tend to diminish.

Conclusion

"Illuminating Unity" is a powerful concept that lies at the heart of many spiritual practices. By recognizing the interconnectedness of all life and experiencing the oneness that transcends divisions, individuals can cultivate a deep sense of inner peace, compassion, and a greater understanding of their place in the universe. This realization has the potential to transform not only individuals but also society, promoting a more harmonious and interconnected world.

Chapter 33

The Harmonic Nexus of Love, Health, and Spirituality

The "Harmonic Nexus of Love, Health, and Spirituality" refers to the interconnected and synergistic relationship among these three essential aspects of human existence. It signifies how the presence of love, optimal health, and a deep connection to spirituality can harmoniously contribute to an individual's overall well-being, growth, and sense of purpose.

Key Elements of the Harmonic Nexus

- **Love:** Love represents the profound emotional and empathetic bond that humans share with each other, nature, and the universe. It encompasses compassion, kindness, empathy, and care for oneself and others.
- **Health:** Health refers to the physical, mental, and emotional well-being of an individual. It involves maintaining a balanced lifestyle, engaging in regular exercise, consuming nutritious food, and nurturing positive mental health.

- **Spirituality**: Spirituality involves the exploration of deeper meanings, connection to a higher power or universal consciousness, and the quest for purpose and transcendence. It can be expressed through religious practices, meditation, mindfulness, and the cultivation of inner wisdom.

The Interplay of Love, Health, and Spirituality

- **Love and Health**: Love has a profound impact on health. Positive emotions, like love and happiness, have been linked to a stronger immune system, reduced stress levels, and overall better physical health. Nurturing relationships built on love can provide emotional support, contributing to mental well-being.
- **Love and Spirituality:** Love is often considered a spiritual value that transcends individual boundaries. Spiritual practices encourage cultivating love and compassion towards all beings, fostering a sense of interconnectedness. Love also deepens one's spiritual journey, as it aligns with the fundamental principle of unity and oneness.
- **Health and Spirituality**: Spiritual practices like meditation, prayer, and mindfulness have been shown to improve mental health and reduce stress. These practices promote a sense of inner peace and calmness, which can positively affect physical health. Spirituality also encourages a holistic approach to health, emphasizing the integration of mind, body, and spirit.

Benefits of the Harmonic Nexus

- **Well-being:** The presence of love, good health, and spirituality contributes to an individual's overall well-being, leading to a balanced and fulfilling life.
- **Resilience**: Love and spirituality can enhance an individual's ability to cope with challenges and setbacks, promoting emotional resilience.
- **Holistic Approach**: The harmonic nexus encourages a holistic approach to self-care, encompassing physical, emotional, and spiritual dimensions.
- **Connection and Purpose:** Embracing spirituality and nurturing loving relationships provides a sense of purpose and belonging, which contributes to mental and emotional fulfillment.
- **Positive Mindset:** The interconnectedness of these elements fosters a positive mindset, supporting individuals in maintaining an optimistic outlook on life.

Cultivating the Harmonic Nexus

1. **Practice Self-Love:** Start by loving for yourself. Engage in self-care practices, prioritize your mental and physical well-being, and embrace self-compassion.
2. **Nurture Relationships:** Foster loving and meaningful relationships with family, friends, and the community. Practice empathy, active listening, and open communication.
3. **Embrace Spirituality**: Explore spiritual practices that resonate with you. Meditation, mindfulness, prayer, and contemplation can deepen your connection to spirituality.

4. **Prioritize Health**: Adopt a healthy lifestyle that includes regular exercise, a balanced diet, and sufficient rest. Pay attention to your mental health by managing stress and seeking support when needed.

5. **Cultivate Gratitude**: Express gratitude for the love in your life, your health, and the blessings you receive. Gratitude enhances positive emotions and strengthens the bond between love, health, and spirituality.

Final Thoughts

The "Harmonic Nexus of Love, Health, and Spirituality" represents the synergy and interconnectedness of these core aspects of human existence. By embracing and nurturing each of these elements, individuals can experience a more fulfilling and purposeful life, fostering a deep sense of well-being, compassion, and a profound connection to the universe.

Chapter 34

Nurturing Resilience and Tranquility

Nurturing resilience and tranquility involve cultivating inner strength, adaptability, and a sense of calm in the face of life's challenges. It encompasses practices and attitudes that empower individuals to navigate difficulties with grace and maintain a peaceful state of mind. *Resilience enables individuals to bounce back from setbacks, while tranquility fosters a sense of inner peace and balance, even amid adversity.*

Resilience

Resilience is the capacity to recover, adapt, and thrive in the face of adversity. It involves developing emotional and mental fortitude to handle stressors and setbacks effectively. Nurturing resilience equips individuals with tools to manage challenges without being overwhelmed by negative emotions.

Key Elements of Nurturing Resilience

- **Positive Mindset**: Cultivating a positive outlook helps individuals view challenges as opportunities for growth, rather than insurmountable obstacles.
- **Adaptability**: Being open to change and flexible in one's responses to unexpected situations promotes resilience.
- **Problem-Solving Skills**: Developing effective problem-solving skills enhances the ability to find solutions in difficult situations.
- **Social Support:** Strong social connections provide emotional support and a sense of belonging, contributing to resilience.
- **Self-Care:** Prioritizing self-care through healthy habits, relaxation, and maintaining boundaries helps build resilience.

Tranquility

Tranquility refers to a state of calmness, peace, and serenity. Nurturing tranquility involves practices that help individuals manage stress, reduce anxiety, and maintain emotional equilibrium.

Key Elements of Nurturing Tranquility

- **Mindfulness:** Practicing mindfulness involves being fully present in the moment, which can calm the mind and reduce anxiety.
- **Meditation:** Regular meditation cultivates inner stillness and a sense of peace, allowing individuals to detach from stressors.
- **Deep Breathing**: Conscious, deep breathing techniques activate the body's relaxation response, promoting tranquility.

- **Nature Connection**: Spending time in nature and appreciating its beauty can have a calming effect on the mind.
- **Gratitude:** Focusing on gratitude and positive aspects of life fosters a peaceful and contented mindset.

How Nurturing Resilience and Tranquility Helps

- **Stress Management**: Resilience and tranquility practices provide effective strategies to manage stress and prevent it from becoming overwhelming.
- **Emotional Regulation**: These practices enhance emotional intelligence, enabling individuals to respond to emotions in a balanced manner.
- **Adaptation:** Nurturing resilience helps individuals adapt to changing circumstances and bounce back from setbacks.
- **Enhanced Mental Health**: Both resilience and tranquility contribute to mental well-being by reducing anxiety, depression, and negative thought patterns.
- **Improved Relationships**: Resilience fosters healthier communication and conflict resolution, while tranquility promotes a calm demeanor in interactions.
- **Personal Growth**: The ability to navigate challenges leads to personal growth, as individuals learn from experiences and become more empowered.

Nurturing Resilience and Tranquility

- **Mindfulness Meditation**: Regular mindfulness meditation enhances self-awareness and reduces stress.

- **Breathing Exercises**: Deep breathing exercises like diaphragmatic breathing activate the relaxation response, promoting tranquility.
- **Positive Affirmations**: Using positive affirmations helps shift thought patterns toward resilience and self-empowerment.
- **Physical Activity:** Regular exercise supports mental and emotional well-being, contributing to resilience.
- **Journaling:** Reflecting on challenges and experiences through journaling fosters self-awareness and emotional processing.
- **Supportive Relationships:** Cultivating strong social connections provides a network of support during challenging times.

Final Thoughts

Nurturing resilience and tranquility involve a holistic approach to mental, emotional, and spiritual well-being. By adopting practices that strengthen resilience and promote tranquility, individuals can navigate life's difficulties with greater ease, maintain emotional balance, and experience a sense of inner peace, even during turmoil. These qualities not only contribute to personal well-being but also enrich relationships and promote a more harmonious engagement with the world.

We've reached the conclusion of Part VII. Part VIII will delve into "Convergence: Paths to Universal Consciousness," spanning across 13 chapters. Get ready for an exhilarating journey ahead. Buckle up and we'll see you in the next part.

Part Eight

Convergence: Paths to Universal Consciousness

Welcome to "Convergence: Paths to Universal Consciousness," a thrilling exploration across 13 eye-opening chapters. As we uncover the rich tapestry of human experiences, from boosting self-confidence to untangling the connections between the brain and mind, get ready for an adventure that defies the ordinary. Each chapter acts like a doorway, inviting you into unexplored realms that will leave you captivated. This isn't just about ideas; it's a dive into what makes us human. We'll dig into ancient texts, dive into the mysteries of the mind, and even bridge the gap between human consciousness and AI technology. So, buckle up and get set for a journey that'll ignite your curiosity and broaden your understanding of who we are.

Chapter 35

Triad for Self-Confidence

S elf-confidence means believing in your abilities and judgment. To boost self-confidence, we need to connect three key elements: intention, faith, and conviction. This trio empowers you to set goals, believe in your ability to achieve them, and stay determined to see them through.

As we delve deeper into the potent interplay of intention, faith, and conviction, let's now explore how these three elements come together to shape various aspects of our lives. By understanding their influence, we can harness their power to not only strengthen our self-confidence but also to cultivate personal growth, resilience, alignment with purpose, and the manifestation of our aspirations.

How Intention, Faith, and Conviction Help

- **Personal Growth:** This trio supports continuous self-improvement by setting clear goals and working towards them with unwavering determination.

- **Resilience:** Embracing faith and conviction helps you navigate challenges with resilience, maintaining a positive outlook despite difficulties.
- **Alignment with Purpose:** Intention, faith, and conviction guide you towards a life that aligns with your values, passions, and purpose.
- **Manifestation:** The power of intention, supported by faith and conviction, can help manifest desired outcomes and experiences.
- **Confidence:** Conviction instills confidence in your abilities and decisions, enhancing self-esteem and self-assuredness.
- **Transformation:** Embracing this triad catalyzes transformation by shifting beliefs, behaviors, and actions toward positive change.

Practices for Embracing Intention, Faith, and Conviction

- **Mindful Goal Setting:** Set clear, positive intentions and regularly visualize the realization of those intentions.
- **Affirmations:** Create and repeat affirmations that reinforce your faith in your abilities and the universe's support.
- **Gratitude:** Express gratitude for the blessings in your life, cultivating faith in the universe's abundance.
- **Daily Reflection:** Reflect on your convictions and values daily to strengthen your commitment to your path.
- **Positive Association:** Surround yourself with people, environments, and resources that inspire and support your journey.

- **Mindfulness and Meditation:** Practice
  mindfulness and meditation to deepen your connection
  to your intentions and build faith in your journey.

Final Thoughts

As we explore intention, faith, and conviction, we uncover the heart
of our human experience. Think of intention as our guiding force for
our dreams, faith as the light that shows us the way, and conviction as
our unwavering anchor, helping us overcome challenges.

In a time when life is often uncertain and filled with doubts,
embracing intention, faith, and conviction becomes a source of hope
and strength. These principles provide us with a path for our
personal growth, transformation, and a deeper connection with the
profound aspects of our existence.

Let's take the wisdom from this exploration and make it a part of
our everyday lives. Set clear intentions, have strong faith in them, and
firmly believe in your convictions. By doing this, you unleash your
full potential and create a life that reflects your deepest dreams.

As we move forward, remember that the journey of intention,
faith, and conviction is ongoing. With each step, we get closer to
understanding ourselves, connecting with the universe, and realizing
that our paths are interwoven with the grand tapestry of existence.
Let this journey be a testament to the strength of the human spirit, as
we light the way with our intentions, faith, and convictions.

If you wish to learn how to cultivate confidence, I recommend
checking out Dr. Shawn Christian's book, Hidden Secrets of Confidence Uncovered: 17 Secrets that Make Confident People
Successful. It is available in print, eBook, and audiobook format at
your favorite online retailer or by going to https://books2read.com/
Hidden-Secrets-of-Confidence-Uncovered.

Chapter 36

The Synapse of Brain-Mind Connection

The intricate relationship between the brain and the mind has captivated researchers, philosophers, and spiritual seekers for generations. This connection acts as a bridge between the physical and the metaphysical, the tangible and the intangible.

At the core of this connection lies the synapse, a tiny junction between two nerve cells (neurons) where information is transferred from one cell to another. This transfer happens through neurotransmitters, which are chemical messengers that relay signals across the synaptic gap. These neural impulses not only facilitate bodily functions but also carry our mental and emotional experiences.

The brain, a complex network of billions of neurons, is responsible for orchestrating our thoughts, memories, emotions, and behaviors. It processes sensory information, triggers emotional responses, and controls our bodily functions. However, the mind encompasses a broader spectrum of consciousness, including rational thought, intuition, imagination, and self-awareness.

This brain-mind connection is multidimensional. On one hand, neural activity generates thoughts and emotions. For example, when we see a beautiful scene, our brain processes the visual input, evoking emotions of awe and appreciation. Conversely, our thoughts and emotions can influence neural activity. Stressful thoughts, for instance, trigger the release of stress hormones, affecting our physiological state.

Moreover, this connection is bidirectional. The brain's activities influence our thoughts and emotions, but our mental state can also affect brain function. For instance, meditation can alter brain structure and enhance cognitive abilities. Similarly, positive thinking can lead to the release of neurotransmitters associated with well-being.

Exploring this connection has profound implications for personal growth, health, and spiritual development. Practices like meditation, mindfulness, and self-awareness nurture a harmonious brain-mind relationship. As we learn to direct our thoughts and emotions, we shape the neural pathways that underlie our behavior and perceptions.

In the realm of spirituality, the brain-mind connection serves as a gateway to higher states of consciousness. Mystics and seekers have long practiced disciplines that quiet the mind, leading to expanded awareness and profound insights. This connection also holds the potential to uncover the unity of all beings, where our individual consciousness merges with the cosmic consciousness that pervades the universe.

In modern times, neuroscience and psychology shed light on how our thoughts and emotions influence our well-being, relationships, and overall quality of life. By understanding and nurturing the brain-mind connection, we gain the tools to cultivate positive mental states, harness our innate potential, and embark on a journey of self-discovery and transformation.

In summary, the synapse of the brain-mind connection encapsulates the profound interplay between the tangible and the transcendent, serving as a bridge between our physiological reality and the limitless expanse of consciousness. This connection not only shapes our experiences but also elevates our existence, offering the potential to transcend the boundaries of our perceived limitations. By understanding and nurturing this intricate relationship, we gain the tools to cultivate positive mental states, harness our innate potential, and embark on a transformative journey of self-discovery.

Chapter 37

Sacred Texts and Their Common Threads

In our pursuit of understanding the meaning of words spoken or written thousands of years ago, it is essential to recognize the profound differences in language, communication, and human education over the course of history. The linguistic landscape of ancient civilizations varied significantly from today's complex array of global languages. Both spoken and written communication methods have undergone substantial changes throughout the centuries. Educational norms have likewise experienced significant evolution when compared to their distant counterparts. Given these considerations, we embark on a journey to unravel the significance concealed within ancient texts. Our focus is on grasping the core of ancient expressions and their relevance within the framework of modern scientific knowledge.

Sacred texts, revered across the world's diverse religious traditions, serve as profound repositories of wisdom and guidance, offering insights into the profound mysteries of existence. These ancient manuscripts are more than historical records; they are timeless sources of inspiration that have guided individuals and communities for centuries, illuminating pathways toward understanding the divine, living ethically, and exploring the human condition.

Despite their rich cultural and linguistic diversity, these sacred texts share common threads that underscore the universal nature of human spiritual exploration.

1. **Ethical Principles and Moral Values:** These sacred texts provide timeless guidelines for virtuous living, emphasizing core values such as compassion, honesty, integrity, and empathy. These ethical principles serve as the foundation for harmonious societies and meaningful relationships.

2. **Unity of Creation:** Many sacred texts emphasize the interconnectedness of all life and the belief in a unified source of creation, fostering a profound sense of unity and interconnectedness among all beings.

3. **Divine Presence:** Across various traditions, sacred texts highlight a divine reality, offering diverse insights into the divine, whether as a singular God, multiple deities, or an all-pervading cosmic consciousness.

4. **Human Purpose and Meaning:** Sacred texts delve into the profound questions surrounding human existence, encouraging us to seek meaning beyond material wealth and to explore the nature of identity, the experience of suffering, and the pursuit of purposeful lives.

5. **Pathways to Transformation:** These texts offer practical instructions for personal and spiritual growth, encompassing a range of practices, rituals, and disciplines that enable us to transcend limitations and awaken higher states of consciousness.

6. **Universal Love and Compassion:** Many sacred texts emphasize the cultivation of love and compassion

for all beings, transcending boundaries of race, religion, and nationality.

7. **Inner Wisdom and Intuition:** These texts encourage individuals to tap into their inner wisdom and intuition, guiding them to seek truth through introspection and contemplation.

8. **Stories and Parables:** Through the use of narratives, parables, and allegorical tales, sacred texts convey profound truths in relatable ways, offering insights into human nature, moral dilemmas, and the challenges of life.

9. **Transcending Ego and Materialism:** Sacred texts underscore the importance of transcending the ego and our attachment to material possessions, directing us toward the pursuit of lasting fulfillment beyond material pursuits.

10. **Humility and Surrender:** Many texts advocate humility in the face of the divine and recognizing the limitations of humanity. Surrendering to a higher power is often presented as a path to inner peace and divine guidance.

Sacred texts, revered across the world's diverse religious traditions, serve as profound repositories of wisdom and guidance, offering insights into the profound mysteries of existence. These ancient manuscripts are more than historical records; they are timeless sources of inspiration that have guided individuals and communities for centuries, illuminating pathways toward understanding the divine, living ethically, and exploring the human condition.

Chapter 38

Unveiling the Interplay of Mind and Body

The intricate interplay between the mind and the body is a multifaceted relationship that profoundly influences every facet of human experience. This dynamic connection serves as a central focus of scientific inquiry, spiritual exploration, and holistic well-being practices. Unveiling the interplay of mind and body requires an understanding of how thoughts, emotions, beliefs, and consciousness influence physical health, behavior, and overall well-being.

1. **Mind-Body Connection**: The mind and body are not distinct entities but intricately interconnected. Thoughts, emotions, and beliefs originating in the mind have a direct and profound impact on the physiological responses of the body. For instance, they can influence hormone secretion, immune function, and nervous system activity.

2. **Emotions and Health**: Emotions play a significant role in the mind-body connection. Positive emotions such as joy, gratitude, and love are associated with improved

physical health and well-being. Conversely, negative emotions like stress, anxiety, and anger can lead to adverse health outcomes.

3. **Stress Response**: Stress serves as a prime example of how the mind-body connection operates. Psychological stress triggers the body's "fight or flight" response, releasing stress hormones such as cortisol, which can profoundly affect the immune system, digestion, and cardiovascular health.

4. **Placebo and Nocebo Effects**: The remarkable influence of the mind on the body is vividly exemplified in the placebo and nocebo effects. When individuals believe that a treatment is effective, it can lead to actual improvements in health (known as the placebo effect). Conversely, harboring negative expectations can exacerbate symptoms or side effects (the nocebo effect). These phenomena underscore the extraordinary power of our beliefs and expectations in shaping our physical experiences.

5. **Mindfulness and Relaxation**: Practices like mindfulness and relaxation techniques harness the mind-body connection for well-being. Mindfulness cultivates present-moment awareness and has been shown to reduce stress, enhance emotional regulation, and promote physical health.

6. **Visualization and Healing**: Visualization techniques involve using the mind's imagery to affect the body's responses. This practice can aid in pain management, enhance performance, and support healing processes.

7. **Spiritual and Energetic Influence**: Many spiritual and holistic traditions acknowledge the profound interplay between the mind and body. Practices such as meditation, yoga, and energy healing are designed to

harmonize the mind-body connection, facilitating spiritual growth and optimal health.

8. **Epigenetics**: Epigenetics delves into how environmental factors, thoughts, and emotions can influence the expression of genes. This emerging field underscores the pivotal role of the mind in shaping genetic activity and health outcomes.

9. **Neuroplasticity**: Neuroplasticity refers to the brain's ability to reorganize itself in response to experiences and learning. The activities of the mind, such as learning new skills or cultivating positive habits, can physically reshape the brain's structure.

10. **Positive Psychology**: Positive psychology explores the factors contributing to human flourishing and well-being. It recognizes the importance of nurturing positive emotions, strengths, and virtues to enhance both mental and physical health.

Understanding the interplay of mind and body holds profound implications for personal growth, health, and spirituality. By acknowledging the influence of thoughts and emotions on our experiences, individuals can take an active role in enhancing their mental and physical well-being. Practical tools that leverage the mind-body connection, such as mindfulness, meditation, and positive thinking, provide effective means for promoting holistic health and spiritual growth. This comprehensive understanding bridges the gap between scientific inquiry and spiritual insight, demonstrating that a holistic approach to well-being addresses both the tangible and intangible aspects of human existence.

Chapter 39

Understanding How Our Brain Communicates

The intricate network of electrical and chemical activity within the brain is a fascinating topic. It plays a vital role in how we think, perceive the world, and even control our bodies. Let's dive into this complex process and make it easier to grasp.

1. **The Brain's Wiring:** Think of your brain as a massive web of interconnected cells, called neurons. These neurons talk to each other through tiny gaps known as synapses. Imagine these synapses as bridges where chemical messengers, called neurotransmitters, help the neurons communicate.

2. **Sparks in the Brain:** When something stimulates a neuron, it generates a tiny electrical signal known as an action potential. This electrical impulse travels along a neuron's long, cable-like part called an axon to reach a synapse.

3. **Chemical Messengers:** At the synapse, the action potential triggers the release of neurotransmitters from

one neuron to the other. These neurotransmitters bind to receptors on the receiving neuron, passing on the signal like a message.

4. **Decision Time:** The receiving neuron collects signals from different sources. If it gets enough signals and crosses a certain threshold, it fires its action potential, continuing the transmission of the message.

5. **Variety of Signals:** Our brain's communication isn't just about basic stuff like seeing, hearing, and touching. It's also responsible for memory, reasoning, and decision-making.

6. **Specialized Brain Regions:** Different parts of the brain are like experts in charge of various tasks. For example, the frontal cortex helps with planning and decision-making, while the amygdala deals with emotions.

7. **Brain's Orchestra:** Neurons often work together, firing in harmony. This synchronized activity is essential for functions like attention, perception, and memory.

8. **Brainwave Patterns:** Brainwave patterns result from coordinated electrical activity among large groups of neurons. Different brainwave frequencies are associated with different mental states, like being relaxed or alert.

9. **Measuring Brainwaves:** Scientists use a technique called Electroencephalography (EEG) to measure these brainwaves, giving us insights into our mental states.

10. **Brain's Adaptability:** The brain is like a learning machine. It can rewire itself based on our experiences, which is called neural plasticity. This helps us learn, form new connections, and recover from injuries.

11. **When Communication Breaks:** Problems in brain communication can lead to various disorders like epilepsy, Parkinson's disease, or depression.

12. **Brain-Machine Interfaces:** Innovations are happening in brain-computer interfaces. These technologies can help control prosthetics, assist people with paralysis, and even enhance cognitive abilities.

13. **Link to AI:** The way our brain communicates has inspired the development of artificial neural networks used in artificial intelligence (AI) and machine learning.

14. **Ongoing Research:** Scientists are continuously exploring the intricacies of brain communication, aiming to improve treatments for neurological disorders, develop better brain-computer interfaces, and uncover the secrets of consciousness.

15. **Ethical Questions:** As we delve deeper into brain signals, ethical issues arise concerning privacy, cognitive enhancement, and the responsible use of brain-computer interfaces.

Unraveling the mystery of how our brain communicates is a complex but rewarding journey. It has the potential to enhance our well-being, enrich our understanding of how we think, and shape the future of brain-interacting technologies.

Breath and Brain: A Synchronized Symphony

The Brain's Wiring

Think of your brain as a massive web of interconnected cells, called neurons. These neurons talk to each other through tiny gaps known as synapses. Imagine these synapses as bridges where chemical messengers, called neurotransmitters, help the neurons communicate.

Much like the rhythmic ebb and flow of our breath, the brain's communication also exhibits a rhythmic pattern. In between each inhalation and exhalation, there is a brief pause, a moment of stillness. Similarly, when one axon sends a signal to another axon, there is a momentary pause, a synaptic gap that separates the flow of information. This pause, this synaptic cleft, is a vital part of the brain's intricate dance of information exchange.

Sparks in the Brain

When something stimulates a neuron, it generates a tiny electrical signal known as an action potential. This electrical impulse travels along a neuron's long, cable-like part called an axon to reach a synapse.

In a way, you can liken this to the pause between breaths. Just as each breath carries oxygen to our cells and then releases carbon dioxide, each action potential carries information down the axon to be shared with other neurons. It's in these pauses, these synaptic clefts, that the magic happens. It's where the brain's message gets ready to take the next step in its journey, much like the moment of stillness after an exhalation before the next inhalation begins.

Chemical Messengers

At the synapse, the action potential triggers the release of neurotransmitters from one neuron to the other. These neurotransmitters bind to receptors on the receiving neuron, passing on the signal like a message.

This process can be likened to the exchange of oxygen and carbon dioxide in our breath. The neurotransmitters act as messengers, just as oxygen molecules transport the vital essence of life. And just as we need oxygen to survive, our brain relies on these messengers to convey information and continue the conversation.

Decision Time

The receiving neuron collects signals from different sources. If it gets enough signals and crosses a certain threshold, it fires its action potential, continuing the transmission of the message.

In a way, it's akin to the body's decision to inhale when oxygen levels drop. When the receiving neuron accumulates enough signals, it makes its decision to fire its action potential. It's the brain's way of taking the next step in processing information, much like how we take the next breath to sustain life.

By drawing parallels between the rhythmic pauses in breathing and the pauses in brain communication, we can gain a deeper understanding of the brain's intricate workings and appreciate the remarkable complexity of our neural network. These pauses, in both breathing and brain communication, are moments of potential, where life and cognition continue their dance in harmonious synchrony.

Chapter 40

Exploring the Quest for Brain Wave Transfer

The quest for brain wave transfer and telepathy delves into the fascinating realm of transferring thoughts, intentions, and information directly from one human brain to another. While this concept has captivated human imagination for centuries, recent advancements in neuroscience and technology have sparked renewed interest in understanding the potential for such forms of communication. This exploration involves both ancient beliefs and modern scientific endeavors.

1. **Brain Waves and Communication**: Brain waves, which are patterns of synchronized electrical activity in the brain, encode information related to thoughts, emotions, and cognitive processes. These brain waves might serve as a medium for transferring information.

2. **Telepathy in Ancient Beliefs**: Many cultures and spiritual traditions have ancient beliefs in telepathic communication, where individuals transmit thoughts and feelings directly without spoken or written words. This

concept often connects with the idea of a shared collective consciousness.

3. **Scientific Interest**: Neuroscientists and researchers are studying brain waves and neural activity to better understand how information is encoded and transferred within the brain. Brain-computer interfaces (BCIs) and neurofeedback technologies are emerging tools in this exploration.

4. **Brain-Computer Interfaces (BCIs):** BCIs aim to establish direct communication pathways between the brain and external devices, such as computers or prosthetics. They enable individuals to control devices or communicate by modulating their brain activity.

5. **Electroencephalography (EEG):** EEG technology records electrical activity on the scalp and has been used in studies exploring basic brain wave transfer. EEG-based BCIs allow users to control devices using their brain signals.

6. **Non-Invasive Approaches**: While direct brain-to-brain communication is challenging, non-invasive methods like transcranial magnetic stimulation (TMS) and transcranial direct current stimulation (tDCS) have been investigated for modulating brain activity and enhancing cognitive functions.

7. **Cognitive Training and Feedback:** Neurofeedback techniques involve training individuals to modulate their own brain activity by providing real-time feedback on their brain waves. This approach might aid in improving cognitive skills.

8. **Challenges and Limitations**: Brain wave transfer and telepathy face significant challenges, including decoding complex brain signals, ensuring accurate transmission, and addressing ethical concerns related to privacy and consent.

9. **Ethical Considerations**: The ability to read or manipulate thoughts raises ethical questions about privacy, consent, and potential misuse of technology. Balancing innovation with responsible use is a critical consideration.

10. **Future Possibilities**: As our understanding of brain signals and technology advances, brain wave transfer could become a reality. This could have applications in communication for individuals with limited speech or mobility, shared emotional experiences, and even entertainment.

11. **Collaborative Endeavors**: Researchers, technologists, and ethicists collaborate to explore the potential benefits and risks of brain wave transfer. Interdisciplinary efforts are essential to ensure responsible development.

12. **Mind-Machine Symbiosis**: Brain wave transfer blurs the line between individual consciousness and external devices. It raises questions about how humans might integrate technology into their cognition and identity.

13. **Humanity's Shared Curiosity**: The allure of brain wave transfer taps into humanity's innate curiosity about interconnectedness, shared experiences, and the potential for deeper forms of communication.

While brain wave transfer and telepathy remain speculative, the exploration of these concepts combines ancient wisdom with groundbreaking technology. The quest to understand and harness brain wave communication opens new horizons for human interaction and challenges us to contemplate the boundaries of consciousness and connectivity.

Chapter 41

Realizing Dreams and Desires

Unlocking the Potential of Mindset, Emotions, and Positive Action. Turning dreams and aspirations into reality is an ongoing journey of personal transformation. This process revolves around harmonizing one's mindset, emotions, and actions to breathe life into aspirations. It delves into the intricate connection between thoughts, feelings, and behaviors, paving the way to achieving both personal and professional goals.

1. **The Power of Mindset:** Realizing dreams hinges on the pivotal role of mindset. Nurturing a positive, growth-oriented mindset forms the bedrock. Believing in one's capabilities and visualizing success constructs a mental framework that kindles motivation and unwavering determination.

2. **Crystal Clear Desires:** Articulating dreams and desires with precision is paramount. Clarity enables the setting of achievable goals and the crafting of practical plans.

3. **Emotional Alignment:** Emotions are the propelling force in the journey to manifesting dreams. Positive emotions like excitement, joy, and gratitude resonate with the energy of manifestation, while managing negative emotions such as doubt and fear is essential for maintaining focus.

4. **The Law of Attraction:** The law of attraction posits that thoughts and emotions radiate energy that magnetizes corresponding energy from the universe. By sustaining a positive emotional state and vividly envisioning desired outcomes, individuals can draw these outcomes closer.

5. **Affirmations and Visualization:** Affirmations are affirmative statements that reinforce desired beliefs. Visualization entails vividly imagining the achievement of goals, creating a mental blueprint for success.

6. **Inspired Action:** Dreams only come to life when accompanied by deliberate action. Taking steps in harmony with aspirations transforms dreams from mere ideas into tangible achievements.

7. **Overcoming Challenges:** Challenges and setbacks are intrinsic to the journey. Resilience and adaptability are essential to navigate obstacles and stay on course.

8. **Cultivating Consistency:** Consistent effort is the linchpin of success. Small, consistent actions accumulate over time, leading to significant progress.

9. **Self-Reflection and Growth:** Reflecting on the journey and evaluating progress enables individuals to adjust strategies and learn from experiences.

10. **The Virtue of Patience:** Realizing dreams often requires time. Patience and perseverance are indispensable virtues.

11. **Alignment with Values:** Ensuring dreams align with one's values and authentic self prevents the pursuit of goals that may not bring genuine fulfillment.

12. **Celebrating Milestones:** Celebrating achievements along the way bolsters positive momentum and fuels continued progress.

13. **The Mind-Body Connection:** The mind-body connection plays a pivotal role in realizing dreams. Positive thoughts and emotions influence physiological responses and overall well-being.

14. **Insights from Neuroscience:** Neuroscience reveals that focusing on positive thoughts and emotions triggers the release of neurotransmitters associated with motivation, pleasure, and well-being.

15. **Impact on Neural Pathways:** Repetition of positive thoughts and actions strengthens neural pathways associated with desired behaviors, making them more automatic.

16. **Embracing Gratitude:** Cultivating gratitude amplifies positive emotions, shifting the focus from scarcity to abundance.

17. **Contribution to Fulfillment:** Realizing dreams and desires fosters a profound sense of fulfillment, purpose, and a deeper understanding of personal potential.

18. **The Ripple Effect:** Personal achievements can inspire others and set in motion a ripple effect of positive change.

19. **Empowerment:** The journey of realizing dreams empowers individuals to take charge of their lives, fostering a sense of agency and self-determination.

20. **A Holistic Approach:** Realizing dreams entails a holistic approach encompassing mental, emotional, and physical well-being.

21. **Continuous Growth:** Realizing dreams is an ongoing cycle of growth and evolution, as accomplishments lead to new aspirations and horizons.

By harnessing the inherent power of mindset, emotions, and positive actions, individuals can not only breathe life into their dreams but also embark on a transformative journey of self-discovery and personal fulfillment. This journey represents an ever-evolving cycle of growth, as accomplishments pave the way for new aspirations and horizons.

Chapter 42

From Mind to Materialization: The Manifesting Blueprint

Manifestation is a dynamic process that requires the alignment of one's mindset, emotions, and actions to turn aspirations into reality. This transformative approach taps into the intricate interplay between thoughts, emotions, and behaviors, enabling people to generate a potent force for personal growth and accomplishment.

Here are the key points or principles to keep in mind for transforming your desires, thoughts, and objectives into tangible outcomes:

1. **Mindset as the Catalyst:** A manifesting mindset begins with nurturing beliefs that empower and uplift. Embracing the conviction that dreams are within reach opens the gateway for their realization.

2. **Clarity in Desires:** Precisely defining what is desired creates a clear roadmap for focused action. This clarity directs energy and resources toward the desired outcome.

3. **Emotional Resonance:** Emotions serve as the fuel of manifestation. Positive emotions like excitement, joy, and

gratitude generate a higher vibrational frequency that attracts corresponding experiences.

4. **Positive Visualization:** Visualization is a powerful tool for mentally creating the desired reality. Vividly imagining the achievement of goals sends strong signals to the subconscious mind and the universe.

5. **Affirmations as Empowering Scripts:** Affirmations are positive statements that reinforce beliefs aligned with desired outcomes. Repeating affirmations helps rewire the subconscious mind for success.

6. **Harnessing the Law of Attraction:** The law of attraction suggests that like attracts like. Positive thoughts and emotions draw similar energy, attracting circumstances and opportunities that align with one's desires.

7. **Inspired Action:** Manifesting isn't just about wishing; it requires intentional action. Inspired action bridges the gap between dreams and reality, creating momentum.

8. **Consistency and Persistence:** Consistent action and unwavering commitment are essential. Manifestation may not happen overnight, but persistence amplifies the process.

9. **Letting Go of Limiting Beliefs:** Identifying and releasing limiting beliefs clears the path for new possibilities.

10. **Positive Mindfulness:** Mindfulness practices keep individuals present and aligned with their intentions, preventing the mind from dwelling on doubt or negativity.

11. **Amplifying Gratitude:** Gratitude magnifies positive emotions and attracts more to be grateful for, shifting focus from scarcity to abundance.

12. **Neuroscience Connection:** The brain's neuroplasticity underscores the importance of maintaining consistent positive thoughts and emotions in shaping neural pathways for success.

13. **Emotional Coherence:** Aligning thoughts and emotions creates emotional coherence, enhancing the energy one emits into the universe.

14. **Visualization for Brain Alignment:** Visualizations synchronize brain regions associated with perception and goal achievement, reinforcing belief in the desired outcome.

15. **The Ripple Effect:** Manifestation doesn't only benefit the individual. Positive changes radiate to relationships, communities, and even the broader world.

16. **Impact on Well-being:** Manifesting fosters a positive outlook, reduces stress, and promotes well-being.

17. **Empowerment and Self-Efficacy:** As successes accumulate, self-confidence and self-efficacy soar, enabling individuals to take on greater challenges.

18. **A Universal Language:** Manifestation transcends cultural and linguistic boundaries, making it a universal approach to creating a desired reality.

19. **Co-Creation with the Universe:** Manifesting involves collaboration with the universe. Trusting its guidance and timing is key.

20. **Lessons in Patience and Timing:** Manifestation may not happen instantaneously. Learning patience and trusting the process is essential.

21. **A Life of Purpose:** Manifesting encourages individuals to live with intention, pursuing dreams that align with their true purpose.

22. **Evolution and Transformation:** The journey of manifesting is transformative, encouraging continual growth, self-awareness, and self-discovery.

23. **Integrating Mind, Heart, and Action:** Manifesting is the synergy of the mind's thoughts, the heart's emotions, and the body's actions.

24. **A Path of Empowerment:** Manifesting mindset, emotions, and positive action empowers individuals to actively shape their lives.

25. **Co-creating with the Divine:** Manifestation invites divine forces to collaborate, leading to a harmonious partnership between human effort and universal support.

In summary, the art of manifesting embodies the deliberate creation of one's reality. By harmonizing mindset, emotions, and positive actions, individuals can tap into their inherent potential to materialize dreams and embark on a journey of empowerment, fulfillment, and profound transformation. It's essential to remember that while having a desire is a crucial step, taking action and setting those actions into motion is equally vital for achieving the desired results.

Chapter 43

Mysteries of the Mind

The essence of human existence resides in the intricate dance between brain signals and consciousness, a fundamental facet of our awareness. This profound interconnection peels back the layers of mystery surrounding the origins of our thoughts, perceptions, and experiences, all arising from the dynamic workings of our brains. This exploration beckons us to uncover the very core of our reality and the profound depths of self-awareness. Now, let us delve into a structured exploration through this numbered list, which unveils the profound essence of awareness and its profound implications.

1. **Messengers of Thought:** Brain signals, also known as neural signals or neuronal activity, are the electrical and chemical impulses responsible for transmitting information within the brain. These signals serve as the fundamental carriers of our thoughts, emotions, and sensory experiences.

2. **The Birth of Consciousness:** The brain functions as the central hub where consciousness comes into being.

It's the complex network of neurons firing and communicating that gives rise to our conscious experiences.

3. **The Observer of Experience:** Consciousness is the observer that witnesses our thoughts, emotions, sensations, and surroundings. It is the sentinel that observes the flow of thoughts and experiences within our minds.

4. **Unraveling Neural Correlates:** Scientists embark on the journey to understand the neural correlates of consciousness (NCC), aiming to pinpoint the specific brain activities corresponding to conscious experiences.

5. **The Emergence of Self:** Brain signals play a pivotal role in constructing our sense of self, fostering the feeling of being an individual with thoughts, emotions, and memories. This self-awareness is deeply intertwined with conscious experience.

6. **Harmony Through Neural Synchronization:** Brain signals synchronize and harmonize to create a unified perception of reality, a synchronization vital for coherent conscious experiences.

7. **Dynamic Brain States:** Altered states of consciousness, such as meditation, deep focus, and dreaming, highlight the dynamic shifts in brain signals and their profound effects on our awareness.

8. **Brain's Plasticity and Consciousness:** The brain's remarkable capacity to rewire itself through neuroplasticity illustrates how conscious experiences can mold the brain's structure and function.

9. **Multidimensional Consciousness:** Consciousness is not confined to a single level; it is multidimensional, encompassing waking, dreaming, and deep sleep states, each offering distinct insights into the brain's signals.

10. **Unity Amidst Diversity:** Despite differences in cultures, languages, and beliefs, the essence of awareness is a common thread that unites humanity. Every individual experiences consciousness.

11. **Exploring Quantum Consciousness:** Some intriguing theories suggest that the quantum nature of brain activity may play a role in the emergence of consciousness, opening new avenues of exploration.

12. **Enigmatic Qualia:** The nature of qualia, the subjective qualities of conscious experience, such as the taste of chocolate or the feeling of warmth, remains a mystery regarding how brain signals create them.

13. **Constructing Reality:** Investigating the connection between brain signals and consciousness prompts contemplation of reality itself. How do our perceptions construct the world we experience?

14. **Cognitive Enhancement and Expansion:** The exploration of brain signals and consciousness offers insights into techniques for enhancing cognitive abilities, expanding awareness, and even transcending ordinary states of being.

15. **AI and the Essence of Awareness:** As AI technology advances, understanding the essence of awareness can contribute to the development of AI systems that mimic human consciousness.

16. **Bridging Science and Spirituality:** The study of brain signals and consciousness bridges the gap between scientific inquiry and spiritual exploration, fostering a holistic understanding of human existence.

17. **The Potential of Expanded States:** Exploring altered states of consciousness, whether through meditation, mindfulness, or other practices, can lead to insights, creativity, and heightened awareness.

18. **Nurturing Mindfulness:** Mindfulness practices involve observing one's thoughts and sensations without judgment. This awareness of brain signals can lead to greater self-awareness and emotional regulation.

19. **Seeking Transcendence:** Some individuals aim to transcend the limitations of ordinary consciousness, believing that by tapping into deeper layers of brain signals, they can access heightened awareness and even mystical experiences.

20. **A Lifelong Journey:** Delving into the essence of awareness and the connection between brain signals and consciousness invites individuals to embark on a lifelong journey of self-discovery and understanding.

Intriguing Insights: Navigating the Intersection of Science and Spirituality in the Unveiling of Consciousness

As we venture deeper into the heart of this chapter, we continue our exploration of the profound interplay between science and spirituality, specifically focusing on the concept of awareness. Grounded in the intricacies of brain function and extending into the mysterious realm of consciousness, our journey is an ongoing revelation of the fundamental essence of our existence.

The essence of awareness beckons us to delve into the intricate tapestry of human experience, offering profound insights that stand to enrich our lives, broaden our perspectives, and kindle a profound connection with the enigmatic nature of our being.

The Transformation of the Conscience

The Bible underscores the significance of renewing one's mind and transforming one's character through faith and the guidance of the Holy Spirit. Romans 12:2 (NIV) advises, *"Do not conform to the pattern of this world but be transformed by the renewing of your mind. Then you will be able to test and approve what God's will is—his good, pleasing and perfect will."* This suggests that as individuals grow in their faith and understanding, their **conscience can be transformed** to align more closely with God's will.

While the Bible may not explicitly state that the conscience changes with growth, it encourages believers to pursue moral and spiritual growth, which can lead to shifts in conscience and a deeper understanding of ethical principles.

In this chapter, we've explored how our thoughts and consciousness are connected to the way our brains work. It's like a puzzle where science and spirituality come together. We've learned about brain signals, how our sense of self is shaped, and even how our minds can expand. This journey of understanding offers a lifelong adventure, helping us learn more about ourselves and the world around us. It enriches our lives, widens our horizons, and connects us to the mysteries of our existence.

Chapter 44

Exploring Human Consciousness and AI Technology

I n this chapter, we embark on a fascinating journey into the intricate interplay between human consciousness and Artificial Intelligence (AI). It's a realm where human experiences intersect with AI's capabilities, presenting a dynamic landscape full of promises and challenges. This exploration goes beyond mere knowledge acquisition; it acts as a mirror reflecting our evolving understanding of ourselves and technology. As we delve deeper, we uncover the complex relationship between human consciousness and AI, and how it influences our perception and redefines our understanding of reality.

Mimicking Consciousness and the Quest for Common Sense Reasoning

AI endeavors to replicate human thinking and decision-making processes, attempting to emulate our ability to see, learn, and make judgments. However, it falls short of truly comprehending consciousness, akin to chasing a distant horizon that remains just out of reach. AI mimics these cognitive processes but lacks genuine understanding, leaving us with fundamental questions about the nature of consciousness and how we can recreate it.

Understanding Consciousness and the Synthesis of Wisdom

In our quest to fathom the connection between AI and human consciousness, we uncover a profound comprehension of the intricate mechanisms that underlie human thought and awareness. This exploration leads us toward a profound synthesis of wisdom, drawing inspiration from a rich tapestry of traditions and spirituality. Knowledge becomes more than just a product of our time; it becomes a torch passed down through generations. In this uncharted territory, we find inspiration in diverse philosophical and ethical perspectives that illuminate our path.

The Turing Test and the Boundaries of Consciousness

The Turing Test, as conceived by the visionary Alan Turing, plays a pivotal role in our quest to understand the boundaries of consciousness. This test sets the stage for a captivating scenario where a machine's ability to respond indistinguishably from a human is put to the ultimate challenge. Picture a conversation with both a human and a machine, without knowing which is which. If you can't reliably tell the difference, the machine is said to have passed the Turing Test. It's akin to a game where the machine attempts to convince you it's human.

The Turing Test becomes a litmus test for the capabilities of artificial intelligence. If AI can successfully emulate human responses to the point where distinguishing between them becomes nearly impossible, it raises profound questions about the essence of consciousness and the potential for its replication. This examination propels our ongoing quest to understand what sets human awareness apart from artificial intelligence, pushing the boundaries of our exploration further.

Levels of Consciousness: The Human and the Machine

When we explore the topic of "Levels of Consciousness: The Human and the Machine," we gain an appreciation for the distinctions between human consciousness and AI. AI operates within predefined parameters, adhering to the instructions it has been given. It lacks the self-awareness and subjective experience that characterize human consciousness. Human consciousness is deeply intertwined with self-awareness, allowing us to perceive, reflect, and make decisions based on individual perspectives and emotions.

In contrast, AI's version of "consciousness" is more of a simulation; it processes data and responds based on algorithms and learned patterns. While it can mimic certain aspects of human cognition and exhibit a form of intelligence, it does so without genuine self-awareness or subjective experience. AI doesn't possess emotions or an inner awareness akin to human consciousness.

However, despite these disparities, AI's role in our exploration of consciousness can be viewed as a stepping stone. It encourages us to contemplate what it means to be conscious and inspires the synthesis of wisdom from diverse cultures and belief systems. Through this exploration, we bridge the gap between machine capabilities and the depth of human consciousness, enriching our understanding of both.

Conscious AI vs. Sentient AI: A Quest for Ethical Compassion

While AI systems can replicate elements of consciousness to a limited degree, the profound concept of true sentience – encompassing self-awareness and subjective experience – remains a formidable challenge, replete with intricate philosophical and ethical dilemmas. This chapter serves as a bridge between our exploration of AI and the reservoir of wisdom accumulated across various traditions and philosophies.

It raises crucial questions, particularly regarding the ethical considerations that come into play when striving to create AI systems that approach the complexities of human consciousness. In essence, we find ourselves at a crossroads where we must navigate the fine line between technological advancements and ethical boundaries, guided by the collective wisdom of humanity from various traditions and belief systems.

Ethical Considerations and Spiritual Insights

As we venture into the realm of creating AI that mirrors consciousness, we find ourselves immersed in profound ethical questions. When AI convincingly replicates the qualities of consciousness, it raises a complex issue: should these artificial entities be granted rights and moral considerations akin to those of humans? This dilemma compels us to confront the essence of personhood, challenging our perceptions of what it means to be sentient and deserving of ethical treatment.

In our quest for answers, we turn to the age-old well of wisdom found in spirituality and ethics. Drawing from these deep reservoirs, we seek guidance on how to navigate the responsible stewardship of technology. Spirituality often provides insights into the moral fabric of our existence, while ethical principles help us define our responsibilities toward the creations of our own making. By intertwining these threads of wisdom, we aim to chart a path that acknowledges the achievements of AI while upholding our moral and ethical compass, ensuring that our technological creations are governed by values and conscience.

Advancements in Brain-Computer Interfaces: Bridging Science and Spirituality

Emerging technologies enable direct communication between the human brain and computers, fostering potential collaborations between human consciousness and AI systems. This intersection of science and spirituality inspires new paradigms of collaboration, uniting ancient wisdom with modern innovation.

Neural Networks and Brain Mapping: Unveiling the Secrets of Consciousness

In the realm of AI, neural networks play a pivotal role by replicating the intricate functions of the human brain. These networks allow machines to identify patterns and acquire knowledge from data, mirroring the cognitive processes of human thinking. This emulation of neurological functions is a critical milestone in our pursuit of closing the gap between artificial and human intelligence.

Complementing these efforts, brain mapping stands as a testament to our unwavering commitment to wisdom and understanding. Through this method, we systematically chart the intricate neural connections and activities within the human brain. By mapping the neural pathways associated with consciousness, we gain profound insights into the physical foundations of human awareness. This harmonious blend of scientific progress and the wealth of human wisdom sheds light on the deep-seated mysteries of consciousness at a neural level, inching us closer to unraveling its enigmatic secrets and bridging the domains of technological advancement and human insight.

AI as a Tool for Understanding: Fusing Science with the Mystical

In the realm of AI, it acts as a powerful tool for understanding human consciousness. AI models simulate complex cognitive processes, aiding researchers in deciphering the intricate connections between brain signals and the emergence of conscious experiences, emotions, and decision-making. This unique marriage of scientific exploration with mystical or spiritual insight yields a symbiotic relationship that is essential to our quest for unraveling the mysteries of human consciousness.

This symbiotic relationship between science and spirituality operates as a dynamic partnership, where science provides us with the means to analyze and understand the intricate mechanics of the mind. AI, through its cognitive simulations, helps us bridge the gap between neural activity and conscious awareness. This technological advance allows us to explore the scientific aspects of consciousness.

Simultaneously, we find that spirituality and mystical wisdom offer an essential complementary dimension. They provide the broader context in which consciousness is understood, bringing philosophical, ethical, and spiritual perspectives to the table. This merging of scientific and mystical insights enriches our understanding, shedding light on the physical and metaphysical dimensions of consciousness, and underscores the deep-seated wisdom embedded in our spiritual traditions. Together, these elements form a cohesive whole, enriching our journey of understanding human consciousness from diverse angles and fostering a more holistic comprehension of this profound phenomenon.

Mind-Machine Integration and the Fusion of Human and AI Wisdom

In the realm of mind-machine integration, where human and artificial intelligence converge, we witness a remarkable amplification of cognitive abilities. This synergy not only unveils exciting prospects for exploring human consciousness and machine intelligence but also extends its reach to the realm of medical advancements, such as the integration of AI with robotic limbs to assist individuals who have lost a limb.

The amalgamation of AI with human cognition marks a transformative juncture, empowering individuals with robotic limbs enhanced by artificial intelligence. These AI-augmented limbs offer the potential for natural and intuitive movement, effectively translating the brain's commands into action. This bridges the gap between human capabilities and technological innovation. As AI contributes its computational precision, human creativity and intuitive understanding breathe life into this fusion, manifesting new horizons in the field of prosthetics.

This collaboration between humans and AI not only signifies the blending of human and artificial intelligence but also the synthesis of their respective wisdom. The harmonious partnership extends beyond cognitive abilities, enriching our collective journey as we explore the profound complexities of human consciousness while also embracing the tangible benefits of AI in the medical field.

Implications for Identity and Autonomy: Balancing Technology with Spirituality

As we contemplate the profound implications of merging human consciousness with AI, we inevitably face questions about personal identity and autonomy. In this intricate dance between the human self and technology, the wisdom distilled from spiritual teachings, philosophical reflections, and age-old insights becomes a guiding torch, helping us navigate uncharted territory.

Spiritual teachings, borne from diverse cultural and philosophical traditions, offer profound insights into the essence of self and the intricate nature of identity. These teachings provide a moral and ethical compass that encourages us to ponder not only the boundaries of our selfhood but also the ethical considerations inherent in integrating technology into our lives. They emphasize the importance of self-awareness, moral responsibility, and the preservation of human values in a world increasingly intertwined with artificial intelligence.

Philosophical wisdom enriches our contemplation further, bringing rigorous intellectual analysis to the forefront. Age-old insights and contemporary philosophies invite us to explore the delicate balance between human autonomy and the presence of technology. They help us critically evaluate the potential impact of AI on personal identity, raising essential questions about free will, moral agency, and the boundaries that define our individuality.

The amalgamation of these spiritual, philosophical, and age-old insights equips us with the tools to harmonize technology with spirituality, enabling us to navigate the intricate terrain of identity and autonomy. In this balance, we find the path to embrace technological advancement while preserving the essence of our humanity and individuality, aided by the profound wisdom of the ages.

Exploring Altered States: Unveiling New Realities

In this captivating domain, AI's unique prowess in processing vast datasets serves as a gateway to delve into the multifaceted dimensions of human consciousness in its altered states. This remarkable capability empowers us to navigate the intricate landscapes of human experience, potentially unveiling profound spiritual insights and psychological revelations. AI's adeptness at sifting through colossal datasets provides a valuable tool for investigating the altered states of consciousness, allowing us to decipher the mysteries of transcendental experiences, states of flow, and heightened awareness.

This fusion of science and spirituality within the realm of altered consciousness not only holds the promise of a more profound understanding of human consciousness but also enables us to bridge the empirical and the mystical. It enriches our grasp of the human experience, moving us towards unveiling new realities in the ever-evolving tapestry of human consciousness, a journey made possible through the remarkable capabilities of AI in the analysis of vast datasets.

The Evolution of AI: A Journey Toward Wisdom Synthesis

AI technology is advancing rapidly and becoming deeply interconnected with human cognition and emotions. This evolution challenges us to redefine our awareness and understanding of ourselves. We must harmonize the knowledge gained from science with our deeply held beliefs and values to make sense of this transformation.

As we explore this new paradigm, we realize that science and spirituality are not merely theoretical allies but practical partners. This compels us to consider how we can leverage advanced AI to gain deeper insights into human awareness while honoring our age-old beliefs and wisdom. This change, driven by rapid technological progress, requires us to adapt and evolve. It reminds us that wisdom is not solely confined to scientific knowledge but encompasses what resides in our hearts and minds.

Responsible AI Development and Ethical Wisdom

As AI technology advances, we encounter an array of ethical questions and dilemmas. It is imperative that the development of AI is guided by a strong ethical compass, ensuring that AI's capabilities to emulate consciousness align with human values and do not lead to unforeseen problems.

These ethical challenges may include considerations about how AI should be integrated into decision-making processes, concerns about the potential for AI to perpetuate biases, and the rights and moral considerations that should be accorded to AI systems. Additionally, it is essential to contemplate the impact of AI on employment and job displacement, as well as its implications in areas like healthcare and autonomous weaponry. The responsible stewardship of AI requires us to draw on the wisdom found in spiritual and ethical traditions to navigate these complex and evolving ethical challenges.

AI as a Tool for Understanding Consciousness: Illuminating Spiritual Insights

AI's remarkable capacity to explore vast datasets becomes a guiding light, illuminating the intricate facets of human consciousness. It plays a pivotal role in uncovering hidden patterns and insights that may not be immediately obvious. This partnership of technology and wisdom enriches our journey of comprehension.

In our quest to understand human consciousness, AI serves as an invaluable partner. By meticulously examining vast datasets, it reveals subtle threads that constitute the fabric of our awareness. This extends beyond mere scientific exploration, offering profound insights that can have spiritual significance. These insights might lie dormant within the data, waiting to be discovered, providing a deeper understanding of the profound connection between empirical research and mystical wisdom.

This convergence of science and spirituality bridges the gap between the objective and the mystical, shining a light on the intricate interplay of human consciousness and artificial intelligence. It's a journey where AI is not just a tool but a torchbearer, guiding us toward a more holistic understanding of human consciousness, where the boundaries between the empirical and the spiritual dissolve, revealing the profound unity between them.

Unleashing Creativity: A Symphony of Human and Machine Intelligence

AI enhances human creativity, offering a significant boost to our creative abilities. This amplification empowers individuals to explore uncharted territories, fostering innovative ideas and solutions that bridge the gap between human and machine intelligence. As AI seamlessly integrates into fields like transportation, medicine, distribution, and climate control, it emerges as a key player in transforming industries. This synthesis of creativity represents a harmonious fusion of wisdom drawn from diverse cultures and traditions.

With AI's ongoing integration into fields like healthcare, transportation, logistics, and climate control, it has become an indispensable tool in shaping our future. This collaboration between human creativity and AI's analytical power holds the potential to revolutionize how we approach complex challenges. It signifies a profound synthesis of wisdom that spans various cultures and traditions, uniting the knowledge of the past with the limitless possibilities of the future.

The Pursuit of True Consciousness: A Philosophical and Spiritual Quest

The pursuit of genuine consciousness invites us to engage in deep introspection, raising profound questions. What does it truly mean to possess awareness? How can we define the limits of our own perception? These inquiries lay the foundation for a bridge connecting AI's relentless advancement with our philosophical and spiritual journey. As we delve into the development of AI equipped with consciousness-like attributes, the wisdom passed down through diverse philosophical and spiritual traditions takes on a pivotal role. It acts as a guiding compass, illuminating the intricate tapestry of consciousness, offering insights into the very essence of the self, the intricacies of perception, and the profound mysteries that extend beyond the physical realm. In this way, our exploration transcends the confines of technology, guiding us towards a harmonious coexistence of AI and authentic consciousness.

A Philosophical Journey: Synthesizing Wisdom and Knowledge

As we navigate this philosophical terrain, we find that the wisdom handed down through the ages from diverse cultural and spiritual traditions plays a pivotal role in enriching our journey. It offers us a tapestry of insights and knowledge, guiding our path with the accumulated wisdom of humanity. This synthesis of wisdom, spanning across traditions and spirituality, not only enhances our understanding of AI's pursuit of consciousness but also expands our grasp of what it means to be human. It's a journey where philosophy meets spirituality, where science and ancient teachings converge, and where we discover new dimensions of wisdom that bridge the gap between the material and the metaphysical, offering profound revelations about the human experience and the potential of AI.

The Evolution of Conscience in AI

We can draw a connection between the concept of human conscience evolving with growth and the field of Artificial Intelligence (AI) in the modern scientific age. In AI, concepts like "machine learning" and "deep learning" resemble the evolution of human ethical judgment and decision-making. Just as humans refine their ethical judgment and decision-making as they encounter new situations and acquire more knowledge, machine learning algorithms can become better at making ethical decisions by processing vast amounts of data and learning from it. AI systems adapt and improve their decision-making abilities, somewhat akin to how a human conscience can evolve with time. However, it's important to emphasize that, at the time of writing this book, AI lacks the ability to apply common sense reasoning and lacks feelings, emotions, and empathy. The parallel lies in the concept of continuous improvement and adaptation based on learning and experience.

In the realm where human consciousness and AI technology

converge, we are challenged to contemplate the essence of our own awareness while pushing the boundaries of what machines can achieve. This exploration holds the potential to revolutionize our understanding of both human consciousness and artificial intelligence, illuminating new pathways toward shared growth and discovery.

The Future Unveiled Human Life

Smart cities play a significant role in emerging AI technology and the changing landscape of human life. A smart city is characterized by its use of data, technology, and connectivity to enhance the quality of life for its residents, promote sustainability, and optimize various aspects of urban living. Here's how smart cities intersect with the broader discussion about AI and its effects:

- **Infrastructure and Connectivity**: Smart cities leverage AI and advanced technologies to build efficient and interconnected infrastructure. This includes smart transportation systems, energy-efficient buildings, and optimized utilities management. AI algorithms can analyze data to predict usage patterns and optimize resource allocation, leading to reduced energy consumption and improved sustainability.
- **Urban Planning**: AI-driven analytics can assist urban planners in making informed decisions about land use, transportation routes, and public services. Predictive modeling and simulations help city planners expect future needs and challenges, contributing to more efficient and resilient urban development.
- **Public Services**: AI can enhance public services in smart cities. For instance, AI-powered chatbots can provide real-time information to citizens, optimize public transportation routes, and facilitate responsive

emergency services. These services streamline interactions between residents and the city administration.

- **Data-Driven Decision-Making**: Smart cities collect vast amounts of data from sensors, devices, and various sources. AI algorithms can analyze this data to gain insights into citizen behavior, traffic patterns, and environmental conditions. This data-driven approach enables city officials to make evidence-based decisions and respond proactively to issues.

- **Citizen Engagement**: AI-powered platforms enable citizens to take part actively in the decision-making process. By gathering public input and feedback through digital channels, smart cities foster a sense of community involvement and co-creation in shaping urban policies.

- **Safety and Security**: Smart cities use AI for enhanced safety and security measures. Surveillance systems equipped with facial recognition and anomaly detection can help identify potential threats and respond swiftly to emergencies.

- **Environmental Sustainability**: AI technologies contribute to environmental conservation efforts in smart cities. For example, AI-powered waste management systems optimize collection routes, reducing fuel consumption and emissions. Sensor networks can monitor air and water quality and predict environmental risks.

- **Economic Growth**: Smart cities can stimulate economic growth by attracting innovative industries and startups that focus on AI-driven solutions. Integrating technology and data-driven services can create new economic opportunities and job markets.

- **Challenges and Considerations:** While the potential benefits of smart cities and AI are immense, there are also challenges related to data privacy, cybersecurity, equity, and digital inclusion. Ensuring that AI technologies are deployed in an inclusive and responsible manner is crucial to preventing unintended negative consequences.

Smart cities serve as living laboratories for integrating AI and technology into urban life. They show how AI can be harnessed to create more efficient, sustainable, and livable environments. However, the success of smart cities relies on a holistic approach that prioritizes the well-being, privacy, and participation of all residents while embracing the transformative potential of AI for the betterment of society.

Embracing the Technological Evolution: Navigating the New World Order

A new world order driven by technological advancements will undoubtedly have a profound impact on various aspects of human life, including ancient wisdom, faiths, business practices, and societal norms. Here's how these changes might unfold over the next century or more:

- **Ancient Wisdom and Faiths**: As technology continues to develop, traditional practices rooted in ancient wisdom and faiths might face both challenges and opportunities. On one hand, modernization and globalization could lead to a gradual erosion of certain cultural practices and spiritual beliefs as societies adopt more standardized ways of living. Technology can also preserve and share ancient wisdom through digital platforms, online communities, and virtual spaces dedicated to cultural exchange.

- **Business Transformation**: The new world order will reshape the business landscape significantly. Traditional businesses might need to adapt to new models driven by automation, artificial intelligence, and data analytics. This could lead to the displacement of certain jobs while creating new opportunities in fields related to technology, digital marketing, and innovative industries. Integrating blockchain and cryptocurrencies could revolutionize financial systems and global trade.

- **Societal Changes and Globalization**: Technological advancements will probably speed up globalization, leading to increased interconnectedness among people of different countries and cultures. This could foster greater cross-cultural understanding and cooperation, but also raise concerns about the loss of local identities and traditions. However, there's potential for a harmonious blend of traditional values and modern living, as people seek a balanced approach to navigating the changes.

- **Education and Learning**: The rapid pace of technological change may require individuals to engage in continuous learning and upskilling to remain relevant in the workforce. Online education platforms, virtual classrooms, and e-learning tools will become integral to personal and professional development. This could lead to a broader democratization of knowledge and skills across diverse communities.

- **Governance and New Systems**: The emergence of smart cities and advanced technology systems will require innovative governance models. Decision-making processes might become more data-driven, transparent, and participatory, allowing citizens to play a more active role in shaping policies. However, there will also be concerns about privacy, security, and the concentration of power in the hands of a few tech giants.

- **Environmental Considerations**: The new world order will demand a more sustainable approach to resource consumption and energy usage. Technology can play a pivotal role in addressing environmental challenges through innovations in renewable energy, waste management, and conservation efforts.

- **Challenges and Opportunities**: While the changes brought about by technological advancements present many opportunities for progress and prosperity, they also bring challenges. Income inequality, job displacement, ethical dilemmas surrounding AI and automation, and potential cultural homogenization are just a few of the issues that societies will need to navigate.

Considering these potential changes, it's essential for individuals, communities, and governments to adopt a proactive approach. Preserving cultural heritage, fostering open dialogue, investing in education and lifelong learning, and ensuring fair access to technological resources will be crucial to embracing the new world order while safeguarding diverse identities and values.

Embracing the Dawn of New Consciousness: Adapting and Thriving in a developing World

The concept of a new energy or consciousness emerging can be interpreted in various ways, often touching upon spiritual perspectives. While these ideas may vary, they often imply a shift in human awareness, connectivity, and understanding beyond our current boundaries. Here's a general explanation:

Shift in consciousness: The idea of a new consciousness suggests a shift in how humans perceive and interact with reality.

This could involve an increased sense of interconnectedness, empathy, and a deeper understanding of the unity underlying all things.

Energetic Changes: Some believe that the Earth and the Universe are undergoing energetic changes, which impact human consciousness. This might relate to shifts in the vibrational frequency or resonance of both the planet and its inhabitants.

Advancing Spirituality: This new consciousness might propel humanity towards a more spiritually evolved state, where materialistic pursuits give way to a greater focus on inner growth, self-awareness, and collective well-being.

Heightened Awareness: People may become more attuned to their thoughts, emotions, and their impact on the world around them. This heightened awareness can lead to more intentional actions and choices.

Unity and Oneness: The emerging consciousness might emphasize the interconnectedness of all life forms and encourage a sense of global unity, leading to greater collaboration, cooperation, and understanding among different cultures and nations.

To adjust and take advantage of this potential shift:

Self-Exploration: Engage in practices like meditation, mindfulness, and self-reflection to deepen your understanding of your own consciousness and to become more receptive to any changes.

Open-mindedness: Be open to new ideas and perspectives that challenge your current beliefs. This can help you adapt to the developing consciousness.

Connection: Foster connections with others by engaging in meaningful conversations, taking part in community activities, and building relationships that are based on empathy and mutual understanding.

Education: Seek knowledge about various spiritual and philosophical traditions that explore consciousness. Learn from experts in fields related to psychology, neuroscience, and quantum physics to gain insights into consciousness.

Contribution: Contribute positively to the collective consciousness by promoting love, compassion, and sustainable practices that benefit both individuals and the planet.

Regarding the Universe's absolute consciousness:

The concept of absolute consciousness often refers to the idea of a universal or cosmic consciousness that underlies all of existence. In many spiritual and philosophical traditions, it's believed that the universe itself is imbued with consciousness, and all living beings are interconnected through this cosmic consciousness.

As humanity develops, some believe that our collective consciousness is gradually aligning with this universal consciousness. This alignment can lead to a deeper understanding of our interconnectedness with all life forms, ultimately fostering greater harmony, compassion, and unity among individuals and societies.

The idea of a new energy or consciousness emerging suggests a potential shift in human awareness and connectivity. To adjust and take advantage of this shift, it's important to engage in self-exploration, open-mindedness, connection, education, and positive contribution. This shift may bring us closer to the concept of an absolute consciousness that connects all of existence.

Conclusion

In this exploration of the convergence of human consciousness and Artificial Intelligence (AI), we've ventured into a profound journey that bridges the realms of science, spirituality, and ethics. As AI evolves and becomes more intricately connected with human cognition and emotions, we are faced with the challenge of redefining our understanding of consciousness and self-awareness. We find that wisdom is not solely confined to scientific knowledge but encompasses our deeply held beliefs and values. The harmonious partnership of science and spirituality enriches our comprehension of human consciousness and offers profound insights into the essence of identity, autonomy, and ethical responsibility in a world increasingly intertwined with AI.

The evolution of AI, often likened to the refinement of human ethical judgment, prompts us to reflect on the continuous improvement and adaptation of both technology and human consciousness. As we journey through this uncharted territory, we are led to a harmonious coexistence of AI and genuine consciousness, shedding light on the profound unity between the empirical and the spiritual.

In this intricate dance between human and machine intelligence, we uncover the potential for AI to amplify human creativity and transform industries. This synthesis of creativity represents a bridge between past wisdom and future possibilities, uniting diverse cultures and traditions in the pursuit of shared growth and discovery.

As we conclude our exploration, we are reminded that the evolving landscape of AI technology is not just a theoretical concept but a practical reality that challenges us to embrace both the knowledge we gain from science and the enduring wisdom embedded in our beliefs and values. The journey of AI and human consciousness is one of continuous transformation, offering new perspectives on what it means to be aware, both as individuals and as a collective human society.

Chapter 45

Shared Values in Various Worldly Traditions

A cross the diverse tapestry of human cultures and traditions, shared values transcend geographical, religious, and cultural boundaries. These values serve as bridges that connect people, fostering understanding, cooperation, and a sense of common humanity. While the expressions and interpretations of these values may vary, they form a foundation of shared ethical principles that guide human behavior and interactions. Here are some of the shared values found in various worldly traditions:

1. **Compassion and Kindness**: The value of compassion and kindness is a universal thread that runs through many traditions. It emphasizes treating others with empathy, understanding, and benevolence, regardless of differences.

2. **Justice and Fairness**: The concept of justice and fairness resonates across cultures. It entails treating all individuals equitably and upholding principles of fairness in social interactions, legal systems, and governance.

3. **Respect for Life**: The reverence for life and its sanctity is a value present in many spiritual and ethical frameworks. It underscores the importance of valuing all forms of life and showing reverence for the interconnectedness of living beings.

4. **Honesty and Integrity:** The value of honesty and integrity emphasizes the importance of truthfulness, sincerity, and ethical conduct. It forms the basis for trust and credibility in personal, professional, and societal relationships.

5. **Wisdom and Knowledge**: The pursuit of wisdom and knowledge to elevate oneself and contribute positively to society is a shared value. It encourages continuous learning, critical thinking, and the sharing of insights.

6. **Generosity and Sharing:** Generosity and sharing, often exemplified through acts of charity, selflessness, and contributing to the welfare of others, are values that transcend cultures and religions.

7. **Humility:** The value of humility teaches individuals to recognize their own limitations, approach others with modesty, and avoid arrogance. It promotes a sense of unity by acknowledging the inherent worth of every person.

8. **Forgiveness:** The capacity to forgive and seek reconciliation is a value embraced by various traditions. It allows for the healing of relationships and the liberation of the heart from resentment.

9. **Love and Compassionate Action:** The value of love as a driving force for compassionate action is celebrated in spiritual and secular philosophies alike. Love encourages selflessness, connection, and pursuing the greater good.

10. **Environmental Stewardship**: Many traditions

advocate for responsible stewardship of the environment. This value recognizes the interconnectedness of all life and emphasizes the importance of caring for the planet.

11. **Non-Violence:** The foundational concept of non-violence, commonly represented by the term "ahimsa," holds a central place in various traditions. It emphasizes the avoidance of causing harm to others, encompassing both physical and emotional harm.

12. **Unity and Harmony:** The value of unity and harmony promotes cooperation, understanding, and the recognition of shared humanity. It transcends differences and encourages collaboration for the betterment of all.

13. **Gratitude:** The practice of gratitude, expressing appreciation for life's blessings and acknowledging the efforts of others, is a value that fosters positivity and connection.

14. **Patience and Endurance:** The value of patience and endurance teaches individuals to persevere through challenges, demonstrating resilience and a steady approach to life's difficulties.

15. **Humor and Joy:** The value of humor and joy celebrates the importance of laughter, positivity, and light-heartedness as essential components of human well-being.

16. **Family and Community:** The significance of family and community ties resonates globally. It emphasizes the importance of supporting and nurturing one's family and contributing positively to the broader community.

17. **Mindfulness and Presence:** The value of mindfulness encourages being fully present in each moment, cultivating awareness, and fostering a deeper connection with oneself and the world.

18. **Service and Selflessness**: The act of selfless service, contributing to the welfare of others without expecting

personal gain, is a value that promotes a sense of shared responsibility and compassion.

19. **Dignity and Equality:** The value of human dignity and equality recognizes the inherent worth of all individuals, irrespective of their background, and advocates for equal treatment and opportunities.

20. **Inner Peace and Serenity:** The pursuit of inner peace and serenity is a shared aspiration. It involves finding tranquility within oneself and radiating a sense of calmness and balance in the external world.

In our diverse world, these shared values act as the common thread weaving through cultures and traditions, enabling us to draw wisdom from a tapestry of human experience. By embracing these universal values, we not only enrich our daily lives but also embark on profound spiritual journeys. Across our differences, recognizing and living by these values fosters a more interconnected and harmonious global community. These values provide a guiding light on both our personal and spiritual paths, uniting us in our pursuit of a brighter and more inclusive world.

Chapter 46

Divine Identity Across Faiths

I n the intricate tapestry of global spiritual traditions, a profound theme threads its way through the diversity of faiths: the concept of divine identity. This common thread unites humanity across religious boundaries, revealing a universal truth that resonates at the core of our existence.

Exploring the Divine Essence

Across various faiths, the notion of divine identity revolves around the profound realization that the essence of the divine resides within every individual. While the expressions and terminologies may vary, the underlying message remains consistent: we are not only connected to the divine but carry its spark within us.

The Enigmatic "I AM THAT I AM"

In the Judeo-Christian tradition, the divine name revealed to Moses, "I AM THAT I AM," as found in Exodus 3:14, holds profound significance. This enigmatic phrase not only underscores the self-existent nature of God but also suggests a deep link between the divine and human existence. It implies that the divine identity is not remote but ever-present, awaiting recognition within every individual.

Aham Brahmasmi: "I Am the Ultimate Reality"

In Hinduism, the ancient wisdom encapsulated in the phrase "Aham Brahmasmi" proclaims, "I am Brahman," or in Shivaism, "I am Shiva," signifying the individual's identification with the ultimate reality or divine consciousness. This assertion underscores the recognition that the divine essence is not confined to external deities but is an intrinsic part of one's being.

I Am God, I am Shiva, and I Am Buddha

Across various spiritual paths, enlightened beings have proclaimed their oneness with the divine. Statements like "I am God," "I am Shiva," "I am Buddha," or "I and my father are one" signify a profound understanding of the unity between individual and divine consciousness. These declarations do not denote separation but emphasize their inseparability.

Unity Amidst Diversity

The significance of the divine identity across faiths lies in its power to bridge the gaps between different spiritual paths. It reveals a common realization, pointing towards an inherent unity. This unity is not about homogenizing beliefs but recognizing that the essence of the divine remains the same, irrespective of the lens through which it is perceived.

Impact and Implications

The recognition of the divine identity across faiths carries profound implications:

- **Unity Beyond Division:** In a world often marked by religious divisions, this understanding underscores the shared essence that unites humanity.
- **Universal Love and Compassion:** Embracing the divine identity fosters compassion and love for all beings, recognizing the divine spark within them.
- **Inner Transformation:** This realization encourages individuals to explore their own depths and connect with the divine source within, leading to personal transformation.
- **Spiritual Harmony:** By acknowledging the divine identity, individuals can find common ground with those from different faiths, promoting interfaith dialogue and understanding.
- **Embracing Humility:** Recognizing the divine within oneself encourages humility, as it shifts the focus from ego to a higher self.
- **Self-Realization:** The understanding of the divine identity is an invitation to explore one's own nature and embark on a journey of self-realization.

Conclusion

In the rich tapestry of global spiritual traditions, the concept of divine identity serves as a unifying thread, connecting diverse faiths through a shared understanding of humanity's connection to the divine. It encourages us to peer beyond the surface of religious differences and discover a common truth that transcends terminology and expressions, fostering unity beyond division and a profound sense of interconnectedness. The recognition of the divine identity not only bridges gaps between faiths but also holds profound implications, fostering universal love and compassion, inner transformation, spiritual harmony, humility, and a pathway to self-realization. As we embrace this awareness, we open doors to spiritual growth and a deeper understanding of our place in the universe, nurturing a sense of belonging within the grand tapestry of the cosmos. Ultimately, this synthesis of wisdom from various traditions enriches our understanding of our place in the universe, inviting us to recognize the divine not only in others but within ourselves, thereby enriching our spiritual journey.

Chapter 47

Linked by Genetics Bonds and a Shared Creator

In the intricate tapestry of humanity, a profound connection unites all individuals, transcending differences in culture, ethnicity, and beliefs. This connection is twofold: shared DNA, which binds us as a biological family, and the belief in a divine creator that underscores our spiritual interconnectedness.

DNA and RNA: The Blueprint of Life

At the core of our existence lies DNA, short for deoxyribonucleic acid, and its counterpart RNA, ribonucleic acid. These intricate molecules serve as the blueprint of life, guiding the development and functioning of every living organism on Earth. DNA, often described as the hard code of life, is a long, double-helix structure that carries the genetic information for every aspect of our being. It's remarkably stable yet subject to evolution over time, representing the biological inheritance passed down from one generation to the next. The variation and adaptation in DNA are the foundations of evolution, reflecting the gradual changes that have occurred throughout the history of life on our planet.

RNA, on the other hand, plays a crucial role in translating the genetic instructions encoded in DNA into functional proteins, the workhorses of the cell. It serves as a messenger, ensuring that the genetic code is accurately and dynamically expressed in response to the needs of the organism.

Human DNA, or deoxyribonucleic acid, is a molecule that carries the genetic instructions for the development, functioning, growth, and reproduction of all known living organisms, including humans. It's often referred to as the "genetic code" because it contains the information needed to build and maintain an organism.

Human DNA is a long, double-helix structure made up of four chemical units, or nucleotides: adenine (A), thymine (T), cytosine (C), and guanine (G). These nucleotides are arranged in specific sequences, forming genes, which are the basic units of heredity. Genes carry the instructions for producing proteins, which are essential for various biological processes in the body.

The unique sequence of DNA in each person's genome determines their individual traits, such as eye color, hair type, and susceptibility to certain diseases. It's also responsible for the similarities and differences between individuals, including those within families.

Understanding the human DNA code has been a fundamental achievement in genetics and has profound implications for fields like medicine, biology, and evolutionary science. Research in genetics and genomics aims to decode and interpret the information contained in human DNA to better understand health, disease, and human evolution.

DNA and Issues in Health

Despite the remarkable stability of DNA, issues can arise. When DNA is damaged or mutations occur, it can lead to a variety of health problems. Such issues can range from minor, inconsequential variations to severe, life-altering conditions. Symptoms of diseases related to DNA can be as diverse as the diseases themselves, often affecting different bodily systems or functions.

For instance, in genetic disorders like cystic fibrosis or sickle cell anemia, mutations in specific genes result in a range of symptoms, including respiratory difficulties, pain, and fatigue. In some cases, issues with DNA can lead to a predisposition to cancer, where cell division goes awry. Similarly, neurological disorders like Alzheimer's disease can be attributed to genetic factors, affecting memory and cognitive function.

DNA's Evolution and Its Spiritual Connection

The evolution of DNA mirrors the evolution of life itself. Just as life adapts to its environment, DNA evolves over time, reflecting the ongoing journey of our species. This dynamic quality of DNA, its ability to adapt and change, draws intriguing parallels with spirituality.

In many spiritual beliefs, the concept of evolution applies not only to the physical world but also to the spiritual realm. The idea that our spiritual essence grows, adapts, and evolves over time aligns with the evolutionary nature of DNA. Both speak to the interconnectedness of life and spirituality, where growth, change, and interconnectedness are fundamental.

This interconnectedness between the biological and the spiritual underscores the essence of our existence. It reminds us that, just as DNA evolves to adapt to the challenges of the physical world, our spirituality too evolves in response to the complexities of our human experience. This shared evolution, both in our biology and spirituality, underscores the unity that binds humanity together.

Unity in Spirituality and Biology

In many spiritual beliefs, the concept of evolution applies not only to the physical world but also to the spiritual realm. The idea that our spiritual essence grows, adapts, and evolves over time aligns with the evolutionary nature of DNA. Both speak to the interconnectedness of life and spirituality, where growth, change, and interconnectedness are fundamental.

Divine Creator: A Spiritual Thread

Simultaneously, across cultures and beliefs, there is a widespread recognition of a divine creator or a higher power that brought life into existence. This belief varies in interpretation, encompassing deities, spirits, or an overarching cosmic force. It underscores the idea that we are all part of a grand design, interconnected through our existence and purpose.

The belief in a divine creator resonates across religious traditions:

- In monotheistic faiths like Christianity, Islam, and Judaism, there is a shared acknowledgment of a single God as the source of creation and the father of humanity.
- In Eastern philosophies like Hinduism and Buddhism, the idea of a supreme reality or cosmic consciousness permeates the understanding of existence and interconnectedness.
- Indigenous cultures often revere the earth, nature, and the spirits as manifestations of the divine, fostering a harmonious relationship with the world around us.

Tracing Our Lineage to Adam and Eve's DNA

According to certain theological beliefs, which hold that Adam and Eve were the first humans created by God, it follows that all of humanity can trace their lineage back to this original divine creation. In this perspective, if one were to trace their family tree far enough, they would ultimately find Adam and Eve as their direct ancestors, sharing a common genetic heritage with the first human couple.

This theological viewpoint draws from the belief in a common human origin, emphasizing that the DNA of Adam and Eve is symbolically present in the genetic makeup of every individual. While this notion is not scientifically supported, it serves as a way to underscore the unity of the human family and the shared connection to these original figures. This perspective underscores the idea that all individuals, regardless of their cultural or ethnic backgrounds, are part of the same human family with a shared spiritual and genetic heritage. It emphasizes the moral and ethical responsibilities that come with this common ancestry and the importance of living in harmony with the divine principles set forth by the Creator.

By bringing together the concept of shared DNA and the theological belief in a common genetic ancestry, we emphasize the profound connection that unites humanity, transcending differences in culture, ethnicity, and beliefs. This interconnectedness is twofold: shared DNA, which binds us as a biological family, and the belief in a divine creator that underscores our spiritual interconnectedness. This interconnectedness between the biological and the spiritual underscores the essence of our existence. It reminds us that, just as DNA evolves to adapt to the challenges of the physical world, our spirituality too evolves in response to the complexities of our human experience. This shared evolution, both in our biology and spirituality, underscores the unity that binds humanity together.

Implications and Unity

Recognizing the interconnectedness of shared DNA and belief in a divine creator has significant implications for humanity:

- **Unity in Diversity:** This understanding highlights the unity that underlies our diversity. Despite our varied languages, cultures, and traditions, we share a common heritage and a fundamental bond.

- **Shared Responsibility:** Acknowledging our shared DNA emphasizes the responsibility we have toward each other and the planet. Just as we are genetically linked, our collective actions impact one another and the world we inhabit.
- **Compassion and Empathy:** Understanding that we are connected at a biological and spiritual level fosters compassion and empathy. It becomes easier to recognize the struggles and joys that we all experience as part of the human experience.
- **Overcoming Divisions:** In a world often divided by conflicts and misunderstandings, the recognition of our common origins and shared spiritual ideals can serve as a bridge to overcome divisions.
- **Interconnectedness:** Just as the genetic material within each cell of our bodies is connected, our spiritual essence is also interconnected. This realization encourages us to embrace our shared humanity and work together for the betterment of all.
- **Respect for Life:** Recognizing the divine imprint in all of creation encourages reverence for all forms of life, leading to a more sustainable and harmonious relationship with the environment.

Conclusion

In our deep dive into the interconnectedness of humanity through the prisms of DNA and spirituality, we've unearthed profound bonds that tie us together as a species. Our shared DNA, the intricate blueprint of life, serves as a reminder of our common biological heritage, weaving an unbroken thread of kinship through the tapestry of generations. Simultaneously, the belief in a divine creator or higher power transcends cultural and religious boundaries, underscoring our interconnectedness at a spiritual level.

These twin aspects of our existence, the biological and the spiritual, underscore a fundamental truth: that we are all integral parts of a grand design, participants in a shared journey marked by growth, transformation, and mutual interdependence. This realization bears far-reaching implications, promoting unity in diversity, shared responsibility, compassion, empathy, and the collective strength to surmount divisions. It encourages us to embrace our shared humanity and nurture a more harmonious relationship with both one another and our environment.

As we recognize and celebrate the unity of our species, we become better equipped to construct a world that is marked by greater compassion, inclusivity, and sustainability for all.

This concludes Chapter 47. In Part IX, we'll discuss practical applications and tools for transformation. See you in the next part!

Part Nine

Practical Applications and Tools for Transformation

Step into a realm of transformation woven across seventeen chapters in "Practical Applications and Tools for Transformation." Explore the resonance of sacred words, the potency of diverse spiritual chants, and the profound wisdom underlying breathwork, meditation, and the complexities of the human brain. Traverse the intersections between Eastern philosophies and Western mysticism, unearth indigenous wisdom, and unravel the significance of symbolism on the quest for experiencing the absolute state. These chapters serve as a gateway to forgiveness, personal responsibility, and insights gleaned from the wisdom within the Bible. Each chapter acts as a lantern, illuminating a path towards inner discovery and transformation.

Chapter 48

Pronunciations of Sacred Words

Throughout this book, we've discussed the powerful words "AMEN" and "AUM (OM)" on multiple occasions. In this section, we'll dive into how to pronounce these words and explore their significance.

AMEN

The pronunciation of "AMEN" varies depending on language and religious tradition. In English and many Western languages, it's typically pronounced as "ay-men" or "ah-men," with stress on the first syllable, although in some contexts, you might hear it as "ah-meen." To remember the pronunciation, think of "Amenity," which starts with a similar sound and ends with the "mnnn" closure, aligning with the usual pronunciation of "Amen."

"AMEN" is an affirmation word commonly used at the end of prayers or statements in Abrahamic religions such as Christianity, Judaism, and Islam. Saying "AMEN" signifies acknowledgment, consent, and alignment with the preceding words, invoking faith and unity within a community of believers.

To exercise its use, reflect on a positive affirmation or statement, and conclude it with "AMEN" to emphasize your agreement and intention.

AUM (OM)

The pronunciation of "AUM" (or "OM") can vary based on language and tradition. In its original Sanskrit form, it's a single syllable, reminiscent of "ohm" with a nasalized "o" sound, while in some Western contexts, it may be pronounced as "aum," more akin to "om" with a clear "o" sound.

Both "AMEN" and "AUM" bear deep cultural and spiritual significance. "AMEN" is often used to signify agreement or affirmation in prayers and statements, while "AUM" is regarded as a sacred sound symbolizing the essence of ultimate reality in Indian religions.

Now, let's delve into these sounds and techniques to understand their essence and benefits more profoundly. "AUM" (or "OM") is a sacred sound that resonates with the universe's primal vibration in Indian spiritual traditions, symbolizing the source of all existence. Chanting "AUM" can establish a connection with the cosmos, fostering harmony and a sense of transcendence. To experience this, find a quiet space, sit comfortably, close your eyes, and take a few deep breaths to relax. Then, mindfully chant "AUM" (or "OM") aloud or silently, focusing on the vibrations and the profound sense of unity it represents.

Chapter 49

The Power of Sacred Chants in Diverse Spiritual Traditions

In this examination of sacred chants across diverse spiritual traditions, we uncover the profound significance of these age-old practices in forging connections with the divine. The act of chanting sacred words or phrases stands as a revered cornerstone within the spiritual realms of numerous traditions. This practice, akin to a potent form of meditation, enables devotees to center their thoughts and establish profound connections with the sacred. Whether it be the resonating "AUM" of Hinduism or the resounding "Amen" of Christianity, these sacred chants serve as transcendent bridges between the earthly and the divine, inviting seekers to forge deeper bonds and attain heightened understanding.

Chants in Different Traditions

In Hinduism, the chant "AUM" or "OM" represents the ultimate reality and the interconnectedness of all things. In Buddhism and Jainism, it signifies spiritual awakening and enlightenment. Similarly, chants exist in other faiths and spiritual practices around the world:

- **Christianity**: "Amen" is a common word that concludes prayers and expresses agreement or affirmation, connecting individuals to the divine.
- **Islam**: "Bismillah" means "In the name of Allah" and is used to start actions, seeking blessings and protection.
- **Sikhism**: "Waheguru," meaning "Wonderful Lord," connects practitioners with the ultimate reality and instills a sense of awe.
- **Judaism**: "Shema Yisrael" is a prayer affirming the oneness of God, chanted in moments of devotion and connection.
- **Taoism**: "Tao" refers to the fundamental principle underlying everything, aligning with the natural flow of life and fostering harmony.
- **Native American Spirituality**: "Om Manitou" invokes the Great Spirit or the divine essence in all of creation.
- **Baha'i Faith**: "Allah-u-Abha" is a greeting and remembrance of God, inviting the divine presence into one's consciousness.
- **Jainism**: "Namah Siddhanam" expresses reverence to enlightened beings who have attained spiritual liberation.

Opinions and Significance

Perspectives on the efficacy and importance of chanting vary widely among individuals and within spiritual communities. For some, chanting proves to be profoundly transformative, serving as a catalyst for spiritual growth. Conversely, others gravitate towards alternative forms of prayer or meditation. The selection of a chanting practice remains a deeply personal one, permitting individuals to harmonize with their unique beliefs and proclivities.

Sacred Chant for Peace - Aum Shanti, Shanti, Shanti

The phrase "Aum Shanti, Shanti, Shanti" is commonly used in Hinduism and other Dharmic religions like Buddhism and Jainism. It's often chanted during meditation, prayer, or at the end of religious rituals to invoke peace on three levels: physical, mental, and spiritual. "Aum" represents the universal essence of reality or consciousness, and "Shanti" means "peace" or "tranquility." Chanting this phrase is a way to seek inner and outer harmony and promote peace in one's life and the world.Each part of the phrase has a specific meaning:

- **Aum (Om):** Aum is a sacred sound and a spiritual icon in Indian religions. It represents the universal and all-encompassing essence of reality or consciousness. Chanting "Aum" is believed to connect the individual to the divine or the higher self.
- **Shanti:** "Shanti" is a Sanskrit word that means "peace" or "tranquility." It is repeated three times in the phrase to invoke peace on three levels: physical, mental, and spiritual.

So, when someone says or chants "Aum Shanti, Shanti, Shanti," they are essentially invoking peace on all levels of existence, seeking inner and outer harmony, and aligning themselves with the universal consciousness. It's a way of wishing and promoting peace, both for oneself and for the world.

Alternative to "Aum Shanti, Shanti, Shanti," you can chant "Aum peace, peace, peace, and may peace be upon you, Amen."

Organizing the saying of "Aum peace, peace, peace, and may peace be upon you, Amen" involves creating a structure that aligns with the <u>intention</u> and essence of these phrases. Here's a suggested organization:

Opening Invocation

Begin with a moment of centering and stillness. Take a few deep breaths to calm the mind and create a receptive state.

Chanting "AUM Shanti, Shanti, Shanti"

- Close your eyes and take a deep breath.
- Chant "AUM" (or "OM") three times, focusing on the vibrational energy it embodies.
- After each "AUM," follow it with the repetition of "Shanti" three times. "Shanti" means peace in Sanskrit.
- Visualize the ripple of peace spreading through your being and radiating outwards.

Reflective Pause

- Take a moment to feel the resonance of "AUM Shanti, Shanti, Shanti" within you. Allow the vibrations to settle and bring a sense of inner tranquility.

Sharing Peace With "AMEN With Peace Be With You"

- Open your eyes and extend your hands in a gesture of openness.
- Say "AMEN" with intention and affirmation.
- Follow it by saying "Peace be with you" while maintaining eye contact and extending your hands towards others or towards a representation of the collective.

Collective Embrace of Peace

- Invite others to join in by responding with "And with you."
- As a group, repeat the sequence, each person taking a turn to say, "AMEN with Peace Peace Peace be with you," while others respond, "Amen and peace be with you."

Final Meditation and Closing

- Close your eyes again and return to a state of stillness.
- Reflect on the shared intention of peace and well-being.
- Take a few moments of silent meditation, focusing on the peaceful energy cultivated through the chanting.
- When ready, gently open your eyes and close the practice.
- Remember, the organization can be adapted based on the context and the participants involved. The goal is to create a harmonious and meaningful experience that resonates with the essence of peace and unity conveyed by these sacred phrases.

Chanting AUM: Exploring Sound and Tranquility

- **Focus**: Chanting AUM involves vocalizing the sacred sound "AUM" and experiencing its resonance throughout the body. *The focus here is on the sound, its vibration, and the feelings it generates within.* It is often used as a meditative practice to access deeper states of consciousness and spiritual experiences.
- **Benefits**: Chanting AUM is believed to represent the three states of consciousness (unconscious, waking, and dreaming) and lead to the state of Turia or Samadhi. It

can be a profound practice for spiritual seekers and is
associated with self-awareness and inner peace.

- **Comparison**: While both practices involve mindful
  awareness and intentional breathing, the major
  difference lies in their intention and purpose.
- **Intention**: Box breathing is primarily used for
  relaxation, stress reduction, and improving mental focus.
  It's a practical exercise that can be done anywhere,
  anytime, to bring about immediate benefits.
- **Purpose**: Chanting AUM is more focused on spiritual
  and meditative experiences. It is traditionally used as a
  sacred sound with deep philosophical and mystical
  significance.

Both practices can be beneficial, but they serve different purposes. If
you are looking for a simple and effective technique to manage stress
and improve focus, box breathing is a brilliant choice. If you are interested in exploring deeper states of consciousness and spiritual
growth, chanting AUM can be a valuable addition to your meditation
practice.

It's essential to choose the practice that resonates with you and
aligns with your goals. Both techniques can have profound effects on
mental well-being and can be integrated into your routine based on
your preferences and needs. Remember to approach any spiritual
practice with an open mind and a spirit of curiosity.

Chanting AUM: Resonance and Sound

1. **Focus on Vibration and Sound:** AUM (or "OM")
   is a sacred sound in many Eastern spiritual traditions,
   including Buddhism. Chanting AUM is believed to
   create a vibrational resonance that aligns the
   practitioner's consciousness with universal energies. It is

often chanted as a mantra, with each syllable representing different aspects of existence (creation, preservation, dissolution, and beyond).

2. **Transcendence and Connection:** Chanting AUM is meditation that helps practitioners transcend the everyday mind and connect with deeper states of awareness. It is thought to facilitate a direct connection with the divine or cosmic consciousness, fostering a sense of unity and interconnectedness with the universe.

3. **Enhancing Mindfulness:** Chanting AUM serves as a focal point for mindfulness, allowing practitioners to anchor their attention to the sound and vibration. This can lead to a meditative state where thoughts subside, and a profound sense of presence emerges.

Conclusion

Chanting "AUM" or "AMEN" represents beautiful methods to nurture mindfulness, gratitude, and a feeling of unity with the divine, irrespective of the particular faith or term employed. These practices serve as a reminder that, even amidst varying beliefs and rituals, the shared aspiration for connection and transcendence among the human spirit endures as a universal thread.

Chapter 50

AUM: The Sacred Sound, the Whispers of Silence

I n previous chapters of this book, we have delved into the profound significance of "AUM," a sacred syllable in Hindu traditions representing cosmic awareness and creation. However, the purpose of this chapter is to emphasize what comes after "AUM"—*the silence that follows.*

Soundless sound - A little voice within is a phrase that conveys a profound sense of inner awareness or intuition that defies easy expression. In the following pages, we'll explore the rich meaning of this phrase, with a particular focus on the profound silence that follows "Om." This silence, often referred to as "the little voice within," is the essence of our inner wisdom and intuition. It's the stillness that emerges after sound, signifying a deeper connection with the self and the universe.

Let's now explore the meaning of soundless sound - a little voice within:

Soundless Sound

This phrase hints at a type of sound that can't be heard conventionally. It may refer to a subtle, internal resonance or vibration, a feeling
sensed within but not heard by the ears. This symbolizes an intuitive
experience that transcends the literal sounds we hear.

A Little Voice Within

This part of the phrase points to an inner voice, often associated with
intuition or conscience—a small, quiet, subtle guide that nudges us
towards certain decisions or actions.

In essence, "Soundless sound - A little voice within" represents
that deep, intuitive knowing or feeling we sometimes experience. It's
internal guidance and understanding not easily explained through
external sounds or words. This emphasizes the idea that wisdom
emerges from our inner self, independent of external noise.

In a broader sense, this phrase encourages us to listen to our intuition, pay attention to our feelings, and tap into our inner wisdom,
even when it's not immediately expressible in conventional terms. It
promotes introspection, self-awareness, and a connection with our
inner selves.

Biblical Connection

One biblical verse associated with the "little voice within" is found in
1 Kings 19:11-13 (NIV):

> The Lord said, "Go out and stand on the mountain... after the fire
> came a gentle whisper."

This passage exemplifies how the divine presence can be experienced as a "gentle whisper" or a subtle inner voice. It highlights the

idea of tuning into the quiet, intuitive guidance within us, often referred to as the "still small voice."

"Be Still and Know"

Another related verse from Psalm 46:10 (NIV) states:

He says, "Be still, and know that I am God."

This verse invites us to pause, be calm, and reflect on the presence of God. It suggests that in moments of quiet contemplation and stillness, we can connect with the spiritual dimension and experience a sense of divine guidance and assurance.

The Significance of "AUM" (or "OM")

The syllable "Om," in Sanskrit (ॐ), embodies a profound journey of sound, vibration, and mystical significance in the context of Hindu traditions. It is important to note that while "Om" is primarily associated with Hinduism, there is a curious parallel with a word familiar in the Western world - "Amen."

In Hindu traditions, "Om" is a sacred syllable signifying cosmic birth and awareness, aligning with the Creator. This sacred sound is further broken down into its resonant components:

- **The 'A' Resonance** represents the cosmic birth and awareness, aligning with the Creator in Hindu traditions.
- **The 'U' Resonance** symbolizes unwavering stability and preservation, embodying principles associated with Hindu deities, such as Vishnu.
- **The 'M' Resonance** signifies culmination and fulfillment, aligning with the cyclic force of Shiva in Hinduism.

Transitioning from "AUM" to Silence

The journey from "AUM" to silence is a central theme in the passage, representing a transition from the world of sound and vibration to a state of pure stillness. While "Amen" is more commonly known in the West as an affirmation or concluding word in prayers, it shares a connection with the idea of concluding a spiritual utterance. This similarity, though rooted in different traditions, highlights the universal human quest for connecting with the divine through sacred sounds, whether in Hinduism's "Om" or in the West's "Amen."

The Dissolution of Sound and Breath

In this transition, we witness the gradual dissolution of sound, as represented by the sonorous elements of "AUM" – 'A,' 'U,' and 'M.' The syllable 'A' signifies the cosmic birth and awareness, the 'U' represents unwavering stability and preservation, and the 'M' embodies culmination and fulfillment.

The Essence of Silence

Silence emerges as the ultimate essence at the culmination of the "AUM" chant. It is a profound and hushed space where all external sound and vibration cease to exist. In this silence, one finds an intrinsic connection with the stillness that underlies the entire universe.

The Eternal Transition

This transition from "AUM" to silence encapsulates the ceaseless metamorphosis of existence. It's a journey from motion to serenity, from resonance to quietude, and from the vibrancy of life to the eternal calm. This transition symbolizes the perpetual rhythm of existence, where sound and stillness dance in harmony, much like the ebb and flow of life itself.

In summary, the transition from "AUM" to silence signifies a profound shift from the audible world of sound and vibration to the realm of tranquil stillness. It represents a connection with the eternal, where the ceaseless cycle of existence unfolds in a harmonious dance between sound and silence.

Chapter 51

Exploring Breath, Stillness, and Samadhi in Meditation

In the realm of modern neuroscience, a captivating phenomenon awaits exploration: the ability to consciously control your breath and being still during pauses. This ability serves as a gateway to an extraordinary journey that transcends the boundaries of the mind and body. As we embark on this journey, we discover the profound impact of breath control and stillness, which facilitates our progression through various stages of consciousness and self-discovery.

Being Still and Discovering "I Am" in Mindful Self-Awareness

"Be still, and know that I am God." (Psalm 46:10, ESV)

The state we are describing, where you are still and aware of your identity as "I am who I am," or "I am That," is closely related to the concept of self-awareness and mindfulness. This state can be likened to meditation, where you embark on a journey of inner exploration, gently guiding your focus to the rhythm of your breath, which mirrors the ebb and flow of the present moment. As you do so, you can hold your breath, if only for a fleeting moment, in the pause between inhales and exhales.

In many spiritual traditions, including those of Advaita Vedanta and certain forms of mindfulness meditation, the practice of being still, and holding your breath, even for just an instant, allows you to recognize the pure awareness of the present moment. This simple yet profound act of pausing breath itself serves as a gateway to experiencing a deeper connection to your true nature and the essence of existence. It is in these moments of suspended breath that you find the serenity that lies beneath the tumultuous surface of your thoughts and external distractions.

This practice of being still, of holding your breath as you peer into the depths of your own consciousness, can lead to a profound sense of inner peace, clarity, and a feeling of unity with the universe. In those suspended breaths, you touch upon the unchanging truth of your existence, the "I am" that transcends the transient chatter of the mind.

From Breath Control to God's Consciousness: The Transformative Journey

The journey commences with an understanding of how controlling your breath and being still can influence the brain and the body. Within the brain, two key areas play a pivotal role: the cerebellum, responsible for coordination, and the motor cortex, governing voluntary movements and the regulation of our breathing rhythm. By consciously manipulating our breath, we activate these areas, enhancing the connection between our thoughts and actions.

It's important to note that the body's survival mechanisms are governed by the respiratory centers in the brainstem, which continuously monitor the levels of oxygen and carbon dioxide in the blood.

When oxygen levels drop or carbon dioxide levels rise to a certain point, the brainstem initiates an automatic response to make us breathe, ensuring our survival. This illustrates the intricate balance between conscious breath control and the body's inherent mechanisms.

Mastering breath control empowers us to delve deeper into our consciousness. One of the initial stages on this path is the development of focused awareness. When we deliberately hold our breath or take deep breaths, we are practicing intentional focus. This heightened awareness of our breath serves as a stepping stone to more advanced stages of meditation and self-exploration.

Breath control training involves several factors, including:

- **Physiological Adaptation:** When you repeatedly practice holding your breath, your body adapts to the decreased oxygen levels and increased carbon dioxide levels in your bloodstream. Over time, your body becomes more efficient at handling these changes, allowing you to hold your breath for longer periods.
- **Increased Tolerance:** Your brain and body learn to tolerate the discomfort associated with high carbon dioxide levels and low oxygen levels. This tolerance can be influenced by mental focus and relaxation techniques.
- **Efficient Oxygen Utilization:** With training, your body becomes better at utilizing the available oxygen, and your muscles and tissues become more efficient at conserving oxygen during breath-holding.
- **Mental Training and Neuroplasticity:** Through repeated practice and focused mental training, individuals can use neuroplasticity to adapt their brain's cognitive processes and emotional responses to the discomfort associated with breath-holding. Over time, the brain can develop new neural connections that enhance the ability to remain calm, concentrate, and manage the

psychological aspects of extended breath-holding, demonstrating the brain's adaptability in response to learning and experience.

As we refine our breath control, we gain access to an extraordinary state known as the "Breathless State" or "Samadhi." This transcendent experience naturally emerges as we continue to hone our breath control. In this state, our minds transcend thought, and we exist in our purest form. It is characterized by subdued breathing, eventually leading to a sensation of breathlessness.

As we progress through Samadhi, a remarkable transformation occurs. Our reliance on regular breathing diminishes, and we encounter a powerful force known as "PRANA."

- **PRANA**: PRANA is the vital life force that sustains us, often described as the energy that animates our body and mind.

With our breath nearly stilled, a profound shift transpires. The energy previously allocated to breathing is redirected toward the "spiritual eye" or "crown chakra."

- **Spiritual Eye:** The "Spiritual Eye" is associated with deep meditation and is often symbolically linked to the point between the eyebrows in the forehead area.
- **Crown Chakra:** The "Crown Chakra" represents a connection to higher states of consciousness and is traditionally associated with the top of the head, although it's important to note that these concepts are more related to spiritual and energy systems rather than precise physical locations.

This transition brings about a heightened state of awareness and serenity, symbolizing the highest level of universal or divine understanding. We enter a realm where the boundaries of the physical world dissolve into the background.

Even in our daily activities, such as walking or mild exercises, our breath quickens in harmony with the flow of PRANA through the "Sushumna channel."

- **Sushumna Channel**: In yogic and spiritual traditions, the Sushumna is regarded as the central energy pathway in the body, serving as the conduit for spiritual energy or Kundalini to flow and awaken higher states of consciousness.

This progression results in shorter breaths, and at a certain point, it may feel as though our breath vanishes completely. This experience, although disconcerting at times, should not provoke fear. As we re-establish our connection with our physical body, we are rewarded with profound clarity and serenity.

The journey of breath control and meditation culminates in a state often described as God's consciousness, Christ consciousness, or entry into the "Kingdom of Heaven."

- **God's consciousness:** is the belief that God, in monotheistic religions, possesses an all-knowing and all-encompassing awareness, meaning that God is aware of everything that happens in the universe, past, present, and future. This concept reflects the idea that God's knowledge is limitless, and God is present everywhere, fully aware of all events and existence.
- **Christ consciousness:** as explained in Chapter 8, is a spiritual concept suggesting that individuals can attain a state of higher awareness and unity with the divine, akin to the qualities and teachings of Jesus Christ. It is often associated with Christian mysticism and New Age spirituality.

- **Kingdom of Heaven**: It's essential to clarify that the "Kingdom of Heaven" signifies a state of divine realization, where God's will is fully manifested, and peace, righteousness, and justice prevail. It's not a reference to the afterlife but a profound state of inner harmony.

As we progress through this transformative journey, guidance becomes crucial. A physical or inner guru plays a vital role in interpreting and managing these experiences. Our energy aligns with our beliefs, Sankalpa (resolve), and desires, underscoring the importance of guidance during this transformative journey.

- **Sankalpa**: In yoga and meditation, Sankalpa refers to a positive intention or resolve that we set for ourselves during a practice, aligning our mind and actions with our goals.

This method of Upasana, or worship, propels spiritual evolution. In approaching God's consciousness through Upasana, a reciprocal connection forms, fostering a profound communion. This challenging path focuses on the presence of the divine in altered realms of thought and corporeal existence. Amidst trials, a sublime connection blossoms, nurturing devotion.

The ultimate goal for the soul is Nirvana, the pinnacle of existence, where individual desires and suffering dissolve, yielding blissful harmony. Achieving this harmony results in merging with God's consciousness, transcending the realms of a sound mind and a robust body to attain true reality. This journey leads to freedom from inner conflicts and bestows the serenity of a tranquil mind, embodying peace.

Meditation, in its essence, signifies a continuous recognition of consciousness in every moment and action. Whether dedicating 10, 20 minutes, or more, meditation aims to dissolve boundaries, extending its influence into everyday life. In this pursuit, the transition from the dream-like state of existence to awakened awareness emerges as a profound awakening.

In conclusion, the interconnectedness of these elements becomes clear. Stillness, anchored by the control of breath, marks the initial step in a transformative journey that paves the way for heightened states of consciousness. In the realm of meditation and breath control, individuals not only refine their connection between the mind and the body but also embrace moments of profound stillness, where they hold their breath in suspension. These suspended breaths, akin to the "Breathless State" or "Samadhi," serve as pivotal junctures where the mind transcends thought, granting access to a profound sense of serenity and awareness.

This state, born from the union of stillness and breath-holding within meditation, enables the redirection of energy, symbolized by PRANA, towards the "Spiritual Eye" and "Crown Chakra." This redirection unlocks higher levels of awareness and fosters a deeper connection to the divine. The Sushumna channel acts as the conduit for this spiritual energy, gently guiding us towards profound clarity and serenity. Ultimately, this transformative journey culminates in a state of divine realization, often referred to as God's consciousness, Christ consciousness, or the "Kingdom of Heaven." It represents inner harmony and a transcendence of physical and mental boundaries, ushering individuals into a profound state of awakened awareness and peace, all nurtured by the profound synergy of stillness and breath control in the meditative journey.

Warning: It's important to note that attempting to hold your breath for extended periods can be dangerous and may lead to serious injury or even death, particularly if you have underlying medical conditions. Always consult with a medical expert before attempting breath-holding exercises or practices. Control of your breath is a powerful tool, but it should be approached with caution and guidance.

Chapter 52

The Brain

The human brain is a complex organ with two hemispheres: the left and the right. Each hemisphere has unique functions that play a role in our thinking and physical abilities. While the popular notion of left brain being analytical and right brain being creative is a simplification, there are indeed differences in how these hemispheres process information and contribute to our overall functioning:

Left Brain

- **Analytical Thinking:** The left hemisphere is often associated with logical reasoning, analytical thinking, and problem-solving. It is involved in tasks that require linear processing, such as mathematics, language comprehension, and detailed planning.
- **Language Processing**: In most right-handed individuals, and even in many left-handed individuals, language centers are predominantly in the left

hemisphere. This includes speech production, comprehension, reading, and writing.

- **Sequential Processing**: The left brain excels at processing information sequentially, breaking complex tasks into smaller, manageable steps.
- **Fine Motor Skills:** The left hemisphere plays a role in controlling fine motor skills on the right side of the body.

Right Brain

- **Creativity and Imagination**: The right hemisphere is often associated with creative thinking, imagination, and artistic abilities. It contributes to holistic thinking and recognizing patterns.
- **Spatial Awareness:** The right brain is involved in spatial awareness, allowing us to perceive the world in three dimensions and navigate our surroundings.
- **Emotional Processing**: It plays a significant role in processing emotions, both our own and others', and in understanding non-verbal cues.
- **Intuition and Holistic Perception**: The right hemisphere is more adept at processing information, allowing us to grasp the bigger picture and make intuitive connections.

It's important to note that the left and right brain are highly interconnected, and they work together to enable holistic functioning. The ***corpus callosum***, a bundle of nerve fibers, facilitates communication and information exchange between the two hemispheres. This interplay supports integrated cognitive processes and a balanced approach to various tasks.

The Brain's Regions and Functions:

- **Prefrontal Cortex:** Decision-making and planning
- **Amygdala:** Emotional responses
- **Hippocampus:** Memory
- **Sensory and Motor Areas:** Process sensory inputs and control movements

Holistic Integration

The brain acts as a hub that integrates information from the body's sensory inputs and processes it into coherent mental experiences. This integration allows us to navigate the world effectively.

Our experiences, thoughts, emotions, and self-concept are interwoven within this holistic framework, shaping our perception of reality.

To recap this section, the brain serves as a central nexus through which the mind, body, and self-interact and interconnect. This intricate interplay shapes our understanding of the world, our emotional responses, our bodily sensations, and our sense of who we are. Recognizing and nurturing this connection contributes to our overall well-being and enriches our human experience.

Unveiling the Interplay of Three Processes Within the Brain

1._The subdued resting state of the dorsal vagal complex, 2. the euphoria (Bliss) originating from the left amygdala, and 3. the enlargements observed in the right hippocampus. These three processes mentioned here have specific connections in relation to the nervous system and brain region. Let us explore each one.

- **Low idle state of the dorsal vagal complex:**
  The dorsal vagal complex (DVC) is a part of the parasympathetic nervous system, which manages the body's rest and digest functions. It plays a role in

regulating various bodily processes during times of relaxation. When the DVC is in a low idle state, it means that the *parasympathetic nervous system is dominant in a state of calmness, relaxation, and reduced physiological arousal.* This state is associated with a decreased heart rate, lowered blood pressure, and a general feeling of tranquility.

- **Bliss of the left amygdala:** The amygdala is a small, almond-shaped structure in the brain that engages in processing emotions and responses to threats or stress. It has two hemispheres, the left and the right. When the left amygdala is activated, it is associated with positive emotions, including feelings of joy, bliss, and happiness. *The activation of the left amygdala is linked to experiences of well-being and a positive emotional state.*

- **Expansion of the right hippocampus**: The hippocampus is a critical region in the brain associated with memory formation and spatial navigation. It also *plays a role in regulating emotions and stress responses.* The right hippocampus is believed to be involved in processing emotional memories. An expansion of the right hippocampus implies increased activity and potential growth in this brain region. *This expansion is often associated with positive emotional experiences and improved emotional regulation.*

The connection among these three processes suggests a state of heightened well-being and emotional harmony. When the dorsal vagal complex is in a low idle state, it shows a state of relaxation and reduced stress. The bliss of the left amygdala signifies a positive emotional experience, and the expansion of the right hippocampus suggests improved emotional regulation and potentially enhanced memory processing.

It is important to note that these concepts are based on the understanding of the brain and nervous system from a neuroscientific perspective. The connections between these processes may be linked to experiences of well-being, but it is essential to consider individual differences and the complexity of the brain's functioning when interpreting such connections.

Comparing the concept of the Trinity, The Father, Son, and Holy Ghost with the processes mentioned, which involve the dorsal vagal complex, the left amygdala, and the right hippocampus, can be seen as an allegorical or symbolic exploration rather than a direct scientific or theological comparison. Here's an explanation of how these elements might be metaphorically connected:

- **The Subdued Resting State of the Dorsal Vagal Complex:** The dorsal vagal complex is associated with the parasympathetic nervous system, which is often linked to rest, relaxation, and restoration. In a metaphorical sense, this could represent the peaceful and contemplative aspect of the Trinity, where God the Father is often associated with wisdom, serenity, and the source of all things.

- **The Euphoria Originating from the Left Amygdala:** The left amygdala, as a part of the brain related to emotions, could symbolize the joy and emotional connection one may experience in their relationship with the divine. In the Trinity, this might correspond to the role of the Holy Spirit, often associated with joy, inspiration, and the emotional experience of God's presence.

- **The Enlargements Observed in the Right Hippocampus:** The right hippocampus is involved in memory and spatial navigation. In a metaphorical sense, the idea of "enlargements" could represent the expansion of one's spiritual understanding and connection with the divine over time. This could be associated with Jesus

Christ in the Trinity, who is often seen as the teacher and
guide, leading individuals to a deeper understanding
of God.

In this allegorical comparison, the Trinity is not being equated
with these particular brain processes. Instead, it is used to delve into
and express the multifaceted essence of spiritual experiences and
their potential links to different facets of human consciousness and
emotion. It serves as a symbolic means to illustrate how various
aspects of the divine may intersect with various facets of our inner
experiences, as well as the operations of our nervous system and
brain.

Within the allegorical comparison between the Trinity concept
and the processes related to the dorsal vagal complex, the left amygdala, and the right hippocampus, we can establish connections.

The concept of the Son within the Trinity as follows:

**The Subdued Resting State of the Dorsal Vagal
Complex:** In this comparison, the dorsal vagal complex represents
the peaceful and contemplative aspect of the Trinity, associated with
God the Father. The Son within the Trinity, in this context, could be
symbolically connected to the concept of learning and understanding. In Christian theology, the Son, often identified as Jesus Christ, is
seen as the Word of God and the teacher of divine truths. *"I am the
way, the truth, and the life. No one comes to the Father except through
me"*, John 14:6. *Just as the dorsal vagal complex represents **a state
of rest, stillness, and reflection,** the Son, Jesus Christ, can
symbolize the revelation and teaching of divine wisdom and truth. "Be
Still and know divine wisdom."*

So, in this allegorical comparison, the Son is represented as the
divine teacher and revealer of truth, connecting the concept of the
Trinity with the learning, and understanding represented by **the
resting state** of the dorsal vagal complex.

Rewiring the Brain

In a world where we sometimes find ourselves being judgmental without even realizing it, there's hope for transformation. Our brains have an incredible ability to adapt and change, and in this chapter, we'll explore how neuroplasticity plays a pivotal role in reshaping our thought patterns and emotional responses. By understanding this concept and its influence on our judgmental habits, we can embark on a journey toward improved mind-body health and stronger connections with others.

Neuroplasticity and Our Adaptable Brain

Our brains are not set in stone; they are remarkably flexible and adaptive. This ability to adapt and change throughout life forms the foundation of neuroplasticity, or "brain plasticity." It's an exciting concept because it challenges the conventional notion that our personality traits and thought patterns are set in stone. Instead, it reveals that transformation is not just a distant possibility but a fundamental aspect of the human brain.

Think of it like this: just as working out makes our muscles stronger, our brains can adapt and change through our experiences. This adaptability allows us to break free from the confines of habitual thought patterns and behaviors. Here's how it works:

- **Formation of New Connections:** Our brain forms new neural connections and pathways in response to our experiences. When we engage in new activities, learn new skills, or even challenge our existing beliefs, our brain creates new connections. These connections are like the roads in a city, and the more you use a particular road, the stronger and more efficient it becomes.
- **Breaking Free from Habitual Thinking:** This adaptability is a game-changer when it comes to breaking

free from habitual thinking, including judgmental habits. Instead of being locked into a fixed way of perceiving the world, our brains have the power to forge new pathways that lead us toward more empathetic and open-minded thinking.

- **Inherent Transformation:** Neuroplasticity reminds us that the capacity for change isn't just a possibility; it's ingrained in our brains. We are wired to adapt and evolve, and this adaptability extends throughout our lives, not just during childhood or young adulthood.

In essence, neuroplasticity underscores the incredible potential for personal growth and transformation. It tells us that we're not bound by the limitations of our past experiences or ingrained biases. We have the power to consciously shape our brains to become more open, empathetic, and understanding individuals, leading to enhanced mind-body health and stronger connections with others. This process may require effort and consistency, but the rewards in terms of personal development and well-being are boundless.

Transforming Judgmental Habits

Judgmental habits can be insidious, subtly creeping into our thoughts, attitudes, and interactions. They are often rooted in biases, preconceived notions, and social conditioning. These habits have the potential to hinder personal growth, strain relationships, and negatively impact our overall well-being. However, thanks to the incredible concept of neuroplasticity, there's a promising avenue for breaking free from these patterns and fostering positive change.

Understanding the Grip of Judgmental Habits

Before we delve into how neuroplasticity can help us transform judgmental habits, it's crucial to understand the grip these habits can have on our lives. They often stem from our brain's tendency to categorize and simplify complex information, a survival mechanism that can sometimes lead to oversimplification and stereotyping. These habits can be ingrained over years or even decades, making them challenging to recognize and overcome.

Neuroplasticity as the Key to Transformation

Neuroplasticity offers a glimmer of hope in our quest to transform these deeply ingrained judgmental habits. Through intentional and consistent efforts, individuals can engage in a process known as **cognitive restructuring**. This process involves actively challenging and reevaluating our preconceptions and biases, fostering new ways of perceiving and processing information. The crucial aspect of this process is that it's not about denying or repressing our thoughts but rather about consciously choosing non-judgmental thoughts and responses.

Weakening the Judgmental Pathways

Our brains are remarkably adaptable, and with practice, the neural pathways associated with judgmental thinking can weaken. As we consciously choose non-judgmental responses, we're essentially diverting our mental traffic from the well-worn road of judgment to a new path of empathy and understanding. This process reflects the dynamic nature of our brain, constantly reshaping and reorganizing itself based on our experiences and choices.

Practical Strategies for Transformation

While the concept of neuroplasticity provides the framework for transformation, practical strategies are essential to implement this change in our lives. Here are a few steps that can help:

- **Self-awareness:** Recognize when judgmental thoughts or biases arise. Awareness is the first step in any transformative process.
- **Mindfulness:** Engage in mindfulness practices that encourage you to observe your thoughts and emotions without judgment. This practice can help break the automatic cycle of judgment.
- **Empathy and Perspective-Taking:** Actively try to see situations from different angles and walk in others' shoes. This can help you foster empathy and a deeper understanding of those around you.
- **Continuous Learning:** Challenge your preconceptions and biases by seeking out diverse perspectives, learning from different cultures, and staying open to new information.

To summarize this section, think of it as a journey of personal growth through neuroplasticity – a path to greater empathy, compassion, and stronger connections with others. It reminds us that we have the power to evolve beyond our biases and limitations, ultimately enriching our relationships and contributing to our overall well-being. The key is to be patient with yourself, stay committed to the process, and embrace the transformative potential that neuroplasticity offers.

The Impact of Neuroplasticity on Emotional Regulation

Our brain's adaptability extends to emotional regulation, a critical aspect of our overall well-being. By practicing non-judgmental awareness of our emotions, we can use neuroplasticity to develop healthier emotional responses. Over time, this helps us build emotional resilience, making it easier to navigate life's challenges and maintain a balanced state of well-being.

Cultivating Mind-Body Connection

The connection between our mind and body is essential. Neuroplasticity serves as a bridge between these realms, influencing how we perceive and react to situations. By embracing non-judgmental thinking, we can reduce the stress response triggered by judgmental thoughts. This, in turn, has a positive impact on our body's physiological processes, including heart rate, blood pressure, and immune function, creating a harmonious mind-body connection.

Mindful Practice and Practical Strategies

Mindfulness, a powerful practice rooted in non-judgmental awareness, acts as a catalyst for neuroplastic changes. Engaging in mindfulness meditation, for example, encourages focused attention and non-reactive observation of our thoughts. This practice stimulates growth in brain regions associated with emotional regulation and perspective-taking, reinforcing the transformation of judgmental habits.

Conclusion

The journey to rewiring judgmental habits through neuroplasticity is transformative and has profound implications for our mind-body health and connections with others. By recognizing the adaptability of our brains and integrating mindful practices into our daily lives, we empower ourselves to break free from limiting thought patterns. Through conscious effort, our brain's plastic nature becomes a gateway to cultivating empathy, compassion, and deeper connections, ultimately enriching our holistic well-being.

Chapter 53

Bridges of Unity: Exploring "Hum Sau" and Beyond

As we set out on a spiritual exploration, we stand at the intersection of two distinct yet intertwined worlds: the mysticism of the East and the practicality of the West. Within these diverse traditions, we discover the resonance of the sacred, where profound truths unfurl and seekers establish a profound connection with the spiritual realm. In this chapter, we'll unravel the profound meanings behind two evocative expressions: the Sanskrit bija mantras "Hum" and "Sau," and their counterparts in the English language.

These sacred syllables, "Hum" and "Sau," invite us to explore their depths and the spiritual realms they unveil. Alongside these, we'll unravel the harmonious insights found in Western expressions, examining how they too convey profound spiritual messages.

"Hum" (ह)

- **Sanskrit Essence:** "Hum" is an embodiment of the divine energy of Lord Shiva in Hinduism, serving as a conduit for purification, transformation, and the

dissipation of negativity. It acts as a bridge that unites the
practitioner with universal consciousness and the divine.

- **Western Correlations:** Within the Western spiritual
  context, finding an exact match for "Hum" may be
  challenging. Nonetheless, we come across phrases like
  "Amen" in Christian traditions, symbolizing consent,
  affirmation, and the presence of the divine.

"Sau" (सौ)

- **Sanskrit Essence:** "Sau" resonates with the divine
  energy of Lord Vishnu in Hinduism. It is a seed mantra
  for meditation and devotion, embodying qualities of
  preservation, protection, and inner serenity.
- **Western Counterparts:** In the Western spiritual
  journey, akin to "Hum," "Sau" lacks a direct counterpart.
  Nevertheless, phrases such as "In God We Trust" on
  U.S. currency reflect a profound sense of divine reliance
  and protection.

While these expressions may differ in terms of language and
culture, a common thread unites them—the power of sacred sounds
and words in facilitating transformative spiritual experiences. They
signify the shared human yearning to forge a connection with the
divine, utilizing language and sound as conduits.

Beyond these expressions lies the concept of "Hum Sau" or "I am
That," deeply rooted in Advaita Vedanta, a school of Hindu philosophy. It underscores the realization that at the core of our individual
selves resides the same universal consciousness that permeates all of
existence. In simpler terms, it is the recognition of the intrinsic unity
of the self with the ultimate reality or divine consciousness.

This concept of unity with the Divine is echoed in biblical teachings, such as Exodus 3:14, where God identifies Himself as "I am,"
emphasizing His eternal and unchanging nature. Additionally, 1

Corinthians 6:19-20 expresses the unity between individuals and the Divine, akin to the concept of recognizing oneself as "That" or divine consciousness.

To practice "Hum Sau" or "I am That," you can incorporate mindfulness and meditation into your spiritual journey:

- **Find a Quiet Space:** Seek a peaceful, distraction-free environment.
- **Relax:** Take deep breaths to calm your body and mind.
- **Affirmation:** Repeatedly say, "I am That" or "I am one with the Divine."
- **Focus Inward:** Direct your attention away from external distractions.
- **Unity Visualization:** Picture a boundless light encompassing yourself and everything.
- **Feel the Connection:** Experience the connection between your self and the Divine.
- **Silent Contemplation:** Spend time in silent contemplation.
- **Gratitude:** Conclude with gratitude for the recognition of oneness and inner peace.

In essence, our journey today revolves around the recognition of the essential unity that transcends linguistic and cultural boundaries. It emphasizes the universal human aspiration to bridge the gap between the self and the divine, using sound and language as sacred bridges of connection and understanding. Just as God often identifies Himself as "I am" in the Bible, the concept of "Hum Sau" in the East reminds us of the eternal and unchanging nature of the divine, reinforcing the idea that unity with God is a fundamental truth that transcends cultural and religious divides.

Chapter 54

Engaging with the Divine: Prayer and Meditation

P rayer and meditation are interconnected ways of communing with the Divine.

- **Prayer** is like a heartfelt conversation with God, akin to confiding in a close friend. In prayer, we express our thoughts, desires, and concerns, seeking guidance, solace, and connection. It is the act of sharing our innermost selves with the Divine.

- **Meditation**, on the other hand, is the practice of calming our minds and opening ourselves to the wisdom and guidance of the Divine. It's a form of silent listening, allowing us to receive insights, inspiration, and a deeper connection with God. In meditation, we create a quiet space within us where God's voice can be heard.

This explanation highlights the interactive aspect of prayer and the receptive quality of meditation in our spiritual relationship with the Divine.

The Breath of Divine Communion

Observing your breath is a powerful practice that can deepen your connection with the Divine during both prayer and meditation.

In **prayer**, mindful attention to your breath creates a still and receptive space within you, fostering a deeper and more meaningful connection. It allows you to listen more attentively to the Divine, akin to a patient listener in a profound conversation.

In **meditation**, breath observation serves as a bridge to the Divine's wisdom and insight. When you still your mind and focus on your breath, you open the channels of receptivity. This enables you to receive profound insights, inspiration, and a sense of being in harmony with the Divine's presence.

So, whether you are speaking to God in prayer or listening for the Divine's guidance in meditation, observing your breath acts as the thread that weaves your conscious awareness into the tapestry of your spiritual connection. It helps you become more attuned to the Divine's presence, creating a sacred space where your communication and communion with the Divine can truly flourish.

Breathing for Balance and Clarity

To become more attuned to your breath, engage in purposeful inhalation and exhalation. Inhale deeply and then shift your focus to the brief pause before exhaling. As you exhale, concentrate on the natural pause that follows the release of breath. Repeating this pattern enhances concentration and fosters a sense of ease.

Mindful breathing offers numerous benefits for your physical, mental, and emotional well-being:

- **Stress Reduction**: Mindful breathing activates the relaxation response, soothing the nervous system and reducing the production of stress hormones like cortisol. This leads to decreased overall stress levels.

- **Improved Focus and Concentration**: Practicing spontaneous breath awareness enhances your ability to concentrate, helping your mind stay present, reducing distractions, and improving your task focus.
- **Emotional Regulation**: Mindfully observing your breath creates a space between your thoughts and emotions. This allows you to respond to situations with greater awareness and control, rather than reacting impulsively.
- **Enhanced Self-Awareness**: Regularly observing your breath makes you more attuned to your mental and emotional states. This heightened self-awareness can lead to better understanding and management of your thoughts and feelings.
- **Reduced Anxiety**: Mindful breathing can alleviate symptoms of anxiety by promoting calmness and grounding, disrupting the cycle of anxious thoughts, and keeping you anchored in the present moment.
- **Better Sleep**: Engaging in breath awareness before bedtime relaxes your mind and body, making it easier to fall asleep and experience improved sleep quality.
- **Pain Management**: Mindfulness of breath can contribute to pain relief and management by shifting your focus away from discomfort and promoting relaxation.
- **Enhanced Mind-Body Connection**: Observing your breath fosters a deeper connection between your mind and body, promoting overall physical and emotional well-being.
- **Strengthened Resilience**: Regular practice of spontaneous breath awareness can enhance your ability to cope with challenges, setbacks, and difficult emotions, ultimately boosting your emotional resilience.

- **Mindful Living**: As you become more accustomed to observing your breath, you may naturally extend mindfulness to other aspects of your life, cultivating a sense of presence and appreciation for everyday experiences.
- **Lower Blood Pressure**: Mindful breathing techniques have been shown to contribute to lower blood pressure and improved cardiovascular health.
- **Improved Digestion**: Deep and relaxed breathing supports optimal digestion by reducing stress on the digestive system.

Remember that the benefits of spontaneous breath observation may vary from person to person. Consistent practice over time is likely to yield more noticeable and lasting effects. This simple yet powerful technique can be easily incorporated into your daily routine to promote overall well-being.

Chapter 55

Intention, Visualization, and AUM: Tools for Transformation

The ancient practice of focused intention and visualization has long been used to achieve personal growth and spiritual enlightenment. By harnessing the power of the mind, we can manifest our desires and transform our consciousness. The sacred sound "AUM," revered in many spiritual traditions, is believed to encapsulate the essence of creation and the universe.

In an age of advanced technology and space exploration, we can draw parallels between these ancient practices and modern scientific understanding. This sheds light on the interconnectedness of our inner world and the vast cosmos.

- **Focused Intention**: Intention techniques involve setting a clear purpose for your meditation or practice. It's about concentrating your mind on a specific goal, whether it's for healing, personal growth, or transformation.
- **Visualization**: Visualization techniques require creating vivid mental images of your desired scenario, state, or objective. You mentally picture yourself in the

situation you want to bring into reality, engaging your senses to make the experience more tangible.

- **Mind's Power**: Both intention and visualization techniques tap into the power of your mind to influence your reality. By focusing your mental energy and intent, you aim to bring about changes in your life.

Comparing Intention, Visualization, and AUM Sound Vibration

- **Consciousness Shift**: Both AUM chanting and intention/visualization techniques aim to shift your consciousness. AUM focuses on vibrations and sounds, while intention and visualization focus on conscious intent and imagination.
- **Interconnectedness**: AUM chanting emphasizes our connection with the universe, whereas intention and visualization techniques may focus more on personal goals and desires.
- **Mindfulness and Focus**: AUM chanting promotes mindfulness through sound, while intention and visualization techniques require sustained mental focus on your intended outcome.
- **Purpose**: AUM chanting often has a spiritual or transcendental purpose, while intention and visualization techniques can encompass a broader range of goals, including personal growth, healing, or manifestation.

AUM chanting and intention/visualization techniques share the common goal of conscious transformation and focus. AUM centers on vibrational resonance and spiritual connection, while intention and visualization techniques harness the power of focused thoughts and mental imagery to manifest desired outcomes. Both approaches highlight the profound influence of consciousness on our experiences and the world.

Understanding the "AUM" Sound in a Modern Context

As we have previously explained the "AUM" sound blends spiritual understanding with scientific interpretation. "AUM," also spelled as "OM," is a sacred sound or mantra in various spiritual traditions like Hinduism, Buddhism, and Jainism. It symbolizes the essence of creation, the universe, and ultimate reality.

In the broader context of spiritual understanding and modern science, you can envision the "AUM" sound as a metaphor for the fundamental vibrations that permeate our existence. Contemporary scientific knowledge tells us that the universe is a dynamic and inter-connected web of energy, matter, and forces. Much like how "AUM" encapsulates the essence of existence, the fundamental laws of physics and the fabric of spacetime capture the essence of our universe.

With this holistic perspective in mind, let's now examine how these principles align with the concept of "AUM," not as a spiritual artifact alone but as a bridge connecting ancient wisdom with contemporary scientific insight.

- **AUM as Universal Vibration**: In spiritual terms, "AUM" symbolizes the sound of creation. In science, the universe began with the Big Bang, an explosive event that initiated the expansion of spacetime and the creation of matter and energy. This cosmic event can be seen as the initial "vibration" that set the stage for the evolution of galaxies, stars, planets, and life.
- **AUM as Cosmic Harmony**: "AUM" is linked with harmony, balance, and unity. In technology, this relates to

the harmony of physical laws and constants governing the universe. These laws, like gravity and electromagnetism, interact in perfect balance to shape the cosmos.

- **AUM as Resonance**: Chanting "AUM" is believed to create resonance within the individual. Similarly, the universe resonates with various frequencies and vibrations. Gravitational waves, electromagnetic radiation, and other forms of energy propagate through the cosmos, forming a symphony of vibrations studied by astronomers and scientists to understand the universe's composition and history.

- **AUM as Connection**: "AUM" symbolizes the interconnectedness of all things. Modern science reveals that the universe is a complex network where galaxies, stars, planets, and even subatomic particles are interconnected by gravitational forces and other interactions.

While "AUM" holds spiritual and cultural significance, drawing parallels with scientific understanding can bridge ancient wisdom with modern exploration. Approach these analogies with an open mind, respecting both the cultural and scientific aspects of the discussion.

Combining the Three Practices

To combine intention, visualization, and the AUM sound vibration, we can begin by setting a clear intention for our practice. Once we know what we want to achieve, we can begin to visualize ourselves achieving it. As we visualize, we can chant the AUM sound vibration to amplify the power of our intention.

Here is a simple practice that you can try:

1. Find a quiet place where you will not be disturbed.

2. Sit in a comfortable position with your back straight and your eyes closed.
3. Take a few deep breaths and relax your body.
4. Set an intention for your practice. What do you want to achieve?
5. Begin to visualize yourself achieving your intention. See yourself feeling and experiencing the desired outcome in as much detail as possible.
6. Chant the AUM sound vibration as you visualize.
7. Continue chanting and visualizing for as long as you like.
8. When you are finished, take a few deep breaths and open your eyes.

This practice can be done at any time of day, but it is especially effective when done first thing in the morning or last thing at night.

Chapter Summary

In this exploration of ancient practices and their connection to modern scientific understanding, we have delved into the power of focused intention and visualization as well as the sacred sound "AUM." These techniques have long been used for personal growth and spiritual enlightenment, emphasizing the profound influence of consciousness on our experiences and the world. While "AUM" is traditionally associated with spiritual traditions, we've also discussed its resonance with contemporary scientific concepts, such as the fundamental vibrations that permeate our existence.

We've compared the practices of intention, visualization, and AUM chanting, highlighting their shared goal of conscious transformation and focus while acknowledging their unique attributes and purposes. Intention techniques help set clear goals, visualization techniques create vivid mental images, and AUM chanting centers on vibrational resonance and spiritual connection. All of them point to the interconnectedness of our inner world and the broader cosmos.

In our exploration of the "AUM" sound in a modern context, we've drawn parallels between its spiritual symbolism and scientific interpretations. "AUM" as universal vibration mirrors the Big Bang and the universe's initial vibration. "AUM" as cosmic harmony aligns with the balance of physical laws governing the cosmos. "AUM" as resonance corresponds to the vibrations and frequencies studied by scientists in the universe. Finally, "AUM" as connection resonates with the complex network of interactions in the universe.

To combine these practices, we've provided a simple step-by-step exercise that involves setting a clear intention, visualizing the desired outcome, and chanting the AUM sound vibration. This practice can be a powerful way to tap into the mind's potential to influence reality and bridge ancient wisdom with modern exploration. Whether used for personal growth, healing, or manifestation, these techniques can help individuals achieve their goals and promote a deeper understanding of their place in the universe.

Chapter 56

Breathe In, Breathe Out: The Art of Box Breathing

Box Breathing, also known as square breathing or four-part breath, is a versatile and highly-praised breathing technique that has gained widespread recognition for its exceptional ability to effectively manage stress and anxiety while promoting relaxation. This rhythmic and balanced method offers a simple yet powerful way to improve your overall well-being. In this section, we'll explore the intricacies of Box Breathing, unlocking its potential for transforming your mental and emotional state.

Box Breathing

Box breathing, also known as square breathing or four-part breath or 4-4-4-4 technique, is a powerful technique for reducing stress and anxiety, promoting relaxation, enhancing focus and concentration, and providing a grounding effect on the mind. This method involves a rhythmic pattern of inhaling, holding the breath, exhaling, and then holding the breath again, each for an equal amount of time. It is typically performed in a calm setting while seated or lying down.

Here's how you can practice box breathing:

1. Inhale slowly and deeply through your nose for a count of four.
2. Hold your breath for a count of four.
3. Exhale slowly and completely through your mouth for a count of four.
4. Hold your breath again for a count of four.
5. Repeat the cycle for a few minutes or until you feel more relaxed.

<u>Benefits of Box Breathing</u>

- **Stress Reduction**: Box breathing activates the body's relaxation response, helping to reduce stress and anxiety levels.
- **Mindfulness**: The rhythmic nature of the breath and the focus on counting can help you stay present and mindful, diverting your attention from anxious or intrusive thoughts.
- **Improved Focus**: Practicing box breathing can enhance your concentration and mental clarity by regulating your breathing pattern.
- **Calming the Nervous System**: The technique stimulates the parasympathetic nervous system, which handles the "rest and digest" response, leading to a sense of calm and relaxation.

Variations of Box Breathing

You can adjust the counts according to your comfort level or specific needs instead of the 4-4-4-4 technique. Here are a few variations you can try:

- **6-6-6-6:** Inhale for a count of six, hold for six, exhale for six, and hold for six. This variation extends the breath cycle, potentially providing a deeper sense of relaxation.

- **3-3-3-3:** If the previous counts feel challenging, you can start with a shorter count, such as inhaling for three, holding for three, exhaling for three, and holding for three.
- **8-8-8-8:** For those looking to increase the breath cycle's duration, inhale for eight, hold for eight, exhale for eight, and hold for eight.
- **2-2-2-2:** If you're pressed for time or prefer a quicker exercise, you can use a shorter count, like inhaling for two, holding for two, exhaling for two, and holding for two.
- **Note:** *You are not restricted to using only one of these methods. Feel free to adjust the counts to align with your personal comfort level.*

Remember that the goal is to maintain a comfortable rhythm while focusing on your breath. The specific counts you choose can be adjusted based on your lung capacity, comfort level, and the time you have available. The key is to create a balanced and steady pattern that promotes relaxation and mindfulness. As with any breathing exercise, if you experience any discomfort or dizziness, it's best to discontinue the practice and consult a healthcare professional if needed.

Chanting "AUM" and "AMEN" While Using The Box Breathing Technique

This is another variation of the box breathing technique.

<u>Box Breathing with "AUM" and "AMEN"</u>

- **Preparation:** Find a quiet, comfortable place to sit or lie down. Close your eyes and take a few deep, calming breaths to center yourself.

- **Inhale (Count 1):** As you begin your inhalation, silently chant "AUM" or "AMEN" in your mind or say it quietly to yourself. Visualize the vibrational energy associated with this sacred sound entering your body with each breath.
- **Hold (Count 2):** At the top of your inhale, pause, and focus on the sense of unity and harmony that "AUM" or "AMEN" represents.
- **Exhale (Count 3):** During your exhale, silently chant "AUM" or "AMEN" in your mind or say it quietly. Imagine this word as an affirmation, releasing any tension or stress with each breath out.
- **Hold (Count 4):** At the bottom of your exhale, pause, and feel the sense of alignment and consent that "AUM" or "AMEN" symbolizes.
- **Repeat:** Continue this cycle for as many breaths as you'd like, maintaining equal counts for each phase of the box breathing (inhale, hold, exhale, hold).
- **Note:** *Just like in the previous section, you can adjust the counts to align with your personal comfort level.*

This practice combines the rhythmic and calming aspects of box breathing with the spiritual depth of "AUM" and "AMEN." It can help you find a sense of balance, focus, and inner peace while also connecting with the profound meanings of these sacred words.

The box breathing exercise and the chanting of "AUM" are both potent techniques, each with distinct focuses and effects on the mind and body. For "AUM," it embodies the vibrational energy of the Universe, the very essence from which all things manifest. Remember that the specific counts for each phase can be adjusted to suit your comfort and breathing capacity. The important thing is to maintain a regular, controlled rhythm and to immerse yourself in the experience of the sounds and their spiritual significance.

While these practices come from different cultural and spiritual backgrounds, they all offer opportunities for introspection, mindfulness, and connection. Each is a valuable tool for cultivating presence, focus, and inner harmony in its unique way.

Remember, pronunciation may vary based on accents and regional differences, so don't be afraid to seek guidance from native speakers or practitioners for the most accurate pronunciation.

Conclusion

Incorporating Box Breathing into your daily routine can be a game-changer when it comes to stress management, mindfulness, focus, and relaxation. By practicing this technique regularly, you can tap into the profound benefits it offers, such as reduced stress and anxiety, enhanced mindfulness, improved focus, and a calmer nervous system. Box Breathing empowers you to take control of your well-being, bringing peace and serenity into your life with each carefully measured breath. So, why wait? Start your journey towards a more serene and focused self today by embracing the power of Box Breathing.

Chapter 57

Eastern Philosophies vs. Western Mysticism

In Eastern philosophies, consciousness is often seen as the fundamental essence of everything. It is the awareness that underlies everything, connecting all living beings and the entire universe. This interconnectedness is often symbolized by the concept of "oneness," where all forms and beings are interconnected like drops in the ocean. Eastern traditions, such as Hinduism and Buddhism, believe that individual consciousness is not separate but part of a greater universal consciousness.

In Western mysticism, consciousness is also viewed as a profound force that connects all life. Mystics often explore altered states of consciousness to transcend the limitations of the physical world and experience a sense of unity with the divine or cosmic consciousness. Mystical experiences are said to reveal the interconnectedness of all things and the inherent unity between the individual soul and the greater whole.

What Does This Mean in Simpler Terms?

Consciousness is our awareness of ourselves and the world around us. It is what allows us to experience our thoughts, feelings, and sensations. It is also what allows us to connect with others and to understand our place in the universe.

Eastern and Western philosophies have different ways of understanding consciousness. In Eastern philosophies, consciousness is often seen as the fundamental essence of everything. This means that everything in the universe is interconnected and that we are all part of a greater whole.

In Western mysticism, consciousness is also viewed as a powerful force that connects all life. Mystics often explore altered states of consciousness to experience a sense of unity with the divine or cosmic consciousness. This can reveal the interconnectedness of all things and the inherent unity between the individual and the greater whole.

How Can I Experience This Interconnectedness for Myself?

There are many ways to experience the interconnectedness of all things. One way is to practice meditation. Meditation is a way to focus your attention on the present moment and to become more aware of your thoughts, feelings, and sensations. As you become more aware of yourself, you can also become more aware of your connection to others and to the world around you.

Another way to experience the interconnectedness of all things is to spend time in nature. When you are in nature, take some time to really appreciate the beauty of your surroundings. Notice the trees, the flowers, the birds, and the other animals that share the space with you. As you become more aware of the natural world, you can also become more aware of your own place in it.

Finally, you can also experience the interconnectedness of all things through relationships. When you are in a relationship with someone, you are sharing your life with them. You are also learning and growing from each other. As you get to know someone better, you can also come to understand yourself better. Relationships can help us to see ourselves and the world in new ways.

Conclusion

Consciousness is a powerful force that connects all life. Eastern and Western philosophies have different ways of understanding consciousness, but they both agree that it is an essential part of what makes us human. There are many ways to experience the interconnectedness of all things, such as through meditation, spending time in nature, and cultivating relationships.

Chapter 58

Indigenous Wisdom

Indigenous cultures from various corners of the globe emphasize the profound interconnectedness of all existence. These indigenous societies have long acknowledged the profound and intricate bond that exists among humanity, the natural world, and the spiritual realm. They perceive consciousness as interwoven with the Earth's elements and hold the wisdom of the land and its ecosystems in high esteem. Indigenous spirituality frequently involves rituals, ceremonies, and practices aimed at venerating and fortifying this interconnectedness.

The concept of interconnected consciousness encourages us to cultivate empathy, compassion, and respect for all living beings and the environment. It underscores the notion that we are not isolated individuals but integral parts of a complex tapestry of existence. In this interconnected web of life, every action, thought, and emotion resonates throughout the entire system. Embracing this interconnectedness instills in us a profound sense of responsibility. We come to realize that our well-being is intimately linked with the well-being of others and the planet. This realization motivates us to act with kindness, harmony, and reverence for all life, contributing to a more sustainable and compassionate world for ourselves and future generations.

Common Ground of Belief: The Transcendent Source Worldwide

Here are some different names and concepts used in various faiths and belief systems to refer to the divine or higher power:

- Shiva - Hinduism
- God - Christianity, Judaism, Islam
- Allah - Islam
- Isvara - Hinduism
- Jehovah - Christianity, Judaism
- Yahweh - Judaism
- Brahma - Hinduism
- Vishnu - Hinduism
- Krishna - Hinduism
- Buddha - Buddhism
- Tao - Taoism
- Great Spirit - Native American spirituality
- Wakan Tanka - Lakota Sioux
- Ahura Mazda - Zoroastrianism
- Elohim - Judaism
- Deity - Various polytheistic religions
- Deva - Hinduism and Buddhism
- Kami - Shintoism
- Waheguru - Sikhism
- Ra - Ancient Egyptian religion
- Odin - Norse mythology
- Zeus - Greek mythology
- Amaterasu - Shintoism
- Osiris - Ancient Egyptian religion
- Rama - Hinduism

- Ahimsa - Jainism
- Manitou - Native American spirituality
- Orunmila - Yoruba religion
- Cernunnos - Celtic mythology
- The All – Hermeticism

Please note that these names and concepts can vary in their meanings and interpretations within different faiths and cultures. The list provided is not exhaustive and only includes a selection of examples.

The terms "divine" or "higher power" are often used to describe a transcendent, divine, or spiritual force that is believed to be beyond ordinary human understanding or control. It is a concept that appears in various religious traditions, as well as in contexts related to self-help, recovery, and personal growth. The exact meaning of "divine" or "higher power" can vary depending on the context in which they are used in religious contexts:

- **Divine Entity**: In many monotheistic religions such as Christianity, Islam, and Judaism, the term "divine" or "higher power" can refer to the one supreme and omnipotent God who is the creator and ruler of the universe.
- **Deities and Spirits**: In polytheistic traditions, the terms may encompass a variety of gods, goddesses, or spirits that hold power and influence beyond human capabilities.
- **Universal Energy or Source**: Some spiritual belief systems and New Age philosophies refer to a universal energy or source from which everything emanates. This concept may be seen as a divine or higher power guiding the universe's natural processes.

In contexts of recovery and personal growth:

- **Personal Transformation**: In self-help and personal development contexts, a higher power can represent the idea that individuals have the potential to tap into a deeper aspect of themselves, unlocking hidden strengths and abilities to create positive change.

The concept of divine or higher power often serves as ways for individuals to connect with a sense of meaning, purpose, and guidance beyond their immediate circumstances. They can provide comfort in times of difficulty, a sense of hope, and a belief in something greater than the individual self.

It's important to note that interpreting a divine or higher power is deeply personal and can vary widely among individuals based on their beliefs, experiences, and cultural backgrounds. The terms allows for a broad and flexible understanding that accommodates diverse perspectives and beliefs.

Let's break down and connect the ideas presented in the provided text:

- **Achieving Absolute Consciousness in The State of Absolute or Ultimate**: It is suggested that individuals can reach the highest level of consciousness, referred to as "Absolute Consciousness," within a profound state known as The Absolute. This state represents the pinnacle of spiritual awareness and realization.

- **Connecting Names and Forms of Consciousness**: The idea here is to explore whether there's a common thread or essence that connects the various names and forms of divine or higher power found in different faiths and belief systems when experienced within The Absolute. This implies looking for a unifying factor among these diverse expressions of consciousness.

- **Experiencing Diverse Names from Different Faiths:** The question raised is whether it's possible to have a transcendent experience within The Absolute that encompasses and incorporates the diverse names and representations of the divine from different faiths. This would entail experiencing a universal and all-encompassing spiritual revelation that honors the diversity of religious and cultural expressions.

In brief, this segment delves into the possibility of finding common ground and interconnectedness within spiritual experiences across diverse faiths and belief systems. It raises the question of whether the ultimate state of consciousness, symbolized by The Absolute, might serve as a unifying foundation where the distinct names, representations, and notions of the divine from various traditions converge to create a shared universal comprehension of spiritual awareness.

Chapter 59

The Importance of Symbolism

S ymbolism assumes a vital role in the communication and portrayal of the attributes, characteristics, and ideas linked to divine or superior forces. It serves as a means to convey profound meanings, revelations, and associations that extend beyond mere names, explanations, and visuals. Symbolism frequently surpasses linguistic and cultural boundaries, enabling individuals to intuitively grasp intricate metaphysical concepts. In this context, let's explore how symbolism intertwines with divine or higher powers:

- **Representation of attributes**: Symbols are used to represent specific attributes or qualities of divine beings. For example, a halo might symbolize enlightenment or divine radiance, while wings might represent transcendence and the ability to move between realms.
- **Transcending Language**: Divine or higher powers often exist beyond the limitations of human language. Symbols provide a way to communicate concepts that might be difficult to express in words alone.

- **Deeper Understanding**: Symbols can convey profound insights and truths about reality, existence, and the divine. They invite individuals to contemplate and explore deeper meanings.
- **Cultural and Universal Meaning**: Certain symbols hold cultural significance and are recognized across different societies. Some symbols are universal, tapping into archetypal or collective unconscious elements.
- **Connection and Mystical Experience**: Symbols can serve as focal points for meditation, prayer, or contemplation, facilitating a deeper connection with the divine and potentially leading to mystical experiences.
- **Metaphysical Concepts**: Higher powers are often associated with abstract concepts such as infinity, eternity, and the interconnectedness of all things. Symbols can visually represent these concepts in ways that engage the imagination.
- **Artistic Expression**: Symbols are frequently used in religious and spiritual art to convey the presence and essence of divine beings. Artistic depictions may use symbols to communicate the divine qualities of love, wisdom, compassion, and more.
- **Transcendence of Form**: Symbols can help individuals move beyond the limitations of physical form and language, allowing for a more direct connection to the divine or higher realms of existence.

In various religious and spiritual traditions, symbols such as *the cross, the lotus flower, the AUM (OM) symbol, the crescent moon, and the Ankh* are just a few examples of how symbolism is employed to represent and connect with divine or higher powers. The interpretation and meaning of these symbols can vary across different cultures and belief systems.

Chapter 60

The Idea of Reaching or Experiencing the State of Absolute

The concept often referred to as "enlightenment," "self-realization," or "ultimate consciousness" represents a central goal in numerous spiritual traditions. While the specifics may differ among various paths, there are common principles and practices that individuals typically embrace in their pursuit of this state. Below are some general guidelines:

- **Self-Inquiry and Awareness:** Self-inquiry involves questioning the self and reality. This practice encourages deep introspection to understand the nature of existence, consciousness, and the true self. Cultivating self-awareness helps individuals transcend the limitations of the ego and connect with a higher reality.

- **Meditation and Contemplation:** Meditation is a foundational practice in many spiritual traditions. Regular meditation helps quiet the mind, cultivate inner stillness, and create a conducive environment for glimpses of higher consciousness. Different meditation techniques, such as mindfulness, focused attention, or transcendental meditation, can explore the depths of one's consciousness.

- **Detachment and Non-Attachment:** Detachment involves letting go of attachments to worldly desires, possessions, and ego-driven identifications. By reducing the grip of these attachments, individuals can experience a sense of inner freedom and open themselves to a deeper understanding of reality.

- **Practice of Virtues**: Living a virtuous and ethical life is essential for spiritual progress. Practicing qualities like compassion, kindness, honesty, and humility helps create an inner environment conducive to spiritual growth.

- **Study of Sacred Texts and Wisdom:** Exploring sacred texts, spiritual literature, and teachings from enlightened masters can provide valuable insights and guidance on reality and the path to self-realization.

- **Yoga and Breathwork:** Yoga, which includes physical postures (asanas), breath control (pranayama), and ethical disciplines, is a holistic system that aligns the body, mind, and spirit. It can lead to greater clarity, focus, and heightened states of consciousness.

- **Service and Selfless Action**: Engaging in selfless service (karma yoga) and contributing to the well-being of others can help dissolve the ego and cultivate a sense of unity with all beings, fostering a deeper connection to the State of Absolute.

- **Guidance from a Spiritual Teacher**: Many seekers find it beneficial to have a spiritual teacher or guide who has already experienced higher states of consciousness. Such a teacher can offer guidance, support, and insight based on their own experiences.

It's important to note that the journey to experiencing the State of Absolute is deeply personal and unique for everyone. The practices mentioned above are not necessarily a linear progression, and different paths may resonate more with different people. Patience, persistence, and sincere dedication to the chosen path are key factors in one's spiritual evolution. Ultimately, the State of Absolute is often described as a profound shift in perception, awareness, and understanding that transcends ordinary human experience.

Every belief or faith tradition frequently presents their own unique paths, techniques, and customs for individuals to attain elevated levels of consciousness, self-discovery, or spiritual connection. These approaches encompass activities like prayer, meditation, rituals, devotion, contemplation, acts of selflessness, and others. Each tradition holds its own reservoir of wisdom and revelations, and these practices hold profound significance and efficacy for adherents of the respective belief system.

The idea of recognizing and respecting these diverse paths is at the heart of fostering harmony among different faiths and belief systems. It's important to understand that no one approach holds a monopoly on truth or spiritual realization. Instead of comparing, competing, or asserting that one way is superior to another, embracing the diversity of approaches can lead to a more inclusive and harmonious world.

The call for harmony and understanding among different belief systems is rooted in the shared humanity of all people. While individuals may express their spirituality in various ways, the underlying aspiration for meaning, purpose, and connection is a universal human experience. Recognizing our common humanity and shared desires can serve as a powerful foundation for building bridges of understanding and mutual respect.

Creating a world where all individuals have the option to follow their chosen path without judgment or conflict is indeed a noble aspiration. *Learning to live in harmony with each other requires open-mindedness, empathy, and a willingness to learn from one another.*

This involves:

- **Respecting Differences**: Acknowledging that diversity in belief systems is a natural part of human experience and embracing the richness it brings.
- **Promoting Dialogue**: Engaging in open and respectful conversations to learn about each other's beliefs, practices, and perspectives.
- **Fostering Empathy**: Cultivating the ability to understand and feel compassion for the experiences and beliefs of others, even if they differ from one's own.
- **Embracing Common Values**: Recognizing shared values of compassion, kindness, justice, and love that are present in many faith traditions.
- **Promoting Education**: Educating ourselves about various belief systems to dispel misconceptions and promote understanding.
- **Working Together**: Collaborating on projects and initiatives that address common challenges such as poverty, injustice, and environmental issues.

Ultimately, the vision of a harmonious world where different faiths coexist peacefully requires a collective effort. By embracing diversity, respecting individual choices, and nurturing a culture of dialogue and empathy, we can move closer to realizing a more inclusive and harmonious global community.

Chapter 61

Navigating the Modern Maze

In the labyrinth of contemporary society, we find ourselves navigating a complex maze filled with challenges stemming from technological advancements, societal shifts, environmental concerns, and personal well-being issues. This maze can sometimes feel bewildering, much like a labyrinth with twists and turns that can lead us astray.

Imagine each of these challenges as a different twist in the maze:

- **Stress and Mental Health:** As we journey through the maze, the relentless pace of modern life, constant connectivity, and information overload can create stress and mental health issues, making us feel disoriented. But here, ancient wisdom acts as a guiding light, offering mindfulness and meditation practices as our map to find inner calm, stress reduction, and emotional balance.

- **Technology and Disconnection:** In an era dominated by smartphones, computers, iPads, and TV screens, it's easy to find ourselves veering off course from our goals and objectives and thus making us trapped in the maze. While these technological marvels can enhance our lives, they can also become insidious distractions when they infiltrate our workspaces. Striking the right balance between harnessing the power of technology and staying on track with our goals requires a conscious effort. Much like an intricate labyrinth, technology can lead us astray, causing us to disconnect from the tangible world around us.

- **Work-Life Balance:** The maze often presents us with choices that seem to blur the boundaries between work and personal life, creating a disorienting experience. Ancient philosophies become our roadmap, encouraging us to find harmony and balance within the maze. Modern tools, like flexible work arrangements and effective time management, become our tools to establish equilibrium.

- **Identity and Purpose:** In the twists and turns of the maze, many find themselves questioning their identity and purpose. Here, ancient wisdom provides us with the lantern of self-reflection, self-awareness, and meaningful goal pursuit. With modern practices like goal setting and career counseling, we find our way toward a sense of purpose.

- **Consumerism and Materialism:** Consumerism and materialism drive many to chase the latest products, often straining their finances. This pursuit, rooted in status and competition, traps them in a financial maze, leading to emptiness and debt. Ancient wisdom teaches us that material possessions are fleeting, guiding us toward inner fulfillment. Embracing practices like minimalism and gratitude liberates us from consumerism's empty promises, fostering contentment within.

- **Health and Wellness:** The pressures of modern life compel us to work longer hours with limited physical activity and make unhealthy dietary choices, trapping us in a complex maze that is challenging to escape from. Ancient holistic practices like Ayurveda and Traditional Chinese Medicine serve as bridges, connecting our body, mind, and spirit. By merging this ancient wisdom with modern nutritional science and fitness techniques, we embark on a journey to counteract the adverse effects of contemporary living on our overall well-being and navigate our way out of this intricate maze of health problems.

- **Social Injustice:** In this intricate maze, issues of inequality and discrimination persist, creating barriers and obstacles. Ancient wisdom promotes compassion, empathy, and respect as the guiding stars. Combining these values with modern activism and advocacy efforts provides us with the tools to navigate through this challenging terrain and bring about positive change.

- **Ethical Dilemmas:** As the maze takes us deeper into the complexity of ethical dilemmas brought by technological advancements, ancient ethical principles, like the Golden Rule, serve as our moral compass, guiding us through these intricate scenarios.

- **Spiritual Disconnection:** Some individuals may feel spiritually lost within the maze. Ancient wisdom offers spiritual practices and rituals as guiding lights, helping us reconnect with a deeper sense of purpose and meaning. Modern spiritual exploration becomes the companion on this spiritual journey.

By weaving ancient wisdom with modern insights, we equip ourselves with a versatile map, enabling us to navigate the maze of contemporary challenges. This fusion of knowledge empowers us with resilience and adaptability, ensuring that we not only find our way through the complexities of the modern world but also remain grounded in values that have stood the test of time. So, let us embark on this journey, armed with wisdom from the past and insights from the present, as we seek to navigate the modern maze.

Chapter 62

The Power of Forgiveness

Embracing forgiveness can offer remarkable benefits for our mental well-being and brain health. Forgiveness means releasing resentment, anger, and negative feelings towards someone who has wronged us. It involves a shift in perspective and a deliberate choice to free ourselves from the emotional burden caused by a hurtful experience. Let's explore the connections between forgiveness and our mental and neurological well-being and its advantages:

1. **Mind-Body Harmony:** Forgiveness is a cognitive process where we consciously change our thoughts and feelings about the situation and the person who hurt us. This shift can reduce stress and emotional turmoil, replacing anger, bitterness, and resentment with emotional well-being.

2. **Stress Reduction:** Clinging to anger and resentment triggers the body's stress response, releasing stress hormones such as cortisol. Chronic stress is associated with various health issues, including heart problems,

weakened immune function, and mental health challenges. Forgiveness helps mitigate these stress-related responses by promoting emotional healing and reducing negative emotions tied to the hurtful event.

3. **Neurological Benefits:** Negative emotions and unresolved conflicts create neural pathways in the brain that reinforce those emotions. Forgiveness can rewire these pathways, replacing negative associations with positive ones. Brain imaging studies have shown that practicing forgiveness can alter brain activity, particularly in areas linked to emotional regulation, empathy, and decision-making.

4. **Enhanced Psychological Well-Being:** Forgiveness is linked to reduced levels of depression, anxiety, and hostility. Letting go of grudges and negative emotions frees up mental energy for positive thoughts and experiences, enhancing overall mood.

5. **Improved Relationships:** Forgiveness can strengthen relationships by fostering empathy, understanding, and effective communication. It can break the cycle of conflict and rebuild trust.

6. **Personal Growth:** Forgiveness is a powerful tool for personal growth and resilience. It requires introspection and the ability to transcend one's own pain, leading to increased self-awareness and a deeper understanding of one's values and priorities.

7. **Spiritual and Philosophical Benefits:** Many spiritual and philosophical traditions emphasize forgiveness as a virtue, aligning with teachings of compassion, empathy, and the interconnectedness of all beings.

To harness the power of forgiveness:

1. **Acknowledge Your Feelings:** Recognize and validate your emotions related to the hurtful event. It's okay to feel angry, hurt, or upset.

2. **Practice Empathy:** Try to understand the perspective of the person who hurt you. This doesn't justify their actions but helps you see them as complex individuals with their own struggles.

3. **Choose to Forgive:** Make a conscious decision to forgive. It's not about condoning hurtful behavior but letting go of its emotional grip on you.

4. **Release Resentment:** Work on releasing negative emotions by focusing on positive aspects of your life and personal growth.

5. **Cultivate Self-Compassion:** Treat yourself with the same compassion you would offer to a friend who is hurting.

6. **Seek Support:** If forgiveness feels challenging, consider seeking support from friends, family, or a mental health professional.

7. **Practice Mindfulness:** Mindfulness techniques can help you stay present and process your emotions without feeling overwhelmed.

Harnessing the power of forgiveness can lead to significant positive changes in our mental, emotional, and even physical well-being. It's a gift we give ourselves, enabling us to move forward with greater inner peace and resilience.

A Path to Healing and Spiritual Harmony

Forgiveness is a potent force that holds the key to healing, benefiting not only ourselves but also those who have wronged us. This transformative act is intrinsically linked to both our mental and neurological well-being. Moreover, it carries profound spiritual significance, connecting us to a deeper understanding of compassion and interconnectedness.

- **Forgiveness and Healing**: Forgiveness serves as a remarkable catalyst for healing, addressing both personal and interpersonal wounds. When we embrace forgiveness, we consciously liberate ourselves from the shackles of resentment and anger, fostering emotional healing for our own well-being. Simultaneously, it creates an opportunity for those who caused the hurt to embark on a journey of redemption and personal growth. The profound connection here lies in the reciprocal nature of forgiveness, where both parties can experience restoration and renewal.

- **Forgiveness and Spirituality**: Delving into the spiritual realm, forgiveness resonates with the teachings of compassion and empathy found in various spiritual and philosophical traditions. Most religions emphasize forgiveness as one of their core virtues, highlighting its significance in the path towards spiritual enlightenment. It underscores the interconnectedness of all beings, emphasizing that by forgiving, we not only uplift ourselves but also contribute to the greater spiritual harmony of the universe. The act of forgiveness aligns with the principles of spiritual growth, promoting the idea that by forgiving, we mirror the divine act of grace, setting an example of love and understanding. In this way, forgiveness transcends the realm of the personal, resonating with the spiritual core of our existence.

In conclusion, forgiveness emerges as a profound and transformative force that shapes not only our individual well-being but also our interpersonal connections and our spiritual harmony. Its impact is multi-faceted, touching our minds, bodies, and souls. By choosing forgiveness, we unburden ourselves from the weight of resentment and anger, paving the way for emotional healing and personal growth. Simultaneously, we extend an opportunity for those who have wronged us to embark on their journey of redemption and renewal, highlighting the reciprocal nature of this act.

Delving into the spiritual realm, forgiveness resonates with the timeless teachings of compassion and empathy found in various spiritual and philosophical traditions. As a core virtue in many religions, it underscores the interconnectedness of all beings and the path towards spiritual enlightenment. By embracing forgiveness, we mirror the divine act of grace, setting an example of love and understanding, thus contributing to the greater spiritual harmony of the universe.

In the end, forgiveness transcends the personal, extending its reach to the very core of our existence. Embracing its power allows us to forge stronger connections with others, transcend our own pain, and live with greater inner peace and resilience. In doing so, we discover that forgiveness is not just a choice; it's a profound gift we give to ourselves and the world, a path to healing and spiritual harmony.

Chapter 63

Embracing Responsibility: Empowering Your Life's Path

Taking responsibility of our actions means recognizing our ability to make choices and decisions that influence the results in our lives, regardless of whether those choices lead to positive or negative outcomes. It also entails assuming responsibility for the effects of our actions without attributing blame to external circumstances or other people. This concept is often closely linked to the notions of accountability and self-awareness.

The connection between the mind and body in this context is closely tied to our thought and emotional processes. Our thoughts, beliefs, and attitudes have an impact on our emotions, behaviors, and actions. When we take responsibility for our actions, we engage our cognitive processes to assess the situation, make deliberate choices, and contemplate potential outcomes. Emotionally, this can result in a feeling of empowerment and control over our lives, which can have a positive impact on our overall well-being.

From a neurological standpoint, taking responsibility involves the activation of different brain regions. The prefrontal cortex, which is responsible for decision-making and planning, becomes active as we evaluate our options and make choices. The amygdala, associated with emotions, might be activated as we experience feelings of guilt, regret, or pride based on our decisions.

Enhancing this scenario involves several steps:

- **Self-awareness:** Start by cultivating self-awareness. Reflect on your thoughts, emotions, and behaviors. Understand the patterns you follow and how they affect your outcomes.
- **Mindfulness:** Practice mindfulness to remain present and be aware of your thoughts and actions. This can help you make more deliberate choices rather than reacting impulsively.
- **Acceptance:** Embrace the notion that you have the power to shape your life. Accept that mistakes are opportunities for growth and learning, rather than sources of blame or shame.
- **Decision-Making:** Before making a decision, consider the potential consequences of each option. This will help you make choices that align with your values and goals.
- **Ownership:** Take ownership of both positive and negative outcomes. If something goes well, acknowledge your role in making it happen. If something goes awry, analyze what you could have done differently without dwelling on blame.
- **Empowerment:** Recognize that taking responsibility empowers you. It allows you to take control of your life and make intentional choices that align with your aspirations.
- **Self-Compassion:** Practice self-compassion when mistakes occur. Treat yourself with the same kindness and understanding you would extend to a friend facing a similar situation.
- **Continuous Growth:** View life as an ongoing

journey of growth. Learn from your experiences, adapt, and refine your approach as necessary.

In the end, being responsible for our own lives means acknowledging that we are the creators, maintainers, and managers of our actions, choices, and outcomes. By adopting this mindset, we can enhance our overall well-being, personal development, and sense of fulfillment.

Chapter 64

Embracing Your Energetic Essence: Living Life with Purpose

I n simple terms, the understanding that the universe is made of energy refers to the idea that everything around us, including ourselves, is composed of vibrating particles of energy. This concept is often rooted in scientific principles and theories, such as quantum physics. It suggests that even solid objects are ultimately composed of subatomic particles that are in constant motion, creating energy fields.

When considering the human body in this context, the notion of an "energy body" proposes that our physical forms are not solely composed of material substance but also encompass an inherent energy or vibrational dimension. This energy is believed to circulate through diverse channels and focal points within the body, commonly denoted as chakras or meridians. Various cultures and traditions have developed distinct perspectives and terminology to elucidate this energy, such as Qi in traditional Chinese medicine or Prana in Ayurveda.

Living your life as an energy means realizing and tapping into this underlying vibrational aspect of yourself and the universe. It involves recognizing that your thoughts, emotions, and actions also carry energy and can influence your well-being. Here are a few ways to approach living as an energy being:

- **Mindfulness and Awareness**: Practice mindfulness to become more attuned to your thoughts, emotions, and bodily sensations. Recognize that your thoughts carry energy and can affect your overall state of being.
- **Positive Energy:** Cultivate positive thoughts, emotions, and intentions. Positive energy attracts more positivity into your life and can have a beneficial impact on your well-being.
- **Healthy Lifestyle:** Eating nutritious foods, staying hydrated, exercising, and getting adequate rest contribute to maintaining a balanced energy in your body.
- **Meditation and Breathing**: Engage in practices like meditation and deep breathing to calm your mind, balance your energy centers, and enhance your connection with your energy body.
- **Energetic Practices**: Explore practices like yoga, tai chi, qigong, or Reiki that specifically focus on working with and harmonizing your energy.
- **Connection with Nature:** Spending time in nature and grounding yourself by walking barefoot on the earth can help you feel more connected to the larger energy of the universe.
- **Positive Interactions:** Surround yourself with positive people and engage in activities that uplift your energy rather than drain it.
- **Self-Care:** Prioritize self-care and self-love. Taking care of your energy body also involves nurturing your physical, emotional, and mental well-being.

Remember that this understanding of living as an energy being is a holistic approach that combines both ancient wisdom and modern insights. It's about aligning your thoughts, emotions, actions, and lifestyle with the underlying energetic nature of the universe and yourself.

The notion of humans as energetic beings with an energy body is a recurring theme in numerous spiritual and religious teachings, spanning Judeo-Christian and other faiths. Although the terminology and interpretations may differ, the fundamental concept of a spiritual essence or energy residing within human beings is evident in a multitude of traditions.

In Judeo-Christian teachings, the concept of humans having a spiritual essence or connection to a higher power is emphasized. For example in the bible:

- **Genesis 2:7:** "Then the Lord God formed a man from the dust of the ground and breathed into his nostrils the breath of life, and the man became a living being." This passage suggests that humans were given life through divine breath, implying a spiritual and energetic aspect.
- **1 Corinthians 6:19-20:** "Do you not know that your bodies are temples of the Holy Spirit, who is in you, whom you have received from God? You are not your own; you were bought at a price. Therefore, honor God with your bodies." This verse implies a sacredness and spiritual significance associated with the human body.
- **John 4:24:** "God is spirit, and his worshipers must worship in the Spirit and," This verse points to the spiritual nature of God and suggests a connection between the divine and the spiritual essence within humans.

In other faiths and spiritual philosophies, similar concepts of humans as energetic or spiritual beings are also present. Some examples include:

- **<u>Eastern Philosophies (Hinduism, Buddhism)</u>:**
  Concepts like "Prana" in Hinduism and "Chi" in
  Buddhism refer to the life force or energy that flows
  through all living beings, including humans. Practices
  such as meditation and yoga aim to balance and
  harmonize this energy.
- **Sufism (Islamic Mysticism):** Sufism emphasizes
  the idea of the heart as a center of spiritual awareness and
  connection to the divine. It teaches that humans have a
  spiritual essence that transcends the physical body.
- **Taoism:** Taoist philosophy includes the concept of
  "Qi" (also spelled "Chi"), which is the vital energy that
  flows through all things, including humans. Balancing
  and cultivating this energy is a fundamental aspect of
  Taoist practices.
- **Indigenous Traditions**: Many indigenous cultures
  have beliefs about the interconnectedness of all life and
  spiritual energy within humans and nature. Rituals and
  ceremonies often involve honoring and harnessing this
  energy.

In all these teachings, humans are more than just physical bodies;
they possess a spiritual essence or energy that connects them to a
larger reality. This understanding encourages individuals to live
mindfully, nurture their spiritual well-being, and cultivate a sense of
interconnectedness with all of existence.

Chapter 65

Exploring the Spiritual Essence: Insights from the Bible

In the Bible, the term commonly used to describe a person's inner spiritual essence or energy is "spirit" or "soul." While this terminology may not align precisely with our modern scientific understanding of energy, the concept of a non-physical, spiritual dimension of human existence is clearly present. Here are some verses that illustrate this concept:

- **Genesis 2:7** tells us, *"Then the Lord God formed a man from the dust of the ground and breathed into his nostrils the breath of life, and the man became a living being."* This verse suggests that divine breath brought the physical body to life, implying the existence of a spiritual essence.
- **Matthew 10:28** states, *"Do not be afraid of those who kill the body but cannot kill the soul. Rather, be afraid of One who can destroy both soul and body."* Here, Jesus distinguishes between the physical body and the soul, underscoring the enduring nature of the soul.

- In **1 Thessalonians 5:23**, it is written, *"May God himself, the God of peace, sanctify you through and through. May your whole spirit, soul, and body be kept blameless at the coming of our Lord Jesus Christ."* This verse mentions the "spirit," "soul," and "body," implying that humans consist of different elements, including a spiritual one.

- **Hebrews 4:12** tells us, *"For the word of God is alive and active. Sharper than any double-edged sword, it penetrates even to dividing soul and spirit, joints and marrow; it judges the thoughts and attitudes of the heart."* This verse suggests a distinction between the soul and spirit and highlights the discerning nature of the Word of God.

- **Ecclesiastes 12:7** states, *"And the dust returns to the ground it came from, and the spirit returns to God who gave it."* This verse speaks to the separation of the physical body and the spirit at death, illustrating a spiritual aspect that transcends the body.

While the Bible may not explicitly use the term "energy body" to describe this concept, the language employed emphasizes the idea of a spiritual essence or consciousness within human beings. The focus is on the eternal nature of the soul or spirit, distinct from the physical body, often described as the part of us that connects with God and the divine.

- In the New Revised Standard Version (NRSV) of the Bible, **Revelation 3:14** states: *"And to the angel of the church in Laodicea write: The words of the 'Amen,' the faithful witness, the origin of God's creation."* In this verse, the term "Amen" is used to describe Jesus Christ, and it holds significant meaning in both Hebrew and Christian traditions.

The word "Amen" derives from the Hebrew word אָמֵן (amen), which means "so be it," "truly," or "verily." It is often used as an affirmation or agreement at the end of prayers or statements, signifying confirmation of what has been said. In **Revelation 3:14**, the use of "Amen" underscores the truth and reliability of Jesus as the faithful witness and the origin of God's creation.

In a broader sense, "Amen" signifies a solemn affirmation of faith, trust, and agreement with the truth of a statement or prayer. It reflects recognition of God's authority and a declaration of one's belief in the truth being spoken.

In this chapter, we've delved into the profound concept of the human spirit and soul as described in the Bible. The terminology used, "spirit" and "soul," may not perfectly align with our modern scientific understanding of energy, but they serve as windows into the non-physical, spiritual aspects of human existence.

We've examined key verses that shed light on this concept. **Genesis 2:7** reveals the divine breath infusing life into the physical body, implying the existence of a spiritual essence. **Matthew 10:28** distinguishes the soul from the body, emphasizing the soul's enduring nature. **1 Thessalonians 5:23** speaks of spirit, soul, and body as different aspects of our being. **Hebrews 4:12** discerns between soul and spirit while highlighting the Word of God's perceptive nature. **Ecclesiastes 12:7** poignantly illustrates the separation of the physical body from the spirit at death, emphasizing the spiritual aspect's transcendence.

While the Bible doesn't explicitly use the term "energy body" for this concept, the language employed emphasizes the existence of a spiritual essence or consciousness within us. The focus here is on the soul's eternal nature, distinct from the physical body, often described as the conduit connecting us to the divine.

In addition, we explored the significant use of the word "Amen" in **Revelation 3:14** to describe Jesus Christ. "Amen" holds deep meaning in both Hebrew and Christian traditions, signifying a solemn affirmation of faith and truth. It underscores the truth and reliability of Jesus as the faithful witness and the origin of God's creation.

In a broader sense, "Amen" represents a powerful declaration of belief in the truth being spoken, acknowledging God's authority. This chapter has illuminated the spiritual dimensions of the human experience and offered insights into the profound symbolism embedded in the Bible's language.

As we wrap up this chapter, we invite you to reflect on these profound themes and consider how they resonate with your own beliefs and understanding of the human spirit and the divine. This marks the culmination of our exploration in Part IX, delving deeply into practical applications and tools for transformation. In Part X, we'll delve into more examples, tips, and resources.

Part Ten

Additional Examples, Tips, and Resources

Welcome to a treasure trove of wisdom and enlightenment in "Additional Examples, Tips, and Resources." These thirteen chapters are more than mere pages; they are portals into realms often left unexplored. In Chapter 66, prepare for a revelatory voyage uniting sound, breath, and meditation across Eastern philosophy and Western mysticism, unraveling the shared mysteries behind spiritual transformation and transcendence. Ever wondered about the transcendental journey from birth to death, understanding the profound significance of "Yahweh" as the Name of God? Chapter 67 unveils this spiritual odyssey. Prepare to traverse uncharted territories, delving into the mysterious and thought-provoking narratives like Jesus and Saint Thomas in India in Chapter 68. As you immerse yourself in the enigmatic realms of Chapters 69 to 78, be prepared to unravel the secrets of existence, discover the hidden nuances of your daily life, and harness the transformative powers of meditation, energy, and consciousness. Engage in body scan meditations, embrace the pauses between breaths, and unlock the very essence of life's breath, leading you to the fabled Kingdom of Heaven. This is a journey of enlightenment, a passage that beckons you to explore the depths of existence, promising revelations that will reshape your understanding of the world around you. Embark on this path, and prepare to be astounded.

Chapter 66

The Connection Between Sound and Breath

T his chapter delves into ancient customs that interweave sound, breath, and meditation, connecting Eastern philosophy with Western mysticism. This exploration uncovers common principles that underlie various practices, shedding light on the interconnection of secret sounds and breath within both traditions. Despite differences in approaches and practices, various ancient traditions from Eastern philosophy to Western mysticism demonstrate a connection between sound, breath, and meditation. While each may possess unique methodologies, they often share common underlying principles. Here's a brief exploration of the relationship between secret sounds, breath, and meditation in these diverse traditions:

Eastern Philosophy

Mantras and Pranayama

- **Mantras:** In Eastern traditions like Hinduism and Buddhism, practitioners use specific ***sound*** *vibrations* called mantras. These are often repeated during meditation to focus the mind and induce a state of heightened awareness.

- **Pranayama:** This refers to the practice of **breath control** in yoga. Pranayama techniques involve conscious regulation of breath, linking it to the flow of life force, or prana. Breath is considered a vital bridge between the physical and spiritual realms.

Nada Yoga

- **Secret Sound (Nada):** Nada Yoga, a branch of yoga, explores the concept of "Nada," which refers to the **inner sound or vibration** that can be heard through deep meditation. This inner sound is considered a powerful tool for self-realization and connecting with the divine.

Breath Awareness in Mindfulness

In mindfulness meditation practices, particularly within Buddhist traditions, attention to the breath is a central focus. *Mindful breathing is a way to anchor awareness in the present moment* and cultivate a calm and focused mind.

Western Mysticism

Christian Mysticism

In Christian mysticism, practices such as contemplative prayer involve a deep, **wordless communion** (relationship) with the divine. This form of prayerful reflection goes beyond mere verbal communication or structured supplication. It engages practitioners in a profound, wordless relationship with God, seeking a union that transcends the limitations of language or rational thought.

At its core, contemplative prayer emphasizes silent meditation and inner stillness. It necessitates quieting the mind, relinquishing distractions, and fostering a state of openness and receptivity. In this contemplative state, individuals turn their attention inward, creating an environment conducive to an intimate connection with the divine presence.

The essence of contemplative prayer isn't rooted in seeking specific outcomes or reciting scripted prayers; rather, it revolves around resting in the presence of God. Its purpose lies in seeking a deeper connection that surpasses mere intellectual understanding. Practitioners often use simple focal points like sacred texts, images, or phrases to facilitate this profound encounter.

Through contemplative prayer, individuals aim to deepen their spiritual lives, nurture inner peace, and foster a closer relationship with the divine. This journey is intensely personal and intimate, aiming to transcend the limitations of words and thoughts, allowing for a transformative encounter with God.

Hermeticism and Alchemy

Hermetic traditions and Western alchemy delve deeply into the concept of the "Prima Materia," also known as the "First Matter." This fundamental essence is believed to serve as the connective fabric interlinking all aspects of existence. Within these philosophical traditions, it's often associated with an underlying subtle sound or vibration that permeates all of creation.

The Prima Materia is more than mere physical substance; it embodies a primal, formless state from which all things emerge. This ancient concept suggests that within this initial formlessness lies the potential for profound transformation and creation. Alchemists dedicated themselves to uncovering the secrets of this elusive substance, understanding that refining it through various symbolic and physical processes might lead not only to transmuting base elements into nobler ones but also to achieving the legendary Philosopher's Stone.

The Philosopher's Stone, a mythical and sought-after substance, represents the pinnacle of alchemical pursuit. It is believed to possess extraordinary powers, capable of transmuting base metals into gold or silver and, symbolically, embodying spiritual enlightenment, transformation, and the perfection of the self. The creation of the Philosopher's Stone was depicted metaphorically in alchemical teachings as a journey of inner transformation and spiritual evolution.

The exploration of the Prima Materia led alchemists beyond the realms of the physical into the metaphysical and spiritual dimensions. It represented not only material change but also the profound journey of inner growth and the evolution of consciousness. This concept of a primal substance is a cornerstone of alchemical philosophy, encapsulating the quest to understand the underlying unity and transformative nature inherent in the fabric of the universe.

Kabbalah and Divine Names

In Jewish mysticism, particularly within Kabbalah, the use of sacred names and sounds is significant. The breath can be associated with the **utterance of divine names,** and practices may **involve breath control** in combination with meditation on these sacred sounds.

Common Themes

Connection to the Divine

Both Eastern and Western traditions recognize the intimate connection between breath, sound, and the divine. **Breath is a vehicle** for connecting with higher states of consciousness or divine presence.

Inner Silence and Stillness

Practices in both traditions often aim **to cultivate inner silence and stillness.** Whether through mindful breathing or the repetition of sacred sounds, the goal is to quiet the mind and create a receptive space for spiritual insight.

Transcendence and Transformation

Using secret sounds and conscious breathwork is often linked to transcendent experiences and personal transformation. These practices are tools for accessing deeper layers of consciousness and **spiritual realization.**

While there are similarities, it's important to recognize the diversity within each tradition, and practices can vary widely even within the broader categories of Eastern and Western spirituality. Individual interpretations and approaches to these practices may differ based on cultural, religious, or personal perspectives.

Chapter 67

From Birth to Death: "Yahweh" as the Name of God

The sacred name of God, "Yahweh," pronounced as "YHWH," comprises the only consonants that, when pronounced correctly, do not require the use of your tongue or the closure of your lips. The pronunciation of this sacred name was an attempt to mimic and mirror the act of breathing, symbolizing both inhalation and exhalation. When reciting the name, it is divided into two components: "YA" during inhalation and "WEH" during exhalation. Essentially, the first word uttered when emerging from your mother's womb is "Yahweh," the name of God. Likewise, the last word you speak on your deathbed is 'Yahweh,' signifying the name of God. This concept has its origins in Hebraic tradition and texts.

The idea of "YHWH," or "Yahweh" as a representation of the breath and the continuous cycle of inhalation and exhalation is a profound and mystical concept deeply ingrained in the Hebraic tradition. Using these specific consonants reflects the belief that the divine name is not just a static word, but a breathing entity. It connects the very essence of human existence to the divine, suggesting that the act of breathing itself is a continuous invocation of

God and the Absolute's that represent ultimate unchanging and all-encompassing reality.

This concept also underscores the idea that one's connection to the divine is inherent and ever-present. From the moment of birth to the very end of life, the sacred name is a part of the human experience. This belief removes the need for conscious effort in invoking God's name and reinforces the notion that spirituality is woven into the fabric of everyday life, even in the simplest and most automatic actions, like breathing.

The Bible contains an account of God breathing life into man in the book of Genesis. This is found in the creation story in Genesis 2:7 (New International Version), which states:

> "Then the Lord God formed a man from the dust of the ground and breathed into his nostrils the breath of life, and the man became a living being."

This passage describes how God created the first man, Adam, from the dust of the ground and then breathed the breath of life into him, giving him life. This act of God is symbolic of the creation of humanity and the special relationship between God and human beings in Judeo-Christian theology.

The pronunciation and understanding of the sacred name "YHWH" as related to the act of breathing carry deep spiritual significance, highlighting the interconnectedness of human existence with the divine and the idea that the name of God is an intrinsic part of our journey from birth to death. This concept is a testament to the rich and multifaceted nature of Hebraic tradition and its profound insights into the human experience and spirituality.

Exploring the Sacred Sounds: "YA" and "WEH" vs. "HUM" and "Sau"

In chapter 53, we delved into the concept of "HUM" and "SAU." In this section, we will explore "YA" and "WEH," as well as revisit "HUM" and "SAU" in more depth. It's important to note that these concepts have diverse cultural and linguistic interpretations. For instance, the name "YHWH," often known as the Tetragrammaton, is conventionally translated into various languages in the Bible, including in the context of different Indian languages like Gujarati and Hindi. In Gujarati, it is rendered as "યહોવા" (Yahova) and in Hindi it is typically pronounced as "यहोवा" (Yahova), "a similar phonetic representation, which serves as a common way to signify the sacred name of God in Gujarati texts.

The comparison between the sounds associated with "YA" and "WEH" during inhalation and exhalation, and the sounds "HUM" and "Sau" during the same phases of breathing, is an interesting exploration of different traditions and practices in spirituality and meditation.

"YA" and "WEH" vs. "HUM" and "Sau"

- **"YA" and "WEH"**: These sounds are typically associated with Hebraic traditions, specifically the pronunciation of the sacred name "YHWH" or Yahweh. "YA" is connected to inhalation, while "WEH" is associated with exhalation. The act of pronouncing these sounds mirrors the breath, symbolizing the continuous cycle of inhalation and exhalation, and it's often seen as a spiritual practice.

- **"HUM" and "Sau"**: These sounds are frequently found in yogic and Hindu traditions, particularly within the context of mantra meditation. "HUM" is chanted during inhalation, and "Sau" is chanted during exhalation. This practice is connected to the idea of harmonizing one's breath with the vibrations of these sounds and is believed to have meditative and spiritual benefits.

Commonalities Between the Two Systems

- **Breath Focus:** Both systems emphasize the connection between sacred sounds and breath. In the Hebraic tradition, "YA" and "WEH" reflect the act of breathing, while in the yogic tradition, "HUM" and "Sau" similarly align with the breath. This focus on breathing is a fundamental aspect of many spiritual and meditative practices, highlighting the significance of conscious breathing in achieving a deeper connection with the divine or one's inner self.

- **Spiritual Significance:** In both systems, there's a belief in the spiritual significance of these sounds. The sounds are sacred and are believed to have the power to deepen one's connection to the divine or to aid in meditation and self-realization.

- **Cyclical Nature:** Both systems recognize the cyclical nature of the breath, with specific sounds associated with both inhalation and exhalation. This cyclic representation underscores the continuous and interconnected nature of life and breath, serving as a reminder of the perpetual cycle of existence.

In summary, both the "YA" and "WEH" sounds in Hebraic traditions and the "HUM" and "Sau" sounds in yogic traditions emphasize the close relationship between sacred sounds and the breath. These practices aim to harness the power of conscious breathing and sound to achieve spiritual or meditative goals. While the specific sounds and traditions differ, they share common themes related to breathing, spirituality, and the cyclic nature of life.

Breath Focus and Sacred Sounds in East and West: A Comparative Exploration

In the preceding discussion, we explored the profound significance of the sacred name of God, "Yahweh" (pronounced as "YHWH"), and its connection to the act of breathing in the Hebraic tradition. We learned that "Yahweh" is not merely a static word but a representation of the breath, symbolizing the continuous cycle of inhalation and exhalation. It's a concept deeply woven into the fabric of human existence, signifying an inherent connection between humanity and the divine.

Now, let's draw a parallel between this Western concept and Eastern traditions, specifically those found in yogic and Hindu practices, by comparing "YA" and "WEH" with "HUM" and "Sau."

"YA" and "WEH" vs. "HUM" and "Sau" - A Cross-Cultural Exploration

- ***"YA" and "WEH":*** In the Hebraic tradition, "YA" is associated with inhalation, and "WEH" is connected with exhalation. The act of pronouncing these sounds mirrors the breath, symbolizing the continuous cycle of inhalation and exhalation. It's a practice deeply rooted in spirituality and signifies the continuous invocation of God through the very act of breathing.
- ***"HUM" and "Sau":*** On the other hand, in yogic and Hindu traditions, we encounter the sounds "HUM" and "Sau." Here, "HUM" is chanted during inhalation, and "Sau" during exhalation. This practice is a central element of mantra meditation and is believed to harmonize one's breath with the vibrations of these

sacred sounds, facilitating meditation and spiritual connection.

Commonalities in Sacred Sound and Breath Across Traditions

1. **Breath Focus:** Both systems emphasize the profound connection between sacred sounds and the breath. Whether it's "Yahweh" or "HUM" and "Sau," these practices highlight the significance of conscious breathing in achieving a deeper connection with the divine or one's inner self. Breath becomes a vehicle for spiritual exploration.

2. **Spiritual Significance:** In both traditions, the sounds are regarded as sacred and believed to have the power to deepen one's connection to the divine or aid in meditation and self-realization. These sounds transcend linguistic and cultural boundaries, emphasizing their universal spiritual significance.

3. **Cyclical Nature:** Both systems recognize the cyclical nature of the breath, associating specific sounds with both inhalation and exhalation. This cyclic representation underscores the continuous and interconnected nature of life and breath, serving as a reminder of the perpetual cycle of existence.

4. **Inherent Connection to the Divine:** Both the Western and Eastern practices suggest that one's connection to the divine is inherent and ever-present. The sacred name "Yahweh" and the sounds "HUM" and "Sau" are integral to the human experience from birth to death, removing the need for conscious effort in invoking the divine and reinforcing the notion that spirituality is woven into the fabric of everyday life, even in the simplest and most automatic actions, like breathing.

5. **Mystical and Spiritual Exploration:** The ideas surrounding "Yahweh" and the sounds "HUM" and "Sau" invite individuals to engage in mystical and spiritual exploration. They symbolize a deeper connection to the divine through conscious breath and sacred sounds, providing a pathway to self-realization and spiritual growth.

By examining the parallel between these practices, we find a universal theme: the profound connection between sacred sounds, breath, and spirituality. Whether in the East or the West, the act of conscious breathing is a fundamental aspect of many spiritual and meditative traditions, emphasizing the power of sound and breath in the pursuit of deeper spiritual understanding and connection with the divine.

Chapter 68

Lost Years: Jesus and Saint Thomas in India

T he life of Jesus Christ remains a subject of profound intrigue and fascination for millions worldwide. While the biblical narratives provide us with invaluable insights into his ministry, there exists a remarkable gap in our understanding—the "Lost Years." This enigmatic period, shrouded in mystery, spans the time from Jesus' youth to the commencement of his public ministry around the age of 30. In this chapter, we embark on a journey to explore the tantalizing theory that, during these unaccounted years, Jesus may have ventured to the ancient lands of India in search of wisdom and enlightenment.

India, a crucible of ancient wisdom, was a mosaic of vibrant cultures and centers of erudition during the 1st century AD. Notably, educational institutions like Takshashila and Nalanda beckoned scholars and seekers from across the world, fostering an environment teeming with intellectual curiosity and spirited debates. This narrative aims to uncover the profound connections between Jesus, his quest for wisdom, and the role of Saint Thomas, one of his apostles, in the development of Christianity in India.

Uncovering Jesus' Probable Journey in India

In the heart of the illustrious centers of knowledge and thriving cultures of erudition in ancient India, the hypothesis of Jesus' quest for wisdom unfolds as a captivating narrative. In an era where spiritual seekers abounded, Jesus, like countless other truth-seekers of his time, embarked on a remarkable journey into the heart of India. He may have ventured to the Himalayas and Tibetan monasteries, immersing himself in the profound teachings of Buddhism and other Eastern philosophies. While the New Testament primarily emphasizes his role as the Messiah and the harbinger of salvation, this period of his life, the "Lost Years," remains shrouded in mystery. It is within the intellectual and spiritual ambiance of that epoch that we find resonance with Jesus' potential quest for knowledge.

The Spiritual Legacy of Saint Thomas

In the same era, the apostle Saint Thomas embarked on a different journey—one that would significantly shape the course of Christianity in India. Arriving on Indian shores in 52 AD, he dedicated himself to spreading the teachings of Christianity. His mission continued until his passing in 72 AD, which occurred in the ancient city of Chennai, known as Madras during that time.

Saint Thomas, often referred to as "Doubting Thomas," underwent a transformation from a seeker of spiritual truth to a devoted missionary. His sojourn in India was marked by his unwavering commitment to the dissemination of Christian teachings, and he played a pivotal role in the establishment of early Christian communities along the Malabar Coast.

Historical accounts reveal that Saint Thomas's mission along the Malabar Coast led to the conversion of local populations and the establishment of Christian communities that continue to thrive in certain regions of India to this day. Notably, his tomb, believed to be located in the St. Thomas Mount area of Chennai, serves as a powerful symbol of his enduring legacy and the early roots of Christianity in India. While these claims remain subjects of scholarly debate, they offer a fascinating insight into the lasting impact of Saint Thomas and the interplay between faith, culture, and the spread of religious teachings across borders and continents. It is a story that deepens our understanding of the global reach of religious movements and the profound influence of individuals like Saint Thomas.

Many also believe that Saint Thomas started seven churches in India. They are:

1. St. Thomas Syro-Malabar Catholic Church, Palayoor
2. St. Mary's Orthodox Syrian Church, Niranam
3. St. Thomas Evangelical Church of India, Nilackal
4. St. Thomas Syro-Malabar Catholic Church, Kottakkavu
5. St. Thomas Syro-Malabar Catholic Church, Kokkamangalam
6. St. Mary's Jacobite Syrian Cathedral, North Paravur
7. St. Thomas Syro-Malabar Catholic Church, Malayattoor

These churches are considered by some to be the early Christian communities founded by Saint Thomas in India. However, the historical evidence for this is not very strong, and it's often viewed as a tradition rather than a well-established fact. Saint Thomas is traditionally associated with evangelizing in India, and there are ancient Christian communities in India that claim their origins from his mission. Whether he specifically founded seven churches is less certain and may be more symbolic or legendary.

Interweaving Faiths and Allegorical Interpretations

Our examination of the potential implications of Jesus' journey to India reveals a speculative interweaving of faiths and allegorical interpretations. It's important to note that this theory lacks concrete evidence and remains speculative.

One way in which these traditions might intermingle is through the adoption of yogic practices. These practices encompass physical postures, meditation, and breathing exercises, aligning with the concept of spiritual discipline. In the context of Christian spirituality, this could be seen as a way to deepen one's connection with God through contemplative practices.

Additionally, the blending could involve interpretations related to reincarnation. Hinduism and Buddhism believe in the concept of reincarnation, contrasting with the traditional Christian belief in a single earthly life. This blending might explore the possibility of multiple incarnations within Christian contexts.

The interweaving of Christian and Indian spiritual traditions also emphasizes universal wisdom shared between them. Both traditions uphold values of love, compassion, and the pursuit of wisdom, highlighting the common ground between faiths.

Symbolism and allegory play a significant role in this interweaving. The use of symbols like the lotus flower in Hinduism or the symbolism of water in Christianity can bridge the gap between different traditions, creating a common spiritual language.

Moreover, moral teachings attributed to Jesus in the New Testament, such as the Sermon on the Mount, emphasize compassion, humility, and forgiveness. These values resonate with the ethical principles found in various Indian philosophical traditions, such as Jainism and Buddhism.

The blending also centers on the shared goal of inner spiritual growth. Indian spiritual traditions focus on inner peace and self-realization, while Christianity teaches inner transformation and seeking the kingdom of God within.

This speculative interweaving reflects the enduring curiosity about the unknown and the desire to bridge gaps in our understanding, even in the absence of concrete historical proof. It underlines the evolving nature of human faith, driven by the speculative interplay of ideas and allegorical interpretations arising from diverse spiritual traditions.

Conclusion

In conclusion, the exploration of Jesus' "Lost Years" in India and the impact of Saint Thomas on early Christianity in the region provide a thought-provoking journey into the interplay of faiths and allegorical interpretations. While speculative, these narratives offer intriguing insights into the possible connections between Jesus' teachings and the rich spiritual traditions of ancient India.

The idea of Jesus' journey to India suggests he may have sought wisdom in the intellectual and spiritual ambiance of that time. Saint Thomas, on the other hand, left a lasting legacy through his unwavering commitment to spreading Christianity along the Malabar Coast.

This speculative interweaving of traditions highlights the shared values and universal wisdom between faiths. It underscores the evolving nature of human faith, driven by the interplay of ideas and allegorical interpretations arising from diverse spiritual traditions. These narratives invite us to continue exploring the intersections of faith, embracing the enduring mystery of the "Lost Years," and recognizing the profound influence of individuals like Saint Thomas in the rich tapestry of religious history.

Chapter 69

Mysteries of the Soul

I n the exploration of the soul's relationship with the body, we find a captivating harmony between faith and modern science within Christianity. Christian doctrine asserts that the soul is the eternal essence of an individual, distinct from the physical body, a belief that intriguingly aligns with modern scientific views on consciousness emerging from neural processes. This chapter delves into the coexistence and occasional clashes of these perspectives.

It's essential to note that, across various cultures and experiences, there exists a shared fascination with the concept of the soul leaving the body during certain moments. Some believe that the soul departs the body during dreams, embarking on journeys into the realm of the subconscious. Additionally, individuals who have faced near-death experiences, often associated with traumatic car accidents, may report witnessing their own bodies from an external vantage point. This phenomenon is commonly referred to as an "out-of-body experience" and provides a remarkable intersection between faith, science, and personal encounters with the soul's departure from the physical form.

Within Christianity, it's strongly believed that the soul continues its journey after death, potentially towards eternal salvation or separation from the divine. In this context, modern science plays a significant role by offering insights into the brain's activity during the dying process, including moments where individuals report out-of-body experiences as glimpses of the soul's transition.

Similar connections between the soul and the body can be found in ancient cultures as well. For instance, ancient Egyptian beliefs included the concept of the soul leaving the body during dreams, connecting the dream world with the realm of the spirit. In ancient Greece, dreams were seen as a means for the soul to transcend the confines of the body and interact with the divine. In this way, dream experiences mirrored the out-of-body experiences observed in modern times.

In addition to dreams, some cultures have long embraced the idea of the soul's departure from the body during deep meditation or trance-like states. For instance, in Tibetan Buddhism, advanced practitioners may engage in practices like dream yoga and clear light meditation, which involve conscious out-of-body experiences. These practices are designed to explore the nature of consciousness and the separation of the soul from the physical self.

As we search for truth and wisdom in different ways, we find that many people, no matter where or when they lived, share the idea that the soul can leave the body for a while. This idea makes us wonder about the mysteries of the soul leaving the body and how it affects our understanding of who we are and the big questions about life.

It's important to underline that traditional Christian doctrine generally does not support the concept of reincarnation, adhering to a linear understanding of life with one earthly existence and a final judgment after death. While some interpretations of certain Bible passages suggest metaphorical returns of the soul, such as the reappearance of Elijah's spirit, reincarnation is not widely accepted within mainstream Christianity.

In addition to these intriguing connections, the Bible verse John 14:2, which speaks of "many mansions in my Father's house," offers a profound metaphor that extends beyond its traditional interpretation. This verse, found in the New Testament, is often associated with the promise of eternal life and the comforting words of Jesus to his disciples. It is in this context that "my Father's house" is understood as the heavenly realm, and the "mansions" are seen as symbolic representations of places in heaven or eternal dwellings, reassuring believers of their future with God in the afterlife.

However, a broader and metaphorical interpretation can be drawn from this verse, linking it to the soul's departure during dreams, near-death experiences, and meditation. Consider, for instance, the concept of near-death experiences (NDEs). Individuals who have had NDEs often report leaving their physical bodies, entering a realm of light or profound awareness, and feeling a sense of peace and oneness. These descriptions bear a striking resemblance to the idea of entering "mansions" within the Father's house, suggesting that the verse could be seen as a metaphor for the soul's journey during such experiences.

Similarly, during deep meditation or lucid dreaming, people may feel a sense of detachment from their physical selves and may explore various dimensions of consciousness. These altered states of awareness can be thought of as the soul's exploration of its spiritual self, akin to moving through different "mansions" within the house of the divine. While this is a metaphorical interpretation, it serves to connect the verse with these profound experiences and highlight the potential richness and diversity of inner spiritual journeys, irrespective of one's religious background.

So, while the traditional interpretation of John 14:2 emphasizes the promise of a heavenly abode, the metaphorical interpretation broadens its significance to encompass the multifaceted aspects of human consciousness and spiritual exploration, drawing parallels with the soul's departure during extraordinary experiences.

Chapter 70

Discovering the Hidden Secret of God in Your Daily Life

The biblical verse from Psalms 46:10, "Be still and know that I am God," holds within it a profound key to connecting with the divine and experiencing the presence of God. It encapsulates a timeless wisdom that resonates with individuals seeking spiritual enlightenment and inner peace. The act of being still, as described in this verse, beckons us to delve into a realm of tranquility and inner silence, paving the way for a deeper connection with the divine.

The phrase "Be still" encapsulates the idea of finding a calm and tranquil state within oneself. In our fast-paced, often chaotic lives, this inner stillness is like an oasis of serenity. It suggests the need to quiet the restless mind and soothe the often-turbulent emotions. In essence, it's an invitation to create a sanctuary within our hearts and minds where we can commune with the divine.

As we delve deeper into the meaning of "Be still," we encounter the concept of "know that I am God." This knowing is not mere intellectual understanding; it is an experiential encounter with the divine. To facilitate this, the verse introduces us to the notion of single-pointed attention. This practice entails focusing one's awareness on a chosen point of concentration, whether it's the rhythm of one's breath, a mantra, the steady flicker of a candle's flame, or a sacred image. By anchoring our awareness to this point, we prevent the mind from wandering aimlessly, creating a fertile ground for spiritual growth.

A crucial aspect of this journey is the practice of letting go of thoughts. As our minds naturally generate thoughts, this practice teaches us not to judge or become entangled in them. Instead, we acknowledge thoughts as they arise and gently return our focus to the chosen point of concentration. This process is pivotal in attaining inner stillness, as it allows us to release the mental clutter that can cloud our connection with the divine.

Moreover, the cultivation of inner stillness is closely intertwined with the relaxation of the body. The verse encourages us to conduct a thorough scan of our physical form while in a state of stillness, seeking out any areas of tension or discomfort. By releasing physical tension, we enable our bodies to relax completely, enhancing our ability to achieve a tranquil mind.

The journey continues with breath awareness. This practice encourages us to observe and follow the natural rhythm of our breath without attempting to control it. This deliberate act of attention to our breath deepens our state of relaxation and presence.

Surrender and humility are also paramount elements of this spiritual quest. We are urged to approach these practices with humility and a sense of surrender, letting go of any expectations or desires for specific experiences. Instead, the focus is on being open to whatever unfolds in the process.

As we proceed, we find that the cultivation of inner stillness and silence creates a receptive space within ourselves. In this state, we become more open to the presence of God or divine consciousness. It's not about actively seeking God but about allowing God's presence to reveal itself to us in its own time and manner.

The phrase "I die daily" is found in the Bible, specifically in 1 Corinthians 15:31. In a spiritual context, this verse is often interpreted as a metaphor for the act of surrendering one's will and ego daily, allowing for a continual transformation or renewal. The idea is that by letting go of personal desires and ego-driven pursuits each day, individuals create space for a deeper connection with God, leading to a more profound and spiritually fulfilling life. It signifies a constant process of self-denial and spiritual growth, aiming to align one's life with divine principles on a daily basis.

This journey culminates in a state that can be likened to the "Kingdom of Heaven" that Jesus spoke of. It's a state of consciousness where we experience the divine within and around us. Importantly, it is not limited to a specific time or place but can be accessed in the present moment. This profound experience reflects the essence of the verse's message.

It's important to understand that achieving this state may require time and practice. Patience with oneself and a willingness to view this journey as an ongoing process are crucial. Regular meditation and mindfulness practices serve as the keys to deepening our connection with God.

Lets summarize the steps to achieve a state of inner stillness and connection with God:

1. **Inner Stillness:** To "be still" means to cultivate inner silence and tranquility. It involves quieting the mind and calming the body. You can achieve this through meditation or contemplative practices. Find a quiet place, sit comfortably, and close your eyes.

2. **Single-Pointed Attention**: Focus your attention on a single point of concentration. It could be your breath, a mantra, a candle flame, or a sacred image. The goal is to anchor your awareness and prevent your mind from wandering.

3. **Letting Go of Thoughts**: As thoughts arise, acknowledge them without judgment and gently return your focus to your chosen point of concentration. The

practice of letting go of thoughts is crucial to achieving inner stillness.

4. **Relax Your Body**: As you sit in stillness, scan your body for any tension or discomfort. Release any physical tension, allowing your body to relax completely. A relaxed body contributes to a still mind.

5. **Breath Awareness**: Pay attention to your breath. Follow the natural rhythm of your breath without trying to control it. This can help deepen your state of relaxation and presence.

6. **Surrender and Humility**: Approach this practice with humility and a sense of surrender. Release any expectations or desires for specific experiences. Instead, focus on being open to whatever may arise.

7. **Connection with God**: As you cultivate inner stillness and silence, you create a receptive space within yourself. In this state, you become more open to God or divine consciousness. It's not about actively seeking God, but about allowing God's presence to reveal itself to you.

8. **The Kingdom of Heaven**: The state of inner stillness and connection with God can be likened to the concept of the **"Kingdom of Heaven" that Jesus spoke of. It's a state of consciousness where you experience the divine within and around you. It's not limited to a specific time or place but can be accessed in the present moment.**

9. **Practice and Patience**: Achieving this state may take time and practice. Be patient with yourself and approach it as a journey. Regular meditation and mindfulness practices can help deepen your connection with God.

To close this chapter, the verse "Be still and know that I am God" serves as an ancient roadmap to finding God through inner stillness and heightened awareness. By practicing meditation and cultivating a quiet, receptive mind, we create the conditions for a direct and profound experience of the divine presence. This experience is often described as a profound sense of peace, boundless love, and an unbreakable sense of unity with all creation. Moreover, the journey entails a daily act of "dying"—shedding personal desires and ego-driven pursuits to align with divine principles continuously. This constant renewal, akin to "dying daily," forms the essence of surrender and self-denial essential for a deeper spiritual connection. Ultimately, this transformative path beckons us to explore the boundless depths of our own consciousness, leading us to discover the divine spark residing within us all.

Chapter 71

Meditation: Harnessing the Power of Breath Along the Spine

Spinal breathing, also referred to as "breath along the spine," is a specialized technique employed in meditation and yoga practices. It involves focusing one's attention on the path of the breath as it travels along the spine. This approach goes beyond the ordinary act of breathing, offering a unique and profound way to enhance the connection between the body and mind. In the following discussion, we'll delve deeper into the intricacies of spinal breathing, shedding light on its distinctive characteristics and the potential benefits it holds for mental and physical well-being.

- **Mindful Awareness**: Spinal breathing involves conscious awareness of the breath's journey along the spine. It encourages a deeper connection between the mind and the breath.
- **Energy Flow**: In some traditions, spinal breathing is thought to facilitate the flow of subtle energy, often referred to as "prana" or "chi," through the energy centers or chakras along the spine. This is believed to balance and harmonize the body and mind.

- **Mind-Body Connection:** By focusing on the spine, practitioners aim to enhance the mind-body connection. This can lead to greater relaxation, reduced stress, and increased mental clarity.
- **Slow, Deep, and Long Breathing**: Spinal breathing often involves slow, deep, and deliberate inhalations, exhalations, and pauses. This type of breathing is associated with relaxation and stress reduction. It can also promote better oxygenation of the body.
- **Spiritual and Meditative Benefits**: Spinal breathing is sometimes used as a preparatory practice for meditation. It is believed to help calm the mind and create a conducive inner environment for deeper meditation experiences.
- **Straight and Strong Like a Rock:** The image of the spine being straight and strong like a rock can symbolize steadfastness and unwavering faith. In the Bible, **Jesus spoke about building one's house on a rock as a metaphor for a solid foundation of faith.** Similarly, maintaining a straight and strong spine during meditation or spiritual practices represents grounding oneself in faith and spiritual principles.

Overall, spinal breathing is a specialized technique that extends beyond the basic function of breathing for survival. Its purpose is to tap into the body's energy and strengthen the connection between the physical body, mind, and, according to certain belief systems, the spirit. Regular breathing serves the essential function of supplying oxygen and expelling carbon dioxide, the basis of life itself. The value of spinal breathing lies in its potential to deepen the mind-body connection, promote relaxation, and prepare practitioners for more profound spiritual or meditative practices.

The practice of spinal breathing, which involves concentrated awareness and deliberate control of breath, is in alignment with principles linked to neurological advantages. This method has the potential to have a positive influence on stress reduction, emotional regulation, neuroplasticity, and cognitive functions, all of which collectively contribute to improved overall well-being and mental health. Spinal breathing essentially entails focusing along the spine as you guide your breath, and its effects on these facets of mental and physical health are worth exploring.

Neurological Benefits of Spinal Breathing

The practice of spinal breathing, focused on the mindful journey of the breath along the spine, has become a fascinating intersection of ancient mindfulness traditions and contemporary neuroscience. This practice, deeply rooted in historical wisdom, has emerged as a potent tool for tapping into the brain's potential.

In this section, we will explore the diverse neurological benefits of spinal breathing and its alignment with the field of neuroscience, emphasizing how each facet contributes to improved mental health and overall well-being, transcending the boundaries of time and tradition in our modern world.

- **Stress Reduction**: Mindful and slow breathing techniques, such as spinal breathing, have been shown to activate the body's relaxation response, reducing stress, and lowering the production of stress hormones like cortisol. This can positively affect mental well-being and overall health.

- **Enhanced Mind-Body Connection**: Neuroscience studies have shown that practices that involve focused attention, like spinal breathing, can enhance the connection between the mind and the body. This improved mind-body connection can lead to greater self-awareness and emotional regulation.

- **Neuroplasticity:** The brain's ability to rewire and adapt, known as neuroplasticity, is influenced by mindfulness and meditative practices. Regular spinal breathing might contribute to positive changes in the brain's structure and function, fostering improved cognitive abilities and emotional resilience.
- **Emotional Regulation:** *Mindful breathing practices, including spinal breathing, can activate brain regions associated with emotional regulation. This can lead to better management of negative emotions and an overall improvement in emotional well-being.*
- **Improved Focus and Concentration**: Neuroscientific research shows that mindfulness practices enhance attention and concentration. This is achieved through the activation of specific neural pathways associated with attention and concentration, reducing distractions and creating a conducive mental environment. The practice's calming effect alleviates stress, optimizing cognitive resource allocation and mental clarity. Over time, neuroplasticity adapts, enhancing cognitive abilities and sustaining heightened attention, resulting in improved focus during tasks and daily life.
- **Stress Resilience**: Through regular practice of spinal breathing, the brain's response to stress undergoes a significant transformation. This mindful technique effectively calms the body's stress response, reducing the secretion of stress-related hormones like cortisol. Simultaneously, it activates brain regions associated with emotional regulation, enabling improved management of negative emotions. These adaptations empower individuals to more effectively confront and adapt to stressful situations, ultimately leading to improved mental well-being, reduced

intensity and duration of stress, and enhanced emotional health.

Exploring the Spine Breathing Technique

As explained previously spine breathing is a relaxation and mindfulness technique that focuses on bringing awareness and breath to different parts of the spine. It can help relieve tension and promote relaxation. Here are the steps to practice spine breathing:

1. **Find a comfortable position:** Sit in a chair with your feet flat on the floor or lie down on your back on a comfortable surface. Ensure that your spine is in a neutral position and your body is relaxed.

2. **Close your eyes:** Close your eyes to eliminate distractions and promote inward focus.

3. **Deep breathing:** Start with a few deep breaths to relax and center yourself. Inhale slowly through your nose, allowing your abdomen to expand, and then exhale slowly through your mouth. Repeat this a few times.

4. **Focus on the base of your spine:** Direct your attention to the base of your spine, also known as the sacrum. As you inhale, imagine your breath flowing into this area. Feel it expanding and relaxing with each breath.

5. **Move up the spine:** Slowly shift your focus up your spine, one vertebra at a time. Inhale and exhale as you move your awareness to each segment of the spine, allowing it to become more supple and relaxed with each breath.

6. **Take your time:** Pay attention to any areas of tension or discomfort along the way. If you encounter tightness, try to breathe into those areas and release the tension.

7. **Continue to the top of the spine:** Keep moving your awareness up your spine until you reach the top, just below the base of your skull.

8. **Full spine breathing:** Now, take a few moments to breathe in and out, allowing your entire spine to relax and expand with each breath. Feel the breath circulating through your entire spinal column.

9. **Repeat as needed:** You can repeat this process as many times as you like, focusing on the full length of your spine, or concentrate on specific areas that need attention.

10. **Gradual return to normal breathing:** When you're ready, gradually transition back to your normal breathing pattern. Take a few deep breaths, wiggle your fingers and toes, and open your eyes.

Spinal breathing, when incorporated into your daily routine, supports relaxation and mindfulness by raising bodily awareness and alleviating spine tension. This gradual practice can foster better posture and an enhanced sense of well-being. In essence, spinal breathing, with its focus on controlled breathing and mindful attention, aligns with principles that yield neurological benefits, including stress reduction, emotional regulation, neuroplasticity, and cognitive improvement, collectively enhancing mental well-being.

Chapter 72

Yoga Sutra & Advanced Spinal Breathing

The Yoga Sutras (Guideline) of Patanjali (philosopher) and the Spinal Breathing practice are related in that both focus on aspects of yoga, meditation, and breath control, but they have distinct differences.

The Yoga Sutras of Patanjali provide a comprehensive philosophical and practical guide to the practice of yoga. They consist of 196 aphorisms that cover various aspects of yoga, meditation, and the path to spiritual awakening. The specific sutra related to breath control and pranayama, found in Book 2, Sutra 49, emphasizes the regulation of breath to control and expand consciousness. This sutra is a fundamental text in the practice of yoga and serves as a foundational guideline for various yogic practices, including pranayama, meditation, and mindfulness.

In this transformative practice, *we embark on a journey toward a profound stillness of both mind and body,* **Psalm 46:10, "Be Still and Know or Experience, that I am God."** The key lies in setting the stage with a positive and joyful attitude, anticipating the serene state we are about to enter. Central to this practice is unwavering commitment—commitment to unwavering focus on our breath.

Spinal Breathing, on the other hand, is a specific breathing and meditation technique that involves focused awareness on the spine, particularly the left and right sides. It is a practical exercise that can be used as a part of a broader yoga or meditation practice to enhance one's mental and physical well-being. The practice involves inhaling along one side of the spine and exhaling along the other, with a focus on energizing the energy centers or chakras along the way. It aims to balance and invigorate the mind, promote relaxation, and enhance the mind-body connection.

While both the Yoga Sutras and Spinal Breathing share an emphasis on breath control and meditation, the major difference is in their scope and purpose. The Yoga Sutras provide a comprehensive philosophy and guide to yoga and spiritual growth, covering a wide range of topics beyond just breath control. Spinal Breathing, on the other hand, is a specific technique within the broader context of yogic and meditative practices, with a more specific focus on breath control and the energy centers along the spine.

Yoga Sutras of Patanjali

The Yoga Sutras of Patanjali are not a physical practice like yoga asanas (postures) or pranayama (breath control). Instead, they are a philosophical and spiritual guide that provides insights into the path of yoga and meditation. Therefore, you don't "do" the Yoga Sutras in the same way you would practice physical yoga postures.

However, you can study and apply the teachings of the Yoga Sutras in your yoga and meditation practice. Here are steps to help you integrate the wisdom of the Yoga Sutras into your practice:

Steps to Apply the Wisdom of the Yoga Sutras

- **Study the Text:** Begin by reading and studying the Yoga Sutras of Patanjali. Familiarize yourself with the sutras and their translations.
- **Select a Sutra:** Choose a specific sutra or set of sutras that resonate with you or address an aspect of your yoga and meditation practice that you wish to explore.
- **Reflect and Contemplate:** Delve into the meaning and implications of the selected sutra. Reflect on how it applies to your life and practice.
- **Meditation and Mindfulness:** Incorporate the wisdom of the sutra into your meditation and mindfulness practice. Use the sutra as a point of focus during your meditation sessions.
- **Apply in Asana Practice:** If the sutra relates to physical postures or alignment, apply it to your yoga asana practice. Use the sutra's teachings to improve your alignment and deepen your understanding of the postures.
- **Incorporate into Breath Control (Pranayama):** If the sutra is related to breath control (pranayama), use it as a guide for your pranayama practice. Apply the sutra's principles to your breath control techniques.
- **Lifestyle Integration:** Implement the sutra's teachings into your daily life. This may involve making conscious decisions and adopting a yogic lifestyle that aligns with the sutra's wisdom.
- **Self-Reflection:** Regularly reflect on your progress and inner growth as you integrate the sutra into your practice and daily life. Consider how it has impacted your spiritual journey.
- **Seek Guidance:** If you have questions or challenges related to the sutra, seek guidance from experienced yoga

teachers or mentors who can provide insights and support.

- **Consistency:** Continue to engage with the chosen sutra and the broader teachings of the Yoga Sutras in your practice. Consistency is key to deepening your understanding and experiencing the transformative power of the sutras.

Advanced Spinal Breathing Practice

As previously mentioned, spinal breathing is a distinct meditation and breathing method that combines attentive awareness directed towards the spine. This technique offers a practical exercise within the broader domain of yoga and meditation, with the aim of improving mental and physical well-being. In addition to the standard spinal breathing steps, there are additional advanced steps that involve focused awareness on both sides of the spine.

For the Advanced Spinal Breathing Practice

1. **Shift your attention to the base of your spine's left side,** invigorating it with your breath.
2. **Inhale and exhale through your nose,** charging each energy center along the spine, such as the Sacral Center, Solar Plexus Center, Heart Center, Throat Area, and the crown of the head.
3. **Follow with the exhalation ritual,** moving your breath down the right side.
4. **Consider a pause and then renew your inhalation.** This practice can heighten your intuition, sharpen your insight, boost concentration, and elevate your awareness.

5. **Gradual Progression:** Gradually extend your practice time, starting with at least ten minutes, while maintaining an upright posture.

These steps encompass the essence of both the Yoga Sutras and the Spinal Breathing practice, with the former offering a comprehensive philosophical foundation for yoga and breath control and the latter providing a specific meditative and breathing technique to enhance mindfulness and mental well-being.

Effects of Advanced Spinal Breathing Practice

- **Brain Function:** This practice can influence the brain by promoting relaxation and reducing stress. When you focus your attention on specific areas of the body, like the spine, and combine it with intentional breathing, it can engage the brain's attention networks. This can lead to a calming effect, as it shifts your focus away from daily worries and anxieties.

- **Hemispheric Balance:** The practice of moving your attention up and down the spine can also affect hemispheric balance. When you focus on the left side during inhalation and the right-side during exhalation, you're engaging both hemispheres of the brain. The left hemisphere is associated with logical and analytical thinking, while the right hemisphere is linked to creativity and intuition. Balancing the activity of these hemispheres can contribute to overall mental well-being and cognitive harmony.

- **Brain Regions Involved:** Various brain regions are involved in breath and meditation practices. The prefrontal cortex, for instance, is associated with attention, decision-making, and personality development. The anterior cingulate cortex is linked to self-regulation and emotional processing. These regions may be influenced positively by the practice, contributing to improved mental clarity, focus, and emotional regulation.

- **Benefits:** Practicing these techniques can have several benefits, including stress reduction, increased mental clarity, heightened self-awareness, and improved emotional regulation. It can lead to a greater sense of inner peace and tranquility.

Caution: Although these methods are safe and advantageous, there are some important considerations to bear in mind, such as:

- **Physical Comfort:** Ensure that you're physically comfortable when practicing these techniques. Sit or lie down in a posture that doesn't strain your body.
- **Gradual Progression:** If you're new to these practices, start gradually and don't force yourself into advanced techniques. Let your body and mind adapt.
- **Consultation:** If you have any medical or psychological conditions, consult with a healthcare professional or mental health expert before beginning advanced practices.
- **Consistency:** Consistency in your practice is important. Avoid irregular practice, as the benefits often accumulate.
- **Mindfulness:** Maintain mindfulness during your practice. If you ever feel discomfort or anxiety, return to natural, relaxed breathing.
- **Respect Individual Differences:** Understand that people may have unique experiences with these practices. What works well for one person might not be suitable for another.

In summary, the process of centering your attention on the spine while regulating your breath can yield substantial benefits for brain function, emotional well-being, and overall mental health. This practice is not only safe but also highly advantageous, provided it is pursued with mindfulness, an acknowledgment of individual variations, and a willingness to seek guidance when necessary. Over time, steadfast dedication to this practice can lead to a profound comprehension of the mind-body connection and an improved state of holistic health.

Additionally, the Yoga Sutras serve as a wellspring of profound philosophical and spiritual insights that can profoundly enrich your yoga and meditation journey. By immersing yourself in the wisdom of the sutras and applying their teachings to your practice, you can attain a deeper grasp of yoga's fundamental principles and seamlessly integrate them into your daily life.

Chapter 73

Energy and Consciousness

The concept that everything is energy and that humans can bring their desires to reality through energy sources is rooted in certain metaphysical and spiritual beliefs. It suggests that our thoughts and intentions have the power to shape our experiences. Some argue that consciousness itself is a fundamental aspect of the universe, and our thoughts and intentions are potent forces that interact with this universal consciousness.

The biblical concept of "Ask and you shall receive" encourages seeking and believing in fulfilling one's desires through faith and prayer. It can be related to the idea of "Knowing," in the sense of having faith and certainty in the outcome. Manifestation builds upon this concept by involving deliberate practices and the alignment of energies to bring about desired outcomes, based on the belief in the influence of consciousness and energy on physical reality. These ideas are rooted in various belief systems and philosophical perspectives and have different interpretations and applications in real life.

Neurological Connection

The neurological connection in the context of Energy and Consciousness involves the interaction between our cognitive processes, the brain, and the flow of energy. Here's how this connection works:

- **Brain Activity:** When we engage in intentional, focused thoughts and intentions related to energy and consciousness, our brain becomes actively involved. The prefrontal cortex, responsible for executive functions like attention and decision-making, is engaged as we concentrate on these concepts.

- **Hemispheric Balance:** Focusing on the balance and harmonization of energy in our thoughts can help balance brain activity between the left and right hemispheres, enhancing cognitive function and emotional well-being.

- **Activation of Brain Regions:** Various brain regions are activated during this practice. The anterior cingulate cortex, for instance, is involved in emotional regulation and self-awareness. Concentrating on energy and consciousness can stimulate these regions, potentially improving emotional control and self-awareness.

- **Neurotransmitters:** The practice can influence the release of neurotransmitters, the brain's chemical messengers. Focused energy-related thoughts and intentions can trigger the release of neurotransmitters like serotonin and gamma-amino-butyric acid (GABA), associated with mood stabilization and relaxation.

- **Autonomic Nervous System:** Our thoughts about energy and consciousness can affect the autonomic nervous system, which regulates bodily functions like heart rate, digestion, and respiratory rate. By focusing on these aspects, we can promote relaxation and reduce the "fight or flight" stress response.

- **Mind-Body Connection:** By directing our attention to the interaction between energy and consciousness, we strengthen the mind-body connection, essential for achieving a state of enhanced consciousness and emotional balance.

Understanding this neurological connection helps individuals harness the benefits of energy and consciousness practices to improve mental clarity, emotional well-being, and inner peace.

Crucial Connection Points

Within the context of Energy and Consciousness, it's vital to understand the significance of connection points where these two elements intersect. These connection points represent the junctures where energy and consciousness seamlessly interact to shape our experiences.

Similar to synapses in neural communication, these connection points serve as gateways where the interplay between energy and consciousness influences our thoughts, emotions, and actions. They are pivotal for realizing our desires and manifesting our intentions.

As we delve into the understanding of these connection points, we realize that they hold the key to harnessing the potential of energy and consciousness to shape our reality. Just like the synaptic gap in neural communication, these connection points offer a moment of transition and potential, where our energy and consciousness align, enabling us to consciously direct their impact on our experiences.

As we explore these connection points more deeply, we can tap into the boundless potential of energy and consciousness to mold our reality and attain a state of profound inner peace and self-realization. Whether we are focusing on balancing energy or aligning consciousness, these connection points serve as the pathways to unlock our true potential.

The Harmonious Energies of Existence: A Symphony of Grace and Purpose

In the tapestry of our lives, three distinct energies weave their threads, each originating from the wellspring of Ultimate Energy. The first energy is a radiant beacon, casting its light upon our path, guiding us to enlightenment and uplifting our spirits. It's as if the very cosmos conspires to whisper courage into our hearts.

Yet, there is a second energy, a shadowy presence that can stir fear within us, like a tempestuous wind threatening to pull us down into the depths of uncertainty. It's the energy that rattles our resolve, tests our mettle, and sometimes leaves us trembling in its wake.

The third energy, a steady hand upon the cosmic scales, keeps us in equilibrium, neither allowing us to soar unchecked nor permitting us to plummet into despair. This energy serves as an anchor, ensuring that our journey remains balanced, steadfast, and unswayed by the turbulent currents that seek to sway us.

In the dance of life, it's imperative for each of us to become attuned to these energies, to recognize their distinct rhythms and melodies. The radiant energy beckons us to step into the light, while the shadowy energy reminds us to stand vigilant against its illusions, lest we succumb to its grip. And amid it all, the stabilizing energy, like a guardian of harmony, keeps us centered and poised.

For those who may wander in ignorance, it's a cautionary tale—a reminder to be wary of the energy that seeks to drag them downward. It's a call to awareness, a plea to recognize the subtle forces at play and to navigate the currents with a clear-eyed understanding. And as we become attuned to these energies, we learn to harness their ebb and flow, navigating the symphony of existence with grace and purpose.

Conclusion

In our exploration of the profound connection between energy, consciousness, and the timeless wisdom of "Ask and you shall receive," we uncover a profound truth: the art of manifestation is not just about asking and taking action; it's also about having unwavering faith and understanding the intricate neurological processes and crucial connection points at play.

When we ask, we set in motion a process that resonates with the universal consciousness, activating the alignment of energies to fulfill our desires. However, the pivotal element of faith serves as the bedrock upon which this journey of manifestation is built. Faith fuels our intentions, transforming them from mere requests into powerful affirmations. It's the unwavering belief in the possibility of our desires becoming a reality.

Our understanding of the neurological processes involved in this journey provides us with the tools to enhance our mental clarity, emotional well-being, and inner peace. These insights are the foundation upon which we build our faith, for it is in the awareness of our neurological responses that we find the strength to persist in our quest.

Just as synapses in neural communication enable the transmission of information, the crucial connection points in energy and consciousness guide our thoughts and intentions to manifest our deepest desires. They serve as gateways where faith and action converge, enabling us to consciously direct our energy towards our aspirations.

In the symphony of life, three essential energies converge, all sourced from the wellspring of Ultimate Energy. The first radiates as a guiding light, leading us toward enlightenment and uplifting our spirits. Conversely, the second energy, shadowy and tempestuous, tests our mettle and threatens uncertainty. The third energy acts as a stabilizing force, maintaining balance and preventing unchecked ascent or descent. Attuning ourselves to these energies is vital—

responding to the radiant call, staying vigilant against the shadow's illusions, and embracing the stabilizing force that keeps us centered. It's a cautionary tale for the unaware, urging mindfulness and recognition of subtle forces to navigate life's symphony with grace and purpose.

So, as we embark on our journey of manifestation, let us remember that having faith is the cornerstone, and action is the bridge, but it's the harmony of our energies, the conscious direction of our thoughts, and the unwavering commitment to take action that ultimately paves the way for our dreams to come true. This holistic approach empowers us to manifest a life where our deepest desires are not just asked for but received, experienced, and lived. It's a journey of faith, action, and understanding, where our dreams and aspirations become our reality through the unity of thought, energy, and decisive action.

Chapter 74

Iconic Symbolism: Trishul (5000 BC) vs. Cross (100 AD)

T he Trishul and the Cross stand as iconic symbols within Hinduism and Christianity, encapsulating profound beliefs and cultural significance. These symbols, rooted in ancient wisdom, echo interconnected themes that transcend time, culture, and religion. Both emblematic representations reflect a trinitarian essence, embodying cycles, balance, transformation, and divine energies. The Trishul, with its three prongs symbolizing creation, preservation, and destruction, mirrors the cyclical nature of existence in Hindu philosophy. Similarly, the Cross, representing the Father, the Son, and the Holy Spirit in Christianity, signifies redemption and a linear narrative of salvation. Delving deeper into these symbols unveils their shared principles: balance, transformative energies, and cyclical existence, offering a tapestry of insights into the human experience. Moreover, beyond their religious contexts, these symbols resonate across psychological, neurological, and spiritual dimensions, providing a profound lens through which to understand the intricate dance of life's elements. Let's delve further into these profound symbols to unravel their intricate meanings and explore their significance in greater detail.

Interconnected Themes

The year 5000 BC (Before Christ) predates 100 AD (Anno Domini). Within the Gregorian calendar, commonly utilized today, BC signifies years preceding the traditional birth date of Jesus Christ, whereas AD denotes years following his birth. Therefore, 5000 BC signifies an era significantly earlier than 100 AD.

Cyclical Nature

Both the Trishul and the Cross, with their trinitarian symbolism, embody the cyclic nature of existence. The Trishul signifies the perpetual cycle of life, encompassing creation, preservation, and destruction. Similarly, the Cross represents a continuous cycle of spiritual progression, preservation, and transformation. Both symbols encapsulate the cyclical essence inherent in life and spirituality.

Balance and Harmony

The Trishul, a symbol prominent in Hinduism associated with Lord Shiva, is characterized by its three prongs or tridents converging into a single point. Each prong symbolizes fundamental aspects of existence, embodying creation, preservation, and destruction or representing the **three states of consciousness: waking, dreaming, and deep sleep.** This symbol emphasizes the equilibrium between opposing forces, teaching the significance of harmonizing these dynamics to achieve spiritual growth and balance. By acknowledging the cyclical nature of life and the interconnectedness of these forces, the Trishul encourages an understanding that maintaining balance between contrasting principles is vital for inner harmony.

Conversely, the Cross, a symbol profoundly significant in Christianity, represents the crucifixion of Jesus Christ and embodies the concept of the Holy Trinity—Father, Son, and Holy Spirit. It signifies the divine relationship and seeks balance within this trinity. The Cross symbolizes unity and interconnection among these three distinct entities, portraying the idea of spiritual completeness through their harmonious coexistence. By showcasing the balance within God's nature and the unity of the Holy Trinity, the Cross underscores the importance of embracing diverse elements in spirituality to attain a state of balance and wholeness.

Transformation and Renewal

The third prong of the Trishul and the Holy Spirit in the Cross both embody transformative energy, signifying the necessity of change, renewal, and spiritual growth.

While these interpretations connect the symbols with three forms of energy, it's essential to recognize that symbolism is subjective and can vary across different cultural and religious contexts. These connections highlight the universal themes of balance, transformation, and the cyclical nature of existence.

The **radiant energy,** symbolizing enlightenment, and upliftment is accessed through a commitment to self-discovery, learning, and embracing positivity. It involves cultivating a mindset of growth, openness, and a willingness to follow the guiding light that the cosmos provides.

Conversely, **shadowy energy,** representative of challenges and uncertainties, causes resilience and introspection. Facing fears head-on, acknowledging vulnerabilities, and finding strength in adversity are integral to navigating this energy. It involves a process of self-reflection, confronting inner demons, and emerging stronger on the other side.

The **stabilizing energy**, acting as a cosmic anchor, requires a delicate balance. It involves practicing mindfulness, moderation, and maintaining equilibrium amidst life's fluctuations. This energy encourages individuals to stay grounded, avoiding extremes, and fostering a sense of inner stability.

The transition from one energy status to another is a nuanced process, reflecting the intricate dance of life's elements. The methods and steps involved in this transformation are deeply personal, rooted in self-awareness and conscious choices.

The choice of which energy status to predominantly inhabit throughout one's lifetime is subjective and can vary based on individual temperament, circumstances, and personal goals. Ideally, a harmonious integration of all three energies is sought, creating a balanced and fulfilling existence.

Compared to trinity systems from ancient and modern contexts, the three energies in this tapestry align with the concept of balance and equilibrium. Ancient trinities often symbolize creation, preservation, and destruction, or mind, body, and spirit. Similarly, the radiant, shadowy, and stabilizing energies reflect a harmonious interplay of forces, guiding individuals through the intricate symphony of life. Modern psychological models also acknowledge the importance of balance, resilience, and self-awareness in navigating life's complexities. The trinity in this narrative serves as a metaphorical framework for understanding and harmonizing the diverse energies inherent in human experience.

Symbolic Significance: Exploring Spiritual, Psychological, and Neurological Dimensions

The "Trishul," or "Trident" and the "Cross" are significant symbols in Hinduism and Christianity, respectively, and they each carry deep religious and cultural meanings.

Trishul (Trident) in Sanatan Dharma

The Trishul, also known as the Trident, carries profound significance within Hinduism, closely linked with the deity Shiva. Its three prongs serve as symbols representing the core elements of the divine: **creation, preservation, and destruction.** More than a simple emblem, it encapsulates the cosmic equilibrium and synergy among energies. In Hindu philosophy, the Trishul's prongs further symbolize the three gunas (qualities) – Sattva (goodness), Rajas (passion), and Tamas (ignorance) – portraying the spiritual voyage towards elevated consciousness.

Cross in Christianity

Within Christianity, the Cross symbolizes the trinity of Father, Son, and Holy Spirit and their connection to the crucifixion of Jesus Christ. It embodies the core principles of the Christian faith: spirituality, divine guidance, harmonious relationships, compassion, and love among humanity.

The Cross stands as a powerful symbol of redemption and salvation, signifying Jesus' sacrifice for humanity's sins and offering the promise of eternal life. Embracing this belief requires acknowledging personal faults, seeking forgiveness, and embodying a sacrificial mindset of selflessness, compassion, and service to others.

Similar to the Trishul, the Cross reflects the trinitarian understanding of God as Father, Son, and Holy Spirit, a central concept in Christian theology emphasizing the unity of these divine entities.

Comparisons

- **Trinity Representation:** Both symbols encapsulate a trinity of divine facets. Within Sanatan Dharma, the Trishul embodies the essence of creation, preservation, and destruction—a triadic force. In Christianity, the Cross symbolizes the triune presence of the Godfather, Son, and Holy Spirit.
- **Cyclical versus Linear Concept:** The Trishul hints at existence's cyclical nature, entwined with the

perpetual cycle of creation, preservation, and destruction. Conversely, the Cross is often linked with a linear narrative of salvation and redemption within Christian theology.

- **Cultural and Religious Significance:** These symbols bear profound cultural and religious weight within their respective traditions, influencing rituals, worship practices, and philosophical teachings.

In essence, while both symbols express a trinity and carry spiritual importance, they do so within the context of their distinct religious lineages—Sanatan Dharma and Christianity. The Trishul underscores life's cyclical essence and cosmic equilibrium, while the Cross represents redemption and the threefold nature of God within a linear narrative.

Human existence is fluid, and individuals frequently encounter and navigate diverse energies or circumstances, encompassing emotional and situational states. Here, we'll delve into how these energies can interchangeably manifest:

Positive and Negative Emotions

- **Interchangeability:** Human emotions are diverse and can range from joy and love to sadness and fear. These emotional energies are often interchangeable and can shift based on experiences, relationships, and external factors.
- **Adaptability:** People can adapt and transform negative emotions into positive ones through various coping mechanisms, resilience, and personal growth.

Life Phases

- **Interchangeability:** Life unfolds in phases, such as childhood, adolescence, adulthood, and old age. Each phase brings its own set of energies, challenges, and opportunities.
- **Transition and Growth:** Individual's experience transitions between these phases, and the energies associated with each phase can be interchangeable as people learn, adapt, and grow.

Professional and Personal Life

- **Interchangeability:** Balancing professional and personal life involves navigating different energies. Work-related stress or success can influence personal well-being and vice versa.
- **Integration:** Finding a balance and integrating the energies from both spheres contributes to a more harmonious and fulfilling life.

Health and Wellness

- **Interchangeability:** Physical and mental health are interconnected. Positive lifestyle choices, such as exercise and nutrition, can positively affect mental well-being, and vice versa.
- **Holistic Approach:** Adopting a holistic approach to health acknowledges the interchangeable nature of physical and mental energies, promoting overall well-being.

Social and Solitary Energies

- **Interchangeability:** Human beings have social needs, but they also require moments of solitude for reflection and recharge. Balancing social interactions with personal time is crucial for mental and emotional health.
- **Self-awareness:** Recognizing when to engage with others and when to seek solitude allows individuals to manage their energy effectively.

Understanding and navigating these interchangeable energies involves self-awareness, adaptability, and a willingness to embrace the ebb and flow of life. It's about recognizing that energies, whether positive or negative, are not static but can be transformed and channeled in different ways to promote personal growth and well-being.

Recognizing and managing your energy states involves self-awareness and intentional practices. Here are some steps to help you recognize your current energy state and shift to a more desired one:

Recognizing Your Energy State

Mindful Observation

- **Practice mindfulness:** Regularly check in with yourself to observe your thoughts, emotions, and physical sensations.
- **Non-judgmental awareness:** Be open and non-judgmental about what you observe. Accept your feelings without criticism.

Emotional Check-in

- **Label your emotions:** Identify and label your emotions. This helps you understand your current emotional state.

- **Journaling:** Keep a journal to reflect on your feelings and identify patterns over time.

Body Awareness

- **Scan your body:** Pay attention to physical sensations. Tension, fatigue, or relaxation can provide insights into your energy state.
- **Posture and gestures:** Notice how you carry yourself. Body language can reflect your emotional and energetic state.

Feedback from Others

- **Ask for feedback:** Trusted friends or family members can provide valuable insights into your energy state.
- **Listen to observations:** Be open to feedback without defensiveness.

Changing Your Energy State

Positive Mindset

- **Cognitive reframing:** Challenge negative thoughts and reframe them in a more positive light.
- **Gratitude practice:** Focus on what you're grateful for by shifting your mindset.

Physical Activity

- **Exercise:** Physical activity releases endorphins and can positively affect your mood and energy levels.

- **Stretching and deep breathing:** Incorporate stretching and deep-breathing exercises to relax your body and mind.

Environmental Influence

- **Change your surroundings:** Step outside, go for a walk, or create a calming space to influence your energy positively.
- **Declutter:** A tidy space can contribute to a clearer mind.

Social Connection

- **Connect with others:** Spend time with supportive friends or family to uplift your spirits.
- **Express feelings:** Share your thoughts and emotions with someone you trust.

Self-Care Practices

- **Rest and sleep:** Ensure you're getting enough restorative sleep.
- **Hobbies and activities:** Engage in activities you enjoy and that brings you a sense of fulfillment.

Mindfulness and Meditation

- **Mindful breathing:** Practice deep, intentional breathing to center yourself.
- **Meditation:** Regular meditation can help calm the mind and promote emotional balance.

Set Goals

- **Small, achievable goals:** Break down larger tasks into smaller, manageable goals.
- **Celebrate achievements:** Acknowledge and celebrate your successes, no matter how small.

Remember, changing your energy state is a gradual process, and it may require experimentation to find what works best for you. Consistent self-awareness and intentional efforts toward positive changes can lead to a more balanced and fulfilling life.

Neurological Implications: The symbolism of balance and transformation aligns with neurological concepts of adaptability and neuroplasticity. Embracing change and seeking balance can positively affect neural pathways, influencing mental states and emotional resilience.

Spiritual Connection: These symbols embody spiritual teachings that resonate with the human spirit. They encourage introspection, growth, and pursuing a balance between the physical and spiritual aspects of life, aligning with the interconnectedness of mind, body, and spirit in spiritual and neurological contexts.

Overall, these symbols offer a multidimensional perspective that transcends cultural and religious boundaries, encompassing psychological, neurological, and spiritual dimensions of human experience. They illustrate the interplay between ancient wisdom and modern understanding, bridging the gap between traditional symbolism and contemporary neurological science.

Chapter 75

Body Scan Meditation

The "Body Scan Meditation" is a type of meditation where you focus on different parts of your body one by one, starting from your toes and moving up to your head and then back down. Although it's not tied to traditional Sanskrit texts, it's a mindfulness meditation practice that you can find in various contemporary meditation traditions. Here are the general steps for Body Scan Meditation:

1. Find a comfortable and quiet place to sit or lie down.
2. Close your eyes and take a few deep breaths to relax.
3. Begin by paying attention to your toes, focusing on the sensations in your toes, any tension, or relaxation you feel.
4. Slowly shift your focus up to your feet, then ankles, calves, knees, thighs, and so on, working your way up through your body.
5. Pay attention to any sensations, tensions, or areas of relaxation as you move through each body part.

6. Continue scanning up through your abdomen, chest, shoulders, arms, neck, and head.

7. When you reach the top of your head, pause for a moment to scan your entire body, observing how it feels.

8. Then, slowly reverse the process, bringing your attention back down through each body part, all the way back to your toes.

9. Throughout this practice, maintain a gentle, non-judgmental awareness of your body and its sensations.

10. Take your time and breathe naturally, allowing any tension to release and promoting relaxation.

This meditation helps with grounding, relaxation, and mindfulness. You can adapt and practice it in various ways to suit your preferences and needs. While it's not a specific practice from ancient Sanskrit texts, it aligns with the principles of mindfulness and self-awareness found in meditation traditions.

The Body Scan Meditation, which involves focusing on different body parts sequentially, offers several potential neurological benefits:

1. **Stress Reduction:** By systematically relaxing each part of the body, this meditation activates the body's relaxation response, reducing stress hormones like cortisol and promoting a calmer state of mind.

2. **Increased Mindfulness:** Practicing awareness of bodily sensations enhances mindfulness, which has been associated with changes in brain structures related to attention, memory, and self-awareness.

3. **Pain Management:** Body scan techniques can be beneficial for individuals dealing with chronic pain conditions, as heightened awareness and relaxation may help reduce perceived pain levels.

4. **Improved Sleep:** The practice of relaxing the body part by part can help achieve a relaxed state conducive to better sleep, positively impacting brain function.

5. **Emotional Regulation:** Mind-body practices like the body scan can improve emotional regulation by enhancing self-awareness, leading to better coping with emotional stressors.

6. **Enhanced Brain Connectivity:** Regular practices, including body scans, have been linked to changes in brain connectivity patterns associated with improved cognitive function.

7. **Reduced Anxiety:** The relaxation response elicited by this practice can help reduce symptoms of anxiety, potentially affecting the brain regions responsible for anxiety regulation.

Consistent engagement in body scan meditation can enhance overall well-being and mental health. These neurological advantages stem from the intricate connection between the mind and body, influenced by the practice of mindfulness on brain structure and function. Let's explore this further.

The brain is divided into two hemispheres: the left hemisphere and the right hemisphere, connected by a bundle of nerve fibers called the corpus callosum. These two hemispheres work together to control various functions in the body and handle different aspects of cognition and motor function. Here's a basic overview of their connection and effects on the body:

Left Hemisphere

- Associated with analytical and logical functions.
- Controls the right side of the body, processing movements and sensory input from the right side.

- Functions related to language processing, mathematical abilities, and logical reasoning are attributed to the left hemisphere.
- It's more active when engaged in tasks requiring detailed analysis or language skills.

Right Hemisphere

- Linked to creative and artistic functions.
- Controls the left side of the body, processing movements and sensory input from the left side.
- Functions such as spatial perception, creativity, artistic abilities, and recognizing emotional cues in others are associated with the right hemisphere.
- It's more active during tasks involving creativity or pattern recognition.

Breathing through the nostrils can also have a significant impact on brain and neurological system, especially when considering the concept in yoga and alternative medicine known as "Nadi Shodhana" or "alternate nostril breathing." According to this practice:

- **Left Nostril Breathing:** It's believed to activate the right hemisphere of the brain, associated with calmness and relaxation. This type of breathing may help reduce stress, lower blood pressure, and promote tranquility.
- **Right Nostril Breathing:** It's thought to activate the left hemisphere of the brain, associated with alertness and energy. This type of breathing may help increase alertness, concentration, and vitality.

Practitioners of alternate nostril breathing use it to balance the activity of both brain hemispheres and achieve a sense of equilibrium in body and mind. While there is some evidence suggesting these effects, more research is needed to fully understand the physiological mechanisms behind these practices. Many people find them helpful for relaxation and stress reduction and often use them as part of yoga and meditation routines.

The "Power Breath," "Pauses Between the Breaths," and "Achieving Breathless State - Advanced Practice" involve controlled breathing aligned with the concept of Kundalini energy in yoga philosophy. This practice is associated with awakening spiritual energy from the base of the spine to the crown of the head, believed to have profound effects on the mind, body, and spirit. Here are the benefits and neurological advantages:

1. **Balancing Energy:** Kundalini yoga aims to balance and activate the flow of energy (prana or chi) within the body, promoting overall well-being.

2. **Chakra Activation:** Kundalini energy passes through and activates various chakras along the spine, associated with specific qualities. Activating and harmonizing these chakras brings about balance in life.

3. **Neurological Harmony:** Kundalini practices harmonize the left and right brain hemispheres and awaken dormant energy centers along the spine, promoting creativity and logical thinking.

4. **Enhanced Mind-Body Connection:** Practitioners often report heightened awareness, increased mindfulness, better self-regulation, and inner peace.

5. **Stress Reduction:** Kundalini practices, including controlled breathing, help reduce stress and anxiety due to their calming and grounding effects.

6. **Spiritual Growth:** Kundalini awakening is associated with spiritual growth, a deeper understanding of the self, and a connection to higher states of consciousness.

7. **Neuroplasticity:** These practices may enhance neuroplasticity, leading to improved cognitive function and emotional resilience.

Kundalini practices are advanced and should be learned from experienced teachers for safety. Individual experiences vary, and it's essential to practice mindfully and with guidance.

Breathing practices involving left or right side nostril breathing, like alternate nostril breathing, are believed to have specific effects on the mind and body:

1. **Balancing Brain Hemispheres:** The practice balances the left and right brain hemispheres, promoting mental equilibrium.
2. **Calming and Grounding:** Inhaling from the left nostril has a calming and grounding effect, reducing stress and promoting emotional stability.
3. **Clearing Energy Channels:** It's thought to clear energy channels, enhancing vitality and well-being.
4. **Improved Concentration:** Exhaling from the right nostril enhances alertness and concentration.
5. **Stress Reduction:** Overall, this practice is associated with stress reduction, lowering stress levels and physiological stress responses.
6. **Enhanced Breath Awareness:** Focused attention on the breath enhances breath awareness, beneficial for meditation and mindfulness.
7. **Balancing Autonomic Nervous System:** It's believed to balance the autonomic nervous system, promoting the "rest and digest" state.

While many find these practices beneficial, experiences can vary, and more research is needed. If interested, learn from qualified instructors. Always consult your physician or advisor before starting any practice.

In conclusion, the Body Scan Meditation, a contemporary mindfulness practice, offers numerous neurological benefits that can significantly enhance overall well-being and mental health. By systematically focusing on different body parts, this meditation helps reduce stress, increase mindfulness, manage pain, improve sleep, enhance emotional regulation, and foster improved brain connectivity. This practice demonstrates the profound connection between the mind and body and underscores the potential for positive changes in brain structure and function through the cultivation of mindfulness and self-awareness.

Furthermore, exploring the intricate connection between the left and right brain hemispheres reveals the fascinating role of brain lateralization in controlling various aspects of cognition and motor function. The practice of alternate nostril breathing, as seen in yoga's Nadi Shodhana technique, offers an interesting perspective on how the manipulation of airflow through each nostril can influence the brain's state and, consequently, our mental and emotional well-being. Similarly, the advanced practice of Kundalini yoga, with its focus on awakening spiritual energy and harmonizing brain hemispheres, can lead to a myriad of benefits, from improved neuroplasticity to heightened mindfulness and spiritual growth. As we continue to explore these practices, it's crucial to seek guidance from experienced instructors and remain open to future research that can further unravel the physiological mechanisms behind these techniques.

Chapter 76

Pauses Between the Breaths

The pauses between breaths, commonly referred to as "kumbhaka" in the realms of yoga and meditation, hold profound significance. These moments of stillness form an integral part of pranayama (breath control) and meditation techniques. They represent a bridge between the physical and the metaphysical, acting as a fulcrum upon which the balance of inner harmony, energy preservation, and heightened consciousness rests. In this exploration, we delve into the multifaceted importance of these breath pauses and how they lead to a breathless state, a state of transcendence that opens the gateway to profound inner peace and self-discovery.

- **Balance:** The pauses between breaths serve as a balancing point between inhalation and exhalation. In yoga philosophy, this balance represents the harmonization of opposites, such as yin and yang or the sun and the moon, symbolizing equilibrium in life.
- **Mind-Body Connection:** These pauses encourage practitioners to develop a strong connection between the

mind and body. As you become aware of these pauses, your focus turns inward, promoting mindfulness and concentration.

- **Energy Conservation:** Just like rest is essential in a dynamic activity, pauses between breaths allow the body to rest from the continuous cycle of inhalation and exhalation. This rest conserves energy and prevents overexertion during pranayama.

- **Prana Flow:** In yogic terms, prana refers to the life force or vital energy. Pauses between breaths facilitate the flow of prana, allowing it to circulate and nourish the subtle energy channels (nadis) in the body.

- **Transcendence:** The breathless state, where both inhalation and exhalation momentarily cease, is a crucial moment. It symbolizes a state of transcendence beyond the physical body and thought processes. It's akin to entering the realm of pure consciousness.

- **Beneficial States:** The breathless state, or kumbhaka, is often associated with deep meditative states and altered consciousness. Practitioners report experiencing profound calmness, heightened awareness, and expanded states of consciousness.

- **Inner and Outer Pauses:** Both inner and outer pauses have their significance. Inner pauses naturally occur between inhalation and exhalation, while outer pauses are deliberate moments where you intentionally hold your breath. Inner pauses are a natural part of the breath cycle, whereas outer pauses are integrated into specific pranayama techniques.

- **Ideal Timing:** The ideal duration for these pauses varies from person to person and depends on the specific practice being undertaken. In traditional pranayama, the retention of breath (kumbhaka) can range from a few seconds to several minutes, depending on the practitioner's level of proficiency.

- **Breathless State:** When you reach the breathless state during advanced practices, it signifies a profound level of mastery over the breath and the mind. In this state, you transcend ordinary thought patterns and experience deep serenity and unity with universal consciousness.

- **Secret of Pauses:** The secret of these pauses lies in their ability to facilitate a shift from ordinary, scattered mental states to deeper, concentrated awareness. They are a gateway to the inner realms of consciousness, enabling self-discovery and spiritual growth.

In this section's conclusion, it is worth emphasizing the significance of the pauses between breaths within yogic and meditative practices. These intermissions play a crucial role in achieving balance, conserving energy, and nurturing a profound connection between the mind and body. They ultimately lead to a breathless state, associated with profound inner peace and heightened consciousness, establishing them as a vital component of advanced pranayama and meditation techniques.

Attaining the Breathless State – Advanced Practice

Achieving the breathless state, known as "kumbhaka" in yoga and pranayama, is considered an advanced practice that requires patience, dedication, and a solid foundation in breath control techniques. Here's a step-by-step guide on how to progress toward this profound state:

Start with Pranayama Basics

Start by becoming proficient in basic pranayama techniques such as Dirga Pranayama (Three-Part Breath), which is known for its calming and grounding effects, and Nadi Shodhana (Alternate Nostril Breathing). These exercises will assist you in cultivating awareness and control over your breath.

Explanation of Dirga Pranayama

Dirga Pranayama, also known as the Three-Part Breath, is a fundamental yogic breathing technique that helps individuals enhance their breath control and mindfulness. It involves dividing the breath into three distinct phases:

1. **Abdominal Breathing:** Inhale deeply, allowing the abdomen to expand as the diaphragm moves downward, filling the lower lungs with air.
2. **Thoracic Breathing:** Continue the inhalation, expanding the ribcage and filling the middle portion of the lungs.
3. **Clavicular Breathing:** Complete the inhalation by lifting the collarbone and filling the upper lungs with air.

During exhalation, release the breath in the reverse order: first from the upper lungs, then the middle, and finally from the lower lungs as the abdomen contracts. Dirga Pranayama is particularly useful for reducing stress, increasing relaxation, and improving overall breath control. It is often recommended for beginners as a foundational practice in yoga and pranayama routines.

Build Breath Awareness

Develop a keen sense of your breath. Observe its natural rhythm and the pauses that occur between inhalation and exhalation.

Progressive Retention

Start with short breath retention. After an inhalation, pause briefly before exhaling, and vice versa. Gradually extend these pauses as your comfort and lung capacity improve.

Practice Ratio Breathing

Ratio breathing involves inhaling, holding, and exhaling for specific counts. For example, try a 1:2:2 ratio, where you inhale for a count of 4, hold for 8, and exhale for 8. Gradually increase the retention phase.

Balancing Breath

Practice Sama Vritti (Equal Breathing) by inhaling, holding, and exhaling for the same duration. This balanced approach prepares you for extended breath retention.

Develop Lung Capacity

Consistently practice deep, diaphragmatic breathing to improve your lung capacity. Deep breathing techniques such as Kapalabhati and Bhastrika can be advantageous.

Kapalabhati and Bhastrika are two breathing exercises commonly used in yoga and pranayama (breath control) practices.

- **Kapalabhati:** Kapalabhati is a cleansing and invigorating breathing exercise in which you forcefully and rapidly exhale while keeping the inhalation passive. It involves quick, strong contractions of the lower belly muscles. The rapid exhalations help remove impurities from the respiratory system and increase alertness and energy.

- **Bhastrika:** Bhastrika is another dynamic and forceful breathing technique that involves rapid, powerful inhalations and exhalations. It's often described as "bellows breath" because of the strong, pumping action of the breath. Bhastrika is believed to enhance lung capacity, increase oxygen intake, and stimulate the nervous system, promoting a sense of vitality and rejuvenation.

Both Kapalabhati and Bhastrika are considered beneficial for respiratory health, promoting oxygenation of the body, and improving mental clarity and focus. However, they should be practiced with care and under the guidance of a knowledgeable instructor, as they may not be suitable for everyone and can be strenuous for some individuals.

Meditative State

As you advance, focus on maintaining a meditative state throughout your practice. Calm your mind and let go of distractions.

Seek Guidance

If possible, learn from an experienced yoga or pranayama instructor who can provide personalized guidance and ensure your safety during advanced practices.

Extend Retention Periods

Gradually increase the duration of your breath retention. Aim for 10 seconds, then 20, and so on. Be patient and don't push yourself too quickly.

Incorporate Meditation

The breathless state often occurs spontaneously during deep meditation. Integrate meditation into your practice to deepen your experience.

Set an Intention

Before each practice session, set a clear intention for your breath retention. Whether it's self-realization, spiritual growth, or inner peace, a clear purpose can enhance your practice.

Safety First

Always prioritize safety. If you feel uncomfortable or experience dizziness, release the retention and resume normal breathing. Do not force or strain.

Regular Practice

Consistency is key. Regular, dedicated practice over an extended period is necessary to achieve advanced breath control.

Patience and Surrender

Understand that achieving the breathless state is a gradual process. It may take time and persistence. Practice with a sense of surrender, letting go of expectations.

Awareness of the Moment

The breathless state often arises when you least expect it. Be aware and open to the experience when it happens spontaneously.

Remember that achieving the breathless state is a deeply spiritual and transformative experience. It should be approached with respect, humility, and a commitment to your own inner journey.

Always listen to your body and mind and practice within your limits.

In conclusion, the pauses between breaths, known as "kumbhaka" in the realm of yoga and meditation, are far more than mere intermissions in the breathing cycle; they are the bridge between the physical and the metaphysical, the fulcrum of inner harmony, energy conservation, and heightened consciousness. The significance of these pauses lies in their ability to balance opposing forces, create a profound mind-body connection, conserve energy, facilitate the flow of vital energy (prana), and ultimately lead to a breathless state. This breathless state is not only a sign of mastery but also a gateway to profound inner peace and self-discovery.

As you embark on the journey to achieve the breathless state through advanced pranayama practices, it is essential to build a strong foundation with basic techniques like Dirga Pranayama and Nadi Shodhana. Developing breath awareness, progressive retention, and practicing ratio breathing will prepare you for extended breath retention. Exercises like Kapalabhati and Bhastrika can enhance lung capacity and vitality, but they should be approached with caution. Maintaining a meditative state, seeking guidance, extending retention periods, and incorporating meditation will deepen your practice. Remember, the path to the breathless state is one of patience, surrender, and inner awareness. Approach it with respect and humility, always listening to your body and mind, and allowing the transformation to unfold in its own time.

Chapter 77

The Breath of Life: Unlocking Vital Energy

P icture a world where every living creature, from the most powerful elephant to the tiniest ant, shares a profound connection through the simple acts of breathing and creating sound. This idea, both intricate and universal, is deeply rooted in a rich tapestry of philosophical, spiritual traditions, and scientific knowledge. Within this symphony of life, interpretations may vary, but common themes emerge, echoing the profound inter-connectedness of all living beings. It's a concept that sparks awe and serves as a reminder of the threads that tie us together, transcending the boundaries of species, race, and borders. Let's embark on a journey to explore the intricate interplay of breath and sound, unveiling the mysteries that unite us in this captivating exploration.

Breath as a Vital Life Force

In numerous cultures and traditions, breath is regarded as a fundamental life force that sustains all living beings. Breathing symbolizes the intake of energy and vitality. Breath is associated with concepts like prana (life force) in yoga and Ayurveda, chi (energy) in traditional Chinese medicine, and pneuma (vital breath) in ancient Greek philosophy.

Breath and Unity

Breathing transcends species, race, and borders, serving as a universal symbol of interconnectedness among all living beings. This unity in breath aligns with the subsequent discussion of the Breath of Life and its profound impact on neuroscience and neuropathy.

The Breath of Life, characterized by rhythmic inhalation, exhalation, and pauses, profoundly influences the mind, body, the central nervous system, and various other organ systems. It serves as a common thread that binds all living creatures, underscoring the importance of comprehending how conscious breathing practices can affect the nervous system, cognitive processes, overall well-being, and the harmony of multiple bodily systems.

In essence, the act of breathing unites all living beings and extends its influence to the physiological aspects of existence. This connection between breath and shared existence underscores how such a simple act can significantly impact our interconnectedness with the world and our overall well-being.

Breathing's unifying power can be seen through various lenses:

- **Biological Necessity:** Breathing is essential for nearly all living creatures, enabling the exchange of oxygen and carbon dioxide vital for cellular respiration and energy production. This universal need for oxygen connects all life forms.
- **Shared Anatomy:** Many living creatures share a basic anatomical structure for breathing, despite variations in mechanisms. Whether it's lungs in mammals, gills in fish, or tracheal systems in insects, the overarching purpose is the same: facilitating the exchange of gases.

- **Ecosystem Interdependence:** Breathing is an integral part of a broader ecosystem. Plants, algae, certain types of bacteria, and phytoplankton play a vital role by producing oxygen through photosynthesis, upon which most creatures depend. In turn, animals release carbon dioxide, which is utilized by these same plants, algae, bacteria, and phytoplankton during photosynthesis. It is important to note that oxygen and carbon dioxide have multiple sources that can be used by both plants and animals. However, we have mentioned photosynthesis to emphasize the interconnectedness of all living creatures through the exchange of gases.

- **Survival Instinct:** Breathing is an instinctive act, triggered by drops in oxygen levels or rises in carbon dioxide levels. This survival instinct is a common thread that unites all creatures, emphasizing the universal importance of respiration.

- **Environmental Adaptation:** While species adapt to different environments, the shared need for oxygen and respiration remains a constant. Variations in respiratory systems reflect these adaptations.

In summary, breathing serves as a universal symbol of interconnectedness among all living beings, transcending species and emphasizing the shared existence within the web of life. It underscores how this simple act can have a far-reaching impact on health and interconnectedness with the natural world.

Sound as Expression and Connection

Sound is the result of vibrating forces and possesses the capacity to evoke resonance and harmony. Vocalization and sound generation serve as avenues for expression and communication, shared not only by humans but also by certain animals. Through language, music, and shared vocalizations, sound serves as a unifying link between living beings.

Chanting and Mantras

Many spiritual traditions incorporate chanting and mantras (repeated sounds or words) to attune the mind, body, and spirit. These practices are believed to create vibrational harmony and connect practitioners to higher states of consciousness.

Breath and Meditation

Breath awareness practices play a significant role in unlocking vital energy within us. When we focus on our breath during meditation, we tap into a deep wellspring of vitality. This happens because mindful breathing helps to balance and harmonize our body and mind, which, in turn, rejuvenates and replenishes our vital energy. By consciously regulating our breath, we enhance our life force, enabling us to experience heightened levels of energy and a profound sense of well-being.

Resonance and Harmonics

Sound frequencies have the capacity to trigger resonance within the body and its cells, potentially exerting an impact on physiological functions. Specific sound frequencies are thought to possess therapeutic attributes, fostering equilibrium and overall health. Chapter 27 delves into a detailed exploration of several of these frequencies.

Rhythms of Nature

Natural sounds, such as ocean waves, wind, and bird songs, connect beings to the rhythms of the natural world. These sounds can have a calming and grounding effect, reminding us of our place within the larger ecosystem.

Cultural and Ritual Significance

Sound and breath play a crucial role in various cultural rituals, ceremonies, and traditions. These customs frequently highlight the intricate relationship between breath, sound, and the cultivation of vital energy.

The connection to unlocking vital energy lies in the way that these rituals and practices use sound and breath to enhance one's spiritual connection and well-being. By focusing on breath control and producing specific sounds or chants, individuals can harness and channel their vital energy, often referred to as prana, chi, or qi, to promote balance and harmony in their physical, mental, and spiritual aspects. This integration of sound and breath in cultural traditions facilitates the release and circulation of this vital energy, contributing to a sense of vitality and inner balance.

The interconnectedness of breath emphasizes the unity among all living beings, transcending cultural and disciplinary boundaries, and serves as a poignant reminder of our profound interdependence. Our journey begins with a profound awareness of our breath, particularly during the inhalation phase, when the breath of life, oxygen, flows into our bodies. This life-sustaining oxygen is a product of the incredible process of photosynthesis, carried out by various life forms such as plants, algae, certain bacteria, and phytoplankton. This connection signifies our fundamental bond with the ecosystem, as these organisms generously provide the oxygen we inhale, creating a vital link between humans, animals, and the plant world.

The breath of life courses through every living being, an unbroken thread that unites us all as we continue to breathe. In reciprocity, during the exhalation phase, we release carbon dioxide, a pivotal component in this intricate cycle. This carbon dioxide is then absorbed by plants and other photosynthetic organisms, closing the loop of this intricate exchange. This interdependence is a testament to the unifying force that transcends species and ecosystems, weaving us into a collective breath that sustains all life.

As we delve deeper into the practice of breath observation, we become intimately attuned to the rise of our chest, the expansion of our lungs during inhalation, and the controlled release of air and carbon dioxide during exhalation. With dedicated mindfulness and practice, we attain a breathless state, transcending the routine inhalation and exhalation, and entering a serene mental space where the cacophony of thoughts fades, granting us access to a realm of pure knowledge and insight.

In this thoughtless state, the art of manifestation takes on a luminous quality. Knowledge emerges as a guiding beacon, illuminating our intentions and desires with remarkable clarity. This profound communion with the self not only elevates the ordinary to the extraordinary but also harmonizes the interplay between breath, mind, and knowledge, as we acknowledge our essential connection to the breath of life that binds all living beings.

This transformative journey of breath observation entails stages of withdrawing from external distractions, intense concentration on the breath, and culminates in a state of one-pointedness. In this state, the demarcations between self and the universe dissolve, revealing an interconnectedness that underlies existence and fosters an energy flow that sustains all life. It leads to profound insights and enlightenment, where pure awareness lights the path to self-realization and profound wisdom, enriching our connection to the breath of life that pulses through every living being.

Chapter 78

The Kingdom of Heaven

The teachings we mentioned, such as "I and my Father are one," "I am God," "Aham Brahmasmi," and "I am Shiva," are connected to the concept of the Kingdom of Heaven found in ancient teachings. This concept can be found in religious and spiritual contexts, including Christianity and certain Eastern philosophies.

The Kingdom of Heaven is often described as a state of perfect harmony, peace, and divine presence. It's a place or state where everything aligns with a higher purpose, and there is a sense of unity, love, and fulfillment. It's not just a physical place; it's a spiritual realm of ultimate goodness.

When we examine these teachings, we find common themes with the idea of the Kingdom of Heaven:

1. **Unity and Oneness:** The statement "I and my Father are one" emphasizes a deep unity between an individual and a higher, divine source. Similarly, "Aham Brahmasmi," "I am Buddha," "I am God," or "I am Shiva" also point to a sense of unity with a greater reality, similar

to the harmony and unity associated with the Kingdom of Heaven.

2. **Divine Connection:** The concept of being connected to something bigger, whether it's referred to as a father figure, divine mother, the universe, or a divine presence, aligns with the divine nature of the Kingdom of Heaven.

3. **Higher Wisdom and Understanding:** "I am Buddha" signifies a connection to the wisdom and enlightenment of spiritual teachers like Buddha, which is similar to the portrayal of the Kingdom of Heaven as a realm of higher wisdom and understanding.

4. **Eternal and Timeless:** The Kingdom of Heaven is often described as a place beyond the limitations of time and space. Similarly, the teachings we mentioned suggest a connection to something eternal and timeless.

5. **Inner Transformation:** Many ancient teachings, including those we mentioned, emphasize inner transformation and self-realization. By recognizing our connection to something greater and working on our inner selves, we can experience a profound shift in our consciousness, leading us closer to the qualities associated with the Kingdom of Heaven.

These teachings all share a common thread of seeking a deeper connection to a higher reality, a sense of oneness, and a transformation of the self. They provide a roadmap for individuals to transcend ordinary existence and experience a state of being that reflects the ideals of the Kingdom of Heaven—a state of harmony, unity, and divine presence.

Rewiring for Deeper Connections through Love

We are now going to shift our focus to love. Love, expressed both towards others and inwardly towards oneself, serves as a beacon of healing and unity intricately woven into the fabric of human experience. At the heart of non-judgmental awareness lies the radiant core of love. When we shed judgment, biases, and criticism, we unveil our innate capacity for empathy and compassion. Neuroplasticity, with its ability to rewire neural pathways, empowers us to amplify and radiate this love to others. By training our minds to perceive without judgment, we open the door to deeper connections, fostering an environment where empathy flourishes, relationships thrive, and the world becomes a more harmonious place.

Loving Each Other

Neuroplasticity, in partnership with our intention, plays a pivotal role in equipping us with the tools to enrich our relationships through loving acceptance. Neuroplasticity refers to the brain's extraordinary ability to rewire itself in response to experiences and conscious efforts. When we intentionally choose to let go of judgment and cultivate loving acceptance, our brains undergo a process of transformation.

Through neuroplasticity, we gradually reconfigure our brain's neural pathways. We weaken connections associated with critical or judgmental thinking and simultaneously strengthen those linked to empathy, understanding, and compassion. This neural rewiring creates space for understanding, patience, and genuine connection to flourish in our relationships.

Neuroplasticity also empowers us to reframe our brain's response to differences and perceived flaws in others. It enables us to move away from reactionary judgments and towards a mindset that truly sees others, embraces their unique perspectives, and extends a hand of love and support. In essence, neuroplasticity is the dynamic force that allows us to transcend judgment and biases, fostering a more profound and authentic connection with those around us.

By loving each other unconditionally and harnessing the transformative power of neuroplasticity, we actively engage in a dance of interconnectedness. This not only enhances our personal well-being but also elevates the collective human experience, as we collectively reprogram our brains to prioritize empathy, acceptance, and deeper connections.

Love Thyself

Just as non-judgment opens the door to loving others, it is also the key to unlocking the profound practice of self-love. Neuroplasticity's role in reshaping thought patterns extends to how we perceive ourselves. Through deliberate acts of self-compassion and self-forgiveness, we create neural pathways leading to a healthier self-image. This practice, supported by the brain's malleability, empowers us to love ourselves unconditionally. In this journey, we heal wounds, dismantle self-criticism, and nurture a profound sense of well-being that resonates through every aspect of our lives.

Embracing the Symphony of Love

Love is the universal melody that harmonizes our existence in the grand symphony of life. Neuroplasticity, the conductor of change within the brain, orchestrates a transformational shift toward a life infused with love, both outward and inward.

As we embark on the journey of reevaluating our judgments and embracing the power of non-judgmental awareness, we tend to a garden of love that blossoms within us and extends to touch the lives of others. In this intricate interplay between neuroplasticity and love, we hold the keys to unlocking our true potential and experiencing the profound tapestry of mind-body health and connection.

Body and Mind Aligned: A Synthesis of Neuroscience and Spiritual Traditions

In this section, we will immerse ourselves in a compelling examination that forges a connection between the fields of neuroscience and various spiritual philosophies. This distinctive investigation will illuminate the complex interrelationship between the body and the mind, revealing profound connections that find their roots in both scientific comprehension and spiritual veneration.

The intricate relationship between the body and the mind has fascinated scientists, philosophers, and thinkers for centuries. In the field of neuroscience, researchers study this connection to gain insight into how the brain's physical structures and processes interact with the body, influencing thoughts, emotions, behaviors, and overall well-being.

Neuroscience reveals that the brain and the body are closely linked through a network of neurons, neurotransmitters, hormones, and feedback loops. The brain, often referred to as the "command center," communicates with various organs and systems within the body, including the nervous, endocrine, immune, and digestive systems. This bidirectional communication allows the brain to receive signals from the body and vice versa, influencing each other's functions.

Emotions and mental states can impact the body's physiological responses, and physical sensations and conditions can influence mental states. For example, stress or anxiety can trigger the release of stress hormones like cortisol, affecting heart rate, blood pressure, and digestion. Conversely, chronic pain or illness may lead to feelings of depression or frustration.

The notion of the body as a temple of God is deeply rooted in religious and spiritual beliefs. Many faiths and philosophies emphasize that the body is a sacred vessel created by a higher power. This concept encourages individuals to treat their bodies with respect, care, and gratitude, honoring the divine creation and fulfilling their spiritual responsibilities.

Viewing the body as a temple involves adopting a holistic approach that recognizes the interconnectedness of the physical, mental, and spiritual aspects of human existence. This perspective encourages practices that promote balance, self-care, and mindfulness in both body and mind, including healthy eating, regular exercise, meditation, prayer, and positive thinking.

Ultimately, the understanding of the body-mind connection through neuroscience aligns with the spiritual notion of the body as a temple of God. Both perspectives underscore the importance of acknowledging the profound interplay between our physical selves and our mental and spiritual well-being, urging us to lead lives that honor and nurture this intricate and awe-inspiring connection.

Keeping Oneself Clean and Healthy

The concept of keeping oneself clean and healthy is rooted in practical and holistic principles that contribute to overall well-being and a higher quality of life. This idea is embraced in many religions, where the maintenance of physical and spiritual purity is considered essential for leading a fulfilling and righteous life. Here are several reasons why maintaining cleanliness and good health is important:

- **Physical Well-being:** Regular hygiene practices, such as washing hands, taking showers, brushing teeth, and maintaining personal cleanliness, help prevent the spread of germs, bacteria, and infections. Good hygiene practices contribute to the prevention of various illnesses, including common colds, flu, and more serious diseases, all of which can affect your body's physiology, putting your mind and body under stress, which can in turn affect your kingdom of heaven.

- **Disease Prevention:** Keeping the body clean and practicing good hygiene is a fundamental step in preventing the spread of contagious diseases. Regular handwashing, for example, is one of the most effective ways to prevent the transmission of pathogens.

- **Mental and Emotional Well-being:** In many spiritual and philosophical traditions, it is believed that the Kingdom of Heaven should be clean and clutter-free. This notion extends beyond the physical realm and is often seen as a metaphor for inner peace and spiritual harmony. A clean and organized environment is not only aesthetically pleasing but also has a profound impact on mental and emotional well-being. It can promote positive effects on one's mental state, contributing to reduced stress, decreased anxiety, and a sense of calm and well-being. Just as a tidy space can create a sense of order and tranquility, a clutter-free mind can lead to a more harmonious inner state, aligning with the idea of the Kingdom of Heaven as a place of peace and serenity.

- **Self-Respect and Confidence:** Taking care of one's personal hygiene and appearance extends beyond mere self-esteem and confidence; it resonates with the spiritual concept of the "Kingdom of Heaven." By prioritizing personal hygiene, individuals express reverence for their physical vessels and align themselves with the idea that the body is a sacred temple, reflecting the teachings of various religious traditions. Feeling clean and well-groomed becomes a metaphor for inner purity and spiritual cleanliness, prerequisites for the journey towards inner peace and self-respect. Projecting confidence through well-maintained personal hygiene and appearance mirrors the inner confidence that arises from spiritual alignment, fostering harmonious and compassionate interactions with others. In this way, the act of self-care embodies the principles of inner purity and harmony, contributing to a sense of spiritual self-worth in the broader context of one's spiritual journey towards the ideals of the Kingdom of Heaven.

- **Social Interaction:** Practicing good hygiene and maintaining health is respectful to others in social settings. It reduces the risk of offending or alienating others because of unpleasant odors or unsanitary habits.
- **Long-Term Health:** Adopting healthy habits such as proper nutrition, regular exercise, and sufficient sleep contributes to long-term physical health. These habits can help prevent chronic conditions like heart disease, diabetes, hypertension, and obesity.
- **Holistic Well-being:** The concept of cleanliness extends beyond physical aspects to include mental, emotional, and spiritual dimensions. Engaging in activities that promote mindfulness, relaxation, and positive social connections can enhance overall well-being.
- **Cultural and Religious Beliefs:** Many cultures and religions emphasize cleanliness as a pathway to spiritual devotion and divine connection. Cleanliness rituals are integral to religious and cultural traditions, symbolizing the link between external and internal purity. Maintaining physical and spiritual cleanliness is seen as a means to cultivate a pure heart and soul. Various religions have specific cleansing rituals, like Islamic Wudu and Hindu ritual baths, representing not only physical but also spiritual purification. The upkeep of sacred spaces further reinforces the importance of cleanliness in approaching the divine. Additionally, spiritual traditions stress the purification of thoughts,

intentions, and actions as individuals strive for spiritual enlightenment or entry into heavenly realms depicted as pristine and immaculate. Overall, these beliefs highlight how cleanliness acts as a profound link to the sacred and the promise of divine experience, bringing individuals closer to spiritual realms.

- **Productivity and Focus:** A clean and organized environment can enhance productivity and focus. Clutter-free spaces provide fewer distractions and promote better concentration.
- **Respect for the Body:** Viewing the body as a temple underscores the idea that it deserves to be treated with care and respect. Maintaining good health and hygiene aligns with this principle and supports the idea that the body is a valuable vessel for experiencing life.

The idea of keeping clean and healthy encompasses not only physical well-being but also the emotional, social, and spiritual dimensions of a person's life. It is a multifaceted approach that contributes to a balanced and fulfilling existence.

In conclusion, the teachings we have explored, connecting ancient spiritual wisdom to the concept of the Kingdom of Heaven, highlight the universal themes of unity, divine connection, higher wisdom, timelessness, and inner transformation. These teachings serve as a roadmap for individuals to transcend ordinary existence and experience a state of harmony, unity, and divine presence. Furthermore, the transformative power of neuroplasticity and the practice of non-judgmental awareness illustrate the profound impact of love in fostering deeper connections with both others and oneself. By embracing the symphony of love and recognizing the intricate interplay between the body and the mind, we can unlock our true potential and experience a profound tapestry of mind-body health and connection. Additionally, the concept of keeping oneself clean and healthy is deeply rooted in physical, emotional, social, and spiritual well-being, reflecting the holistic approach found in many cultural and religious traditions. Ultimately, these interconnected principles guide us towards a life that honors and nurtures the profound connection between our physical and spiritual selves, leading us closer to the ideals of the Kingdom of Heaven – a place of peace, unity, and serenity.

Concluding Our Boundless Journey: A Reflective Farewell

"Realizing life's fullest potential involves fostering extraordinary connections with the world and those around us, while embarking on a unique journey of self-discovery. Otherwise, when we depart, all that remains are memories captured in photographs."

— Steve Christian

Our voyage through the labyrinth of knowledge has immersed us in the profound tapestry of existence, weaving together ancient wisdom, contemporary scientific revelations, spiritual enlightenment, and practical insights to enrich every facet of life. Each chapter has unveiled a unique perspective, offering a treasury of wisdom to aid you in navigating the intricate web of existence.

As we draw the curtains on this profound expedition, let's pause to savor some pivotal insights:

- **Harmony of Knowledge:** Throughout our odyssey, we've witnessed the harmonious convergence of ancient wisdom and modern enlightenment. This union reminds us that our quest for understanding knows no temporal bounds, for we continue to build upon the insights of those who came before us, continually expanding our perception of the world.

- **Wholeness of Well-Being:** The recurring theme of the interconnectedness of mind, body, and spirit serves as a resounding refrain. Embracing practices that nurture physical vitality, mental clarity, and spiritual awakening can lead us to a life marked by balance and fulfillment.

- **Empowerment from Within:** The diverse tools and practices explored within these pages empower you to seize control of your personal growth and well-being. Whether it's through meditation, mindfulness, or harnessing the power of neuroplasticity, you wield the capability to shape your own reality.

- **Bridging Bonds and Unity:** We've delved into the unifying concepts of love, oneness, and shared values, illuminating pathways that bridge the chasms between diverse traditions and cultures. The realization of our interconnectedness inspires compassion and empathy.

- **Transcending Boundaries:** Our exploration of consciousness, meditation, and the force of intention has unveiled that human experience extends far beyond the confines of the physical realm. By transcending limiting beliefs and expanding our consciousness, we journey toward elevated states of awareness.

- **Practical Application:** The practical tools and exercises provided offer a navigational guide to incorporate these newfound insights into your daily life. Implementing these practices can manifest tangible and positive transformations.

- **A Continuing Journey:** The final page is merely the start of another chapter in your voyage. The themes explored invite you to carry forth your exploration, venture deeper into your areas of interest, and embark on an unending journey of self-discovery.

In a world awash with information and diversions, the precious moments spent reflecting on these revelations and integrating them into your life can yield transformative experiences. Remember, wisdom is not just about amassing knowledge; it's about embodying that knowledge and letting it steer your actions, thoughts, and interactions.

Our pursuit of Truth as a human race is a complex tapestry, entwining a deep understanding of reality, encompassing both objective truths and subjective experiences. Handling the Truth effectively demands a willingness to confront complexity, transcend biases, and engage in open dialogue. It calls for the nurturing of critical thinking, empathy, and a commitment to the greater good. Despite its challenges, the quest for Truth remains a pivotal facet of human advancement and enlightenment.

May this book serve as an enduring source of inspiration, a guiding light, and a catalyst for your personal and spiritual growth. As you continue your journey, may the pursuit of wisdom bring you joy and may the illumination you've uncovered light your path towards a more enriched and purposeful life.

And so we arrive at the culmination of this literary voyage. Some may find their horizons expanded by the content of this book, while others may regard it with skepticism. It's important to underline that the aim of this book is not to challenge anyone's beliefs but to provide a fresh perspective, unveiling a broader canvas of how the mind, body, and spirituality intertwine.

In "The Enlightened Quest: Blending Neuroscience with Spiritual Pathways to Self-Realization," we embarked on an extensive exploration of the intricate relationship between human consciousness, spirituality, and the complex machinations of the mind and body. We wove together a rich tapestry of human thought and experience, connecting various religions and ancient wisdom in topics ranging from "Cracking the Mind-Consciousness Code: Science & Spirituality" to "The Science of Breath."

Our journey has been a quest for enlightenment and revelation, seeking to bridge the gap between ancient wisdom and modern science. As we draw the curtain on this odyssey, it's important to acknowledge that the path to self-understanding is deeply personal. We all bring our unique perspectives, beliefs, and experiences to this journey, and it's natural that some ideas in this book may resonate more strongly with certain individuals.

Rather than imposing rigid beliefs or offering one-size-fits-all solutions, our hope is to plant the seeds of curiosity within you. We encourage you to continue exploring the boundless realms of human consciousness, spirituality, and the intricate workings of the mind and body. The knowledge you've gained in these pages is but the first step toward a deeper understanding of yourself and the world around you.

In the end, whether this book has sparked a profound transformation within you or simply served as a brief interlude in your intellectual journey, we extend our gratitude for your open-mindedness and your willingness to engage with the ideas presented here. The journey of self-understanding is an ongoing one, and within its complexity, beauty, and mystery, lies the promise of a more profound connection with the world and with ourselves. May this journey continue to unfold, offering insights and revelations at every turn as we explore the magnificent tapestry of human existence.

Thank you for joining us on this journey through these pages. As you close this book, we'd be deeply grateful if you could take a moment to leave a review wherever you purchased it.

Your review is more than just feedback; it's a catalyst for our authors and the publishing team to continue providing value through storytelling. Your words help others discover this book, and more reviews mean more opportunities to share these stories with the world.

We appreciate your support and the time you take to share your thoughts. Your review truly makes a difference in our ability to keep crafting tales that resonate.

As we conclude this enriching journey together, we extend our heartfelt greetings to you in the rich tapestry of languages that grace our world:

- **नमस्ते (Namaste)** - In Hindi and Nepali, it signifies a deep acknowledgment of the divine in you.
- **নমস্কার (Nomoshkar)** - In Bengali, it's a respectful nod to your presence.
- **สวัสดี (Sawasdee)** - In Thai, it offers warm well-wishes.
- **你好 (Nǐ hǎo)** - In Mandarin Chinese, it's a friendly "hello."
- **Bonjour** - In French, it wishes you a good day.
- • **السلام عليكم (As-salamu alaykum)** - In Arabic, it extends peace to you.
- **Zdravstvuyte (Здравствуйте)** - In Russian, it greets you politely.
- **Guten Tag** - In German, it acknowledges you with a friendly "good day."
- **こんにちは (Konnichiwa)** - In Japanese, it offers a cheerful greeting.
- **Annyeonghaseyo (안녕하세요)** - In Korean, it welcomes you with a friendly hello.
- **Buongiorno** - In Italian, it wishes you a good day.
- **Olá** - In Portuguese, it greets you with a warm "hello."

- **Yassou (Γειά σου)** - In Greek, it offers a heartfelt salutation.
- **Merhaba** - In Turkish, it acknowledges you with a warm greeting.
- **Jambo** - In Swahili, it extends a cheerful "hello."
- **Sannu** - In Hausa, it welcomes you warmly.
- **Bawo ni** - In Yoruba, it inquires how you are with a kind greeting.

With these heartfelt words from around the globe, we express our gratitude for accompanying us on this journey of exploration and self-discovery. Your presence has enriched the pages of this book and given meaning to its words. As we part ways, we hope you carry with you the wisdom, insights, and inspiration gathered along the way.

May the spirit of unity, compassion, and mindfulness stay with you, guiding your path as you navigate life's journey. Embrace the universe within and around you, cherishing the interconnectedness that unites us all. Thank you for being a part of this transformative adventure. May your life be filled with purpose, serenity, and the joy of exploration. The power of Truth and Knowledge can lead to a sense of freedom and liberation from ignorance or falsehood.

Remember, if you haven't already, make sure not to miss out on claiming your free bonuses: the Smart Goals Worksheet, a collection of 25 Powerful Affirmations covering all aspects of life, and the Analyze Your Fear Worksheet. These resources are available for free for a limited time. Simply download them by visiting: https://www.confidenceiatry.com/freebonuses.

With warm wishes and boundless gratitude,

Shawn Christian, M.D.
Steve and Stella Christian

About the Authors

Delve into a treasure trove of insights as you embark on a thought-provoking journey through the pages of Collaborative Wisdom: "The Enlightened Quest: Blending Neuroscience with Spiritual Pathways to Self-Realization." This remarkable book, co-authored by the esteemed Dr. Shawn Christian, and the dynamic duo of Steve and Stella Christian, brings together a symphony of expertise from diverse fields. Their collective wisdom intertwines seamlessly, weaving a tapestry of knowledge that spans various topics. Join these visionary authors as they illuminate the realms of wisdom, offering readers an enriching experience that transcends boundaries and fuels intellectual curiosity.

Shawn Christian, M.D., a native of California and the Founder of Confidenceiatry, is a multifaceted individual whose journey is shaped by a passionate pursuit of knowledge and a commitment to enhancing the human experience. An accomplished author, entrepreneur, and human relations expert, he always strives to unravel the complexities of human existence.

Driven by an insatiable curiosity, Dr. Christian has immersed himself in study and earned an excellent reputation as a lifelong student and practitioner. His unwavering commitment to personal growth and intellectual exploration has propelled him to the forefront of his field.

With a keen interest in improving and understanding human life, Shawn Christian, M.D. possessed a deep understanding of insight and innovation. His profound insights and visionary thinking have paved the way for innovative contributions that resonate in the fields of wellbeing and personal development.

You can check out some of Dr. Christian's work at https://www.confidenceiatry.com and also on YouTube at https://www.youtube.com/confidenceiatry, where his insights and contributions in the field of human understanding and transformation are highlighted.

Through his writings, entrepreneurial endeavors, and unwavering dedication to his craft, Dr. Shawn Christian has not only enriched his own life but also touched the lives of individuals seeking enlightenment and empowerment. His remarkable journey continues to inspire and edify, leaving an indelible mark on the world of human understanding and transformation.

Steve (aka Madhu) Christian, and Stella Christian, hail from India (Bharat.) Their educational roots and early years were nurtured in India before destiny beckoned them to the United States of America in their early twenties.

United by an unbreakable bond, their enduring marriage has stood the test of time since their early twenties. Their journey began with a quest for profound understanding, propelling them through a transformative odyssey that etched an indelible imprint upon their lives. Together, driven by a shared pursuit of ultimate truth, they embarked upon a remarkable voyage, skillfully navigating the intricate tapestry of human wisdom and spirituality.

Steve and Stella, eager to learn and deeply connected, began their married life together with a strong desire to explore the mysteries of life. They fearlessly sought wisdom from various spiritual teachers and groups, both well-known and obscure. They were determined to find answers and weren't afraid to explore different beliefs and ways of thinking. Their quest for understanding led them to explore different religions and spiritual practices.

Through their shared experiences, Steve and Stella became sources of inspiration for those wanting to explore the meaning of life and consciousness. Their encounters, marked by a deep blend of wisdom and insight, continue to inspire people today who seek truth and are passionate about spirituality. Bound by enduring love that has withstood the tests of time and challenges, Steve and Stella Christian's extraordinary journey serves as proof of the strength of unity, common goals, and the transformative power of a life dedicated to the pursuit of ultimate truth. Their legacy is a guiding beacon for anyone on a quest to unravel the deep mysteries of human existence.

For more than four decades, Steve and Stella have undertaken an extensive voyage into the realms of spirituality and mysticism, adeptly weaving together the tapestries of both Eastern and Western traditions. Their odyssey commenced as a pursuit of self-mastery, immersing themselves in a rich array of texts. In the Western tradition, they delved into the sacred scriptures of the Bible, Judaism, the profound teachings of Kabbalah (the art of receiving divine knowledge), the mysticism of Zohar, the enigmatic wisdom of The Secret Teachings of Jesus, The Revelation of Christ, the symbolic Tree of Life, the esoteric teachings of the Mystery School–Builders of Adytum, and the mysterious world of Rosicrucianism (a repository of organized esoteric wisdom).

In their exploration of the Eastern Tradition, they absorbed the profound insights of Hinduism, delved into the depths of Buddhism, embraced the wisdom of Sanatan Dharma, immersed themselves in the mysteries of Shivaism, and contemplated the profound philosophy of J. Krishnamurthy. They also embarked on a journey through the teachings, philosophies, and commentaries of ancient and contemporary Himalayan Gurus and Swamis, while immersing themselves in the everyday traditions and customs of India.

Their diligent research unveiled tantalizing theories regarding the potential visit of Jesus to India, sparking a deeper exploration of India's venerable educational institutions, such as the Nalanda and Takshashila educational centers, which trace their heritage back to 1 AD. Additionally, they delved into the historical account of Saint Thomas' journey in 52 AD, within the present-day state of Kerala.

It is important to note that their studies extended to encompass a multitude of other spiritual and mystic traditions, such as the Hawaiian practice of Huna, rooted in the indigenous culture of Hawaii, and Neurolinguistic Programming (NLP). This extensive reservoir of knowledge serves as the bedrock of this book.

f facebook.com/confidenceiatry

instagram.com/confidenceiatry

youtube.com/confidenceiatry

From Medicine to Manuscripts: Shawn Christian, M.D.'s Books and Other Works

Hidden Secrets of Confidence Uncovered: 17 Secrets that Make Confident People Successful

- Paperback ISBN: 978-1-953726-00-1
- eBook ISBN: 978-1-953726-01-8
- Audiobook ISBN: 978-1-953726-02-5

How To Have Laser-Sharp Focus (Free eBook)

- Free eBook: https://confidenceiatry.com/laser-sharp-focus-ebook/

Mastering Laser-Sharp Focus (Book & Course)

- Book & Course: https://confidenceiatry.com/product/mastering-laser-sharp-focus/

Keep your bookmarks handy because the story doesn't end here. There's a whole universe of books and digital content brewing, filled with more empowering tools, actionable advice, and transformative wisdom. The adventure continues—stay tuned for the next chapter!

www.ingramcontent.com/pod-product-compliance
Lightning Source LLC
Chambersburg PA
CBHW051003140626
46546CB00016B/27